MEMOIRS OF AN INDO WOMAN

Always remember and honor
your roots
With Love

Marguérite Schuberthum

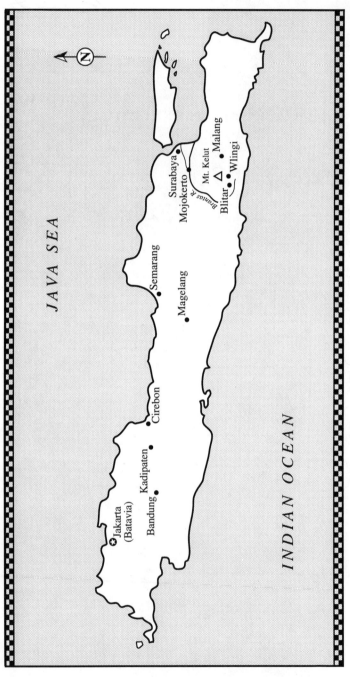

Map of Java showing selected place names.

MEMOIRS OF AN INDO WOMAN
Twentieth Century Life in the East Indies and Abroad

by
Marguérite Schenkhuizen

Edited and translated
by
Lizelot Stout van Balgooy

Ohio University Center for International Studies
Monographs in International Studies

Southeast Asia Series Number 92
Athens, Ohio 1993

99 98 97 96 95 94   5 4 3 2

Printed in the United States of America
All rights reserved

The books in the Center for International Studies Monograph
Series are printed on recycled acid-free paper ∞

Library of Congress Cataloging-in-Publication Data

Memoirs of an Indo woman : twentieth-century life in the
    East Indies and abroad / by Marguérite Schenkhuizen ;
    edited and translated by Lizelot Stout van Balgooy.
        p.   cm. – (Monographs in international studies.
    Southeast Asia series ; no 92)
    Translation from the Dutch.
    Includes bibliographical references.
    ISBN : 0-89680-178-0 (pbk.)
        1. Schenkhuizen, Marguérite, 1907– 2. Eurasians–
    Indonesia. 3. Eurasians–Indonesia–Biography.
    I. Van Balgooy, Lizelot Stout. II. Title III. Series.
DS632.E9S335 1994
959.8'004042'092–dc20   93-30346
                                                CIP

CONTENTS

ILLUSTRATIONS

Map of Java showing selected place names

... frontispiece

1. Marguérite Lanzing, age 20, on a ski slope in Reit im Winkel, Austria, during her stay in Munich 1927-1928 (p. 124).

2. Marguérite Schenkhuizen on her wedding day, age 27, 2 January 1935 in Malang, West Java. From left to right: Paul Lanzing (father), Josje de Kruiff, Marguérite Schenkhuizen, Henk Schenkhuizen, Marga Hanfland (bridesmaid), Emmy Lanzing (mother). The children are Rita and Carla Lanzing, the daughters of Marguerite's brother, Pof.

3. Marguérite Schenkhuizen, age 28, with her first child, Doeshka, in front of the gate leading to the back yard of the house on Slamet Street in Surabaya. The child was born on 15 November 1935 (p. 148).

4. Marguérite Schenkhuizen, age 40, in the fall of 1947 at the end of the Pacific War at the time she and her family left Surabaya for the sugar plantation Kadipaten in Central Java (p. 198).

5. Marguérite Schenkhuizen, age 49, with her family in Bandung 1955-1956. Front row: Henk, Marguérite, and their son, Pax. Back row: Doeshka, Guido, and Joy (pp. 206-12).

6. Marguérite Schenkhuizen, age 85, in Pasadena, California.

... between pages 144 and 145

vii

FOREWORD

Paul W. van der Veur

Men and women of various ethnic backgrounds and cultures have had physical relations with one another since time immemorial. Although stereotypes, prejudice, and racial discrimination confronted the descendants of such unions wherever they were, these differed greatly according to time and place. In a colonial situation, untold numbers of mixed descendants are absorbed within the larger indigenous population. Others become separate from the indigenous mass. How separate they are and how close to the colonizers depends upon the particular colonial power.

In the early period of the Dutch presence in Indonesia (from 1596 onward), the major legal distinction was between "Christians" and "Natives." The Dutch East India Company quite early grudgingly recognized a need to establish orphanages and poorhouses for (in the words of one governor-general) the "numerous poor, roaming hybrids, and orphans of Europeans." Conditions at the elite level of the East India Company officials are vividly described in Jean G. Taylor's *The Social World of Batavia* (Madison: 1983). With practically no women arriving from the Netherlands, an increasing number of high officials married women who were Asia-born and bred, either creole or mestiza. Although the political influence of local-born officials diminished sharply with the demise of the East India Company in 1799, the cultural components of what has been appropriately described as "a Mestizo culture" continued into the twentieth century.

Mestizo culture expressed itself in dress, in a variety of cultural and social characteristics, and in language. In all of these, the local cultural environment played a major role. "Magical powers," for example, seemed an integral part of the Javanese landscape. *Guna-guna* (black magic) early caught the attention of

ix

Dutch journalists and novelists. P. A. Daum wrote knowledgeably on this topic in 1887; Louis Couperus published *De Stille Kracht* in 1900 (which appeared in English as *The Hidden Force* in 1922). A. Th. Manusama's *Njai Dasima* (first published in 1926), a novella, tells the story of a concubine subjected to black magic and then murder. Although Marguérite Schenkhuizen through her strong Christian belief rejects these "dark powers," she details several instances in which *guna-guna* touched her own life experience (pp. 138-41, 157-58, and 207-9).

Mestizo culture also exhibited itself in the development of *pechoh*, a pidgin dialect in which Dutch words and concepts were intertwined with and overgrown by Malay/Indonesian sentence structure, words, grammar, and pronunciation. Marguérite's original manuscript contained a sizeable number of pechoh expressions which for reasons of readability were removed from the final edition. A few remain such as *sudah* (Indonesian for finished, done) and *sudah, al* which expresses the same while combining an Indonesian and an inappropriately used Dutch word. Marguérite also mentions that she never liked to walk slowly, *sloyong-sloyong* (p. 142). Do you hear the sounds of this walk—feet in sandals, barely leaving the ground, shuffling over the tiled floor of a large hall? If you do, you will have caught the flavor and sound of pechoh.

Earlier, reference was made to the importance of religion in creating a separate group of mixed descendants. Separation was further stimulated by a variety of legal provisions. For example, the European father could "recognize" the natural child of a non-European woman. Such an *erkenning* (legal recognition) resulted in European status for the offspring. Letters of legitimization also were used, as was adoption. Finally, the Dutch nationality law of 1892 automatically made Dutch citizens all those who were considered Europeans before 1 July 1893. A. van Marle, writing in the journal *Indonesië* (V, 1951-52: 500), estimates that between 1880 and 1940, the European group increased by some forty-eight thousand persons through erkenning, sixteen thousand through mixed marriages (counting the Asian bride as European), and twenty-nine thousand through children of such marriages. Another two hundred and ten thousand Europeans were born in the colony of "European" parents in which in most cases either one or both of the parents were of mixed descent. The above origins highlight the

x

colorful composition of the European group. Marguérite's family, indeed, shows an extensive degree of interrelationship. Her maternal grandfather was a Dutchman born in the Netherlands married to a Javanese, with whom he had fifteen children (pp. 57 ff). Two of her cousins had an Indonesian mother while some of her uncles were married to Indonesian women or living with them. Marguérite briefly bemoans the fate of concubines (pp. 62-63). Names employed for a particular group frequently are revealing as to the group members' positions in the social hierarchy. The *Mistiezen* (Mestizos) of East India Company times saw themselves referred to in a variety of ways in the nineteenth century. Most common was *Inlandsche kinderen* (Native children) or *Kleurlingen* (Colored). *Indo* and *Indo-Europeaan* (Indo-European) also came to be used. All of these designations developed pejorative overtones. More neutral was *Indisch*, although the addition of *erg* (very) or *echt* (real) quickly made the observers' attitude clear. *Blanken* (whites), obviously received their pejorative share from other groups but generally were referred to by the Malay/Indonesian term, *totok*. Attempts to shy away from racial characteristics produced the terms *Blijvers* (Settlers) and *Trekkers* (Birds of Passage). *Indische Nederlanders* (Indies' Netherlanders) became common in the post-World War II period. At the same time, the term "Indo" got a new reception among those of mixed descent uprooted from their homes in Indonesia. Finding an appropriate *English* designation for "Indo" has always been a problem since "Eurasian" brings with it the Anglo-Saxon prejudice towards the "half caste" and ignored the different and more favorable position of persons of mixed descent in Dutch colonial society. It is fortuitous, therefore, that the present publication uses the term "Indo" in its title and throughout the text.

The "plural society" of twentieth-century Netherlands Indies contained three major legal groupings: the Europeans, the Foreign Orientals (mainly Chinese), and the Natives. The European group consisting of some two hundred and forty thousand individuals in 1930, was minute in size compared to the other two, but held most of the wealth, as well as the economic and political power. To be a European, therefore, held a special aura. But the group itself was carved up into numerous parts determined by education, racial characteristics, occupation, and private wealth. A Dutch education was all-important. J. Th. Koks in his work *De Indo* (1931: 227-28) goes so far as grouping social classes according to graduation from elementary school, high school, or college and university. Access to higher training facilities had become possible at this time in the Indies. To those reared in white societies or thinking in terms of a white caste structure, the upper stratum of the European group provided an unusual sight: local-born Dutch and Indos may well have formed almost one-half of the political top. Indos were found among army generals, provincial governors, city mayors, and heads of departments; some high officials who were pure Dutch had Indo wives. Having made this important point, however, we must quickly note that the majority of Indos held middle and lower positions in government service and private enterprise and, in the words of W. M. F. Mansvelt (*Koloniale Studiën*, 1932: 304), merely formed "an appendix to the apparatus of Western production and administration." These positions, moreover, although only recently gained, were being eroded by increasing competition from recently educated Indonesians. The great depression added another blow to the export-oriented economy of the Indies. Between 1929 and 1935, national income fell by about 57 percent and—limiting attention only to the Europeans—thousands of Europeans became unemployed, with many others in dire straits. East Java's pride, its fabulous sugar industry, faced an almost total collapse. Factories closed down by the dozens and total wages paid by the industry to Indonesian workers plummeted some 85 percent between 1929 and 1936. Marguérite was not directly affected, nor apparently was her family, because the text is silent on the matter.

Rudy Kousbroek in *Het Oostindisch Kampsyndroom* (The East Indies' Campsyndrome) caustically remarks that most European children in the Indies were living the lives of princes and princesses in a tropical paradise (1992: 89). Marguérite's life to a large extent was such a life. She states that her life story is one of "a simple and ordinary but happy woman" (p. 1). Happy, indeed, and remarkably upbeat. Simple and ordinary, no. She refers to her grandfather's living in the countryside and possessing two organs, one shipped from Germany; she also mentions that her parents built three houses in the mountains after leaving Surabaya, where they rented out the house they owned there (p. 135). She herself attended the prestigious Girls HBS (high school) in Surabaya and then—common for well-to-do children—she was sent for further education to

Europe: three years in Switzerland, Germany, England, and Holland. Marguérite does not seem to have faced or been aware of much racial discrimination in spite of her dark features. Her early years in the countryside rather than in the big city may have made a difference. In addition, good looks, vivaciousness, and a certain degree of affluence may have been helpful. She also was able to laugh off comments and even turn the tables in cases in which other Indos might have taken offense or been hurt. Her totok father (jokingly, of course) sometimes called her his "coffeebean," her husband later referred to her as his "black pearl," to which Marguérite immediately responds by noting that black pearls are rare and expensive. She does recall that her mother "felt a bit embarrassed" by having a Javanese mother and the children were told, not unreasonably, "to stay away" from the concubines of their uncles (p. 62). The children's greeting to the Chinese vendor with "a little nonsense rhyme" which they thought "very funny" (p. 42) may have been funny but not totally innocent. But there may have been more discrimination and more hurt feelings than recorded. It is revealing, for example, that in her concluding chapter, while expressing her appreciation for her life in California, Marguérite thanks the Lord for leading Indos where they "can finally be themselves" and no longer are subjected "to the indignity of being regarded as second-class Europeans" (p. 241).

Returning briefly to the 1930s and 1940s, Marguérite recounts her life in Surabaya, her marriage to an Indo bookkeeper, the outbreak of the Pacific war, and the arrival of the Japanese. Indos, as Dutch citizens, had been subject to military service and became prisoners-of-war in March 1942.

The Japanese in Southeast Asia considered persons of mixed European descent as Eurasians in the British context and expected them to be supportive of their Asia for the Asians campaign. Registration forms showing Asian ancestry permitted their holders to stay out of civilian detention camps into which some one hundred thousand European men, women, and children were being herded during 1942-43.

Life outside the camps had obvious advantages and guaranteed a greater survival rate; it was also highly uncertain and unsafe. Schools had been closed, bank accounts had been blocked, salaries and pensions were no longer paid. Frequent re-registrations, raids, searches, and possible arrests by the feared Japanese secret police were traumatic. Some Indo wives and mothers managed to earn a meager salary and supplement it with funds received from support groups and the sale of most of their belongings. Another, more profitable and long-term activity for some, was the sale or trade of second-hand goods. Marguérite reports that it was engaged in by many, but it seems unlikely that others were so successful as she claims to have been (p. 168). She also may have been unusually fortunate in being able to stay in touch with her husband through postcards rather regularly (p. 173). In my own case, one postcard was all I received during my prisoner-of-war period and it had taken two years to reach me.

With the end of the Pacific war an eerie silence settled over Java. No liberators appeared; Japanese authority continued; and rumors referring to an Indonesian proclamation of independence spread. With the arrival of small contingents of British troops and the possibility of a Dutch return, bands of militant youth yelling *bersiap* (get ready) initiated a nightmarish period of arson, kidnapping, and murder. Indos who had not been in camps before were now moved from one place to the next by regular Indonesian army troops to protect them from annihilation. Marguérite recounts this period rather lightly but admits that by the time she was rescued her hair had turned grey.

Indonesian independence was officially recognized by the Netherlands on 27 December 1949. The event was hard to swallow for many Dutch and Indos. Marguérite expresses strong feelings of betrayal and exasperation (p. 201). Her husband, meanwhile, had been re-employed and the couple continued to reside in Indonesia until 1957. At the transfer of sovereignty in 1949, those Dutch and Indos born in the colony, or with close ties to it, had been granted the opportunity to elect Indonesian citizenship during a two-year option period. Only a small minority made a decision in behalf of Indonesia. If the thought of opting for Indonesian citizenship ever entered the minds of Marguérite and her husband, the matter is not referred to in her book.

From 1945 onward, a steady stream of Europeans had been repatriated or evacuated from Indonesia to the Netherlands. Deteriorating relations between the two countries culminated in 1957-58 with the expulsion of practically all Dutch citizens from Indonesia. By the early 1960s, more than two hundred and fifty thousand refugees had arrived in the Netherlands. The only Indos remaining in Indonesia were those who had opted for Indonesian citizenship in the early 1950s and had decided to remain in spite of adverse conditions. Also remaining, of course, were those persons who in spite of their mixed ancestry had always been part of the Indonesian people.

The remarkable economic recovery which the Netherlands experienced from the mid-1950s permitted a reasonably successful absorption of this massive influx. In addition, some migration occurred from the Netherlands. An estimated five thousand or six thousand persons emigrated to Australia and a number of other countries. But the largest recipient was the United States. The Refugee Act of 1953 had allocated an extra seventeen thousand visas for the Netherlands. The Pastore-Walter Act of 1958 allocated 3,136 "units" (some nine thousand persons) and repeated this allocation in 1960. J. E. Ellemers and R. E. F. Vaillant in their *Indische Nederlanders en Gerepatrieerden* (1985: 130-31) estimate that some twenty-three thousand "emigrants from the Indies" entered the United States under these provisions with most of them settling in southern California. B. R. Rijkschroeff in *Een Ervaring Rijker* (One Experience Richer) describes the experiences and fate of these immigrants. He credits their rapid adaptation to their small numbers, the fact that they were not easily recognizable, the absence of a continuous flow of immigrants, and their "high level of aspiration"—they wanted to succeed in this new land of opportunity (1989: 92, 106-8).

Various members of the Schenkhuizen family arrived in Pasadena, California, in the early 1960s. They settled in and got jobs. Marguérite for the first eight years cleaned house for wealthy families, working eight hours a day. She began to draw social security benefits at age sixty-three. Her husband had died shortly after their arrival and Marguérite played the traditional Indo part of maintaining a close-knit family.

In the Netherlands, Indo writer and activist, Tjalie Robinson, had become a dynamic although controversial figure even in Indo circles. Winniefred Anthonio in her unpublished doctoral dissertation on Tjalie for the University of Michigan notes (1990: 113) that Tjalie's magazine *Tong-Tong* not only aimed to educate the Dutch about their former colony but also and "above all" tried "to preserve Indo culture." Tjalie stayed in the United States between

1961 and 1966. In southern California, he was successful in starting the Indo club "De Soos." Marguérite mentions that Tjalie insisted that only subscribers to *Tong-Tong* could serve on the board and that in order to prevent "a dilution of Indo culture" only Indos and their relatives by marriage could become members (p. 232).

Marguérite describes the various activities of the Indo club and the success it had during its early years. But, then, with the old getting older and most of the very young knowing little or no Dutch or the "juicy pechoh," the club withered (p. 237). In what may be seen as an example of sardonic Indo humor, a final play was performed in 1988 with the typical pechoh title *En Toen Al* (And This Is It).

Rudy Kousbroek, cited earlier, remarked that practically all individuals writing about the Indies seemed to have ulterior motives: some had something to hide; others wished to even scores; a third group wanted to embellish the past; and still another wished to rehabilitate the Indo retroactively (1992: 177). This book does not seem to fit any of the above categories. Hella Haasse, speaking about Maria Dermoût (author of *The Ten Thousand Things* and other novels) in a 1989 lecture, noted that Maria was neither Indonesian nor ever or anywhere completely Dutch or European because "her heart and soul had been formed by the world out there." The same could be said about our Marguérite. The years she has recounted most vividly and movingly, as she has noted herself (p. 241), are those of her earliest years, the ones that had to do with her place of birth and her grade school years.

Some Indo writers mournfully express the feeling that Indo culture has vanished for ever. I do not sympathize with that view, since no culture retains its primordial values. Marguérite expresses the hope that her contribution may serve as a legacy to her descendants and those of other Indos. I believe that it also should be seen as proof that mixtures of different races and cultures can live happily and harmoniously in a race-conscious world. Finally, it seems appropriate to note that there has been a remarkable revival of interest in the Indo past among third generation Indos in the Netherlands.

ACKNOWLEDGMENTS

This book has a checkered past. As a student in anthropology at the University of California at Riverside, I discovered that there were relatively few sources available in English on Dutch and Indo culture in the former Dutch East Indies. I resolved to remedy that lack of first-hand information by gathering lifestories from my compatriots residing in California. My idea was to gather enough stories representative of the different cultural strata in the Indies to be able to publish two anthologies, one filled with female voices and the other with male ones.

Soon after I started my quest for reliable sources, Mrs. Schenkhuizen's handwritten pages piling up on my desk made it clear that she was prepared to tell all, something not many of us are ready to do. So, I decided to see if her story could stand on its own. Boy, was she ready for this challenge! And challenge it was, for it took almost three years of cooperation between the two of us and close scrutiny of the data to mold her spontaneous reminiscences into the lifestory presented here. I cannot thank "tante" Rita enough for her trust in me and for her determination to see this through regardless of the many questions and suggestions with which I peppered her. Tante Rita, you're the soul of patience and faith. Thank you.

I also wish to thank my advisor at Riverside, Professor Eugene A. Anderson, whose staunch support was invaluable in the period when few others believed in my project, which was the longest time ever. Thank you, Gene. You played a crucial part in my decision to persevere.

Then there is Professor Paul van der Veur, well-known for his publications on my own group, the Indos, the Eurasians of the former Dutch East Indies. He kindly consented to read the rough draft of my manuscript and made many suggestions, enriching it considerably. Professor Van der Veur, your unstinting support was a great help, and I thank you.

I must also mention my brother-in-law, Dr. Max M. J. van Balgooy, of the Rijksherbarium in Leiden, the Netherlands, who graciously took time—in between his lengthy field trips to the wilds of Indonesia—to edit the descriptions of animal and plant species appended to this work. Max, you're a pal. What more can I say?

Nor should I overlook the helping hand extended by Professor Theo Stevens of the Universiteit van Amsterdam, the Netherlands, when I needed to verify some points.

And thank you Rene Creutzburg, editor and publisher of the monthly magazine *De Indo*, for providing additional information on the early years of the local Indo cultural association, "De Soos."

I'm also grateful to the writing class at the Joslyn Senior Center in Claremont, California, and its guide and mentor, the gracious and knowledgeable Nelle Fertig. Nelle, you and the others provided me with an American audience in which to test this material. Thank you all for your valuable comments.

I would like to end with a bear hug for my patient husband, Cap, and my son, Max A., who stayed supportive and understanding, even when a meal was not on the table on the appointed time once again. Cap and Max, I love you and thank you. I felt you two beside me all the time.

Lizelot Stout Van Balgooy

LANZING AND GEUL

"Be embraced, ye millions!
This kiss is for the whole world!"
    Schiller, *An die Freude* (Ode to Joy)

I was born where the golden rice softly waves in the warm sunshine and the bamboo whispers mysteriously, bending back and forth in an eternal dance, moving with the rhythm of the cool morning breeze, the great expanse of the cloudless sky above—my birth country, my beloved Indonesia—in the town of Wlingi, in the residency Kediri, at the foot of Mt. Kelut or "Broom."

That happened on 1 October 1907. Astrologers say I'm a Libra or Balance. This prompted my husband a long time afterwards to remark that this was true, but that I was a "berserk" balance, who was never exactly in equilibrium. *Sudah!* That might have been true then, but now I have found my equilibrium.

There is so much to tell that I'll probably get sidetracked umpteen times. My thoughts fly from one memory to another at mind-boggling speed: memories strung together like a diamond necklace sparkling with a thousand vividly colored facets.

This is my story—the life story of a simple and ordinary but happy woman—not a biography, such as of Leonardo da Vinci or someone like him, but simply a story about the "10,000 things" of Maria Dermoût, the Dutch fiction writer; the ten thousand things so familiar to people from the Indies; the ten thousand things, which revealed to us the richness and the wisdom of that country and the love that we feel for her.

My name is Marguérite—French *loh*!—Schenkhuizen née Lanzing. My mother is Emma Louisa Geul, one of the fifteen children of *Opa* and *Oma* Geul. "Moes" (Mommy) married Paul Guilaume Antoine Lanzing, my father, who came from a nest of six children.

1

My oma (grandmother) on my mother's side was a simple Javanese *kampong* woman, nothing more exalted, who could neither read nor write, whom my Opa Geul married. Opa (grandfather) was Johannes Jacobus Geul from Brabant, the Netherlands. I remember both of them well. Opa was a Catholic, so Oma was also baptized a Catholic and at that time was given the name Maria. She was a small and slender woman, whom I always knew with her gray hair knotted into a bun, and dressed in a white, lace-edged *kebaya* and the most beautiful *sarongs*. Kebaya are long-sleeved, hip-length or longer, tailored tunics, closed in front with special kebaya pins that are often jeweled. Sarong are lengths of batikked cloth sewn into a tube and used as a wraparound skirt. Oma understood Dutch quite well, but spoke it only haltingly and jam-packed with Javanese.

Opa Geul was an honest-to-goodness *totok*, a Dutchman who had not been born in the Indies, who had gradually turned into an Indiesman. He had thick, gray curls, a drooping mustache, and stern, blue eyes. Opa was as strict as he looked, but he was also fair, and gentle with children. I, for one, was quite fond of him, just as fond as I was of my oma. Opa went around in pajama bottoms cut from a sarong and a pajama top of white cotton, buttoned up with tiny buttons from his throat to below his belly. That was what European men used to wear at home in the good old Indies—it was cool and light.

After a long day's work, Opa would relax in his so-called *krosi males*. This lazy chair consisted of a sort of armchair with an open-weave rattan seat, in front of which you could swing out two hinged, vertical, wooden boards on which you stretched out your legs (these boards turned on two round circles as big as a Dutch two-and-a-half cent coin).

Opa was head forester in Blitar, Kediri residency, in which position he supervised extensive teak forests. I'll tell you more about Opa and Oma Geul and their house in Blitar later on.

Now I'll describe my parents, who are without peer. My mother was an Indo, a Dutch East Indies Eurasian, from head to foot: totok father, Javanese mother. She was brown-skinned with brown eyes and long, wavy, dark brown hair reaching past her hips. She, too, wore sarong and kebaya at home, as did most European women before the 1920s and 1930s, with her hair hanging loose or in a long braid. On her arm, she carried the ubiquitous rattan key basket, in which, besides keys, you could also find a handkerchief, her wallet, and nail scissors. We called her "Moes," a traditional pet name for the more formal "mother."

Moes was a very busy woman, who was primarily educated in Breda in the Netherlands. She could speak English, German and French besides Dutch and could converse easily on historical and geographical matters. But she never mastered subjects such as algebra or physics. You could say that she received an education geared towards the well-to-do young girl of her era. She painted delightfully and made beautiful embroideries; she played the piano and sang; her handwriting was magnificent; later on, she learned photography, including darkroom techniques.

Moes was interested in what happened in the outside world as well as in cooking and crafts. Whenever something new had been invented in the latter areas, she would be one of the first to try it out. Furthermore, she loved gardening and animals, but preferred gardening. I inherited my love of animals from her. She was an orchid expert, had quite a few books about them, and corresponded extensively about these exotic flowers with people all over the world.

My mother was a plucky, energetic and interesting woman. But this "chip" fell quite a ways from "the old block," so, in my case, it didn't turn out as tradition would have it. Moes knew how to count and save money, and her household ran like a well-oiled clock. She did my father's bookkeeping and still found time to help the people in the kampong.

Her one glaring fault (if it was one) was that she couldn't stand dirty jokes. Moes would listen, shake her head disapprovingly, and try not to laugh. But her small *idung pesek*, snub nose, would give away that the joke had amused her anyhow, for then her nostrils would flare out noticeably. We would burst out laughing and yell, "Her nose is slipping. Her nose is slipping. She gets the joke." Moes would eventually give up and join in the laughter. "Isn't Moes's nose slipping yet?" got to be an in-house saying. Once in a while, however, she would truly not get a joke neither do I sometimes, especially when it comes to dirty ones.

This is my mother, from head to toe. Oh yes, she always used sandals at home, just like my father, who even went to the mill in his sandals. As they used to snicker, "You went through life in the Indies in sandals"—and indeed we did, nice and easy as can be!

My father came from a military family—generals and colonels, high hats. But my father, whom I called Mannie, craved adventure

3

when he was young. He left Holland on a sailing vessel as a foot soldier and spent the next three months on the high seas, closeted with live cattle. They encountered stormy weather and, like the biblical Paul on the way to Rome, the crew had to heave the live ballast overboard. It was a horror story that I hated to hear recounted. Father got off the boat in Surabaya, which at that time was still half-drowned by the surrounding marshes. Shortly after arrival, he was sent to Aceh. There he fought under General Van Heutsz, one of the many heroic generals the Indies has known, against the Acehnese. A rifle shot from a fanatical Acehnese left a lasting scar on my father's face. Fortunately it was small and never marred his sweet, handsome face.

By the time peace seemed to have returned to Aceh—seemed, for the proud Acehnese never really surrendered—he tired of the military life and went looking for another job, on Java. Oh yes, my father is not a Dutchman or Hollander; he is a *Limburger*, as he used to emphasize, born in Venlo, Limburg, the Netherlands. (This is an example of the traditional disdain people in the Netherlands have for their compatriots born in a region different from their own.)

I never knew my father other than having silver white, glossy hair and a gray mustache. He was fair-skinned, heavyset, and tall with kind blue eyes. Eventually, he moved from Surabaya to Blitar, where he found a job as a so-called field employee—one of the lower ranks for Europeans—on a plantation in the mountains, where they grew coffee and rubber.

Blitar was surrounded by various coffee and rubber plantations and served as their local rest and relaxation station. One day, walking around at a party, my father heard a lady laugh so charmingly, reminding him of the "cooing of a dove"—I'm just citing my papa—that he decided to find its source. Behind a large shrub, he ran into my future mother, laughing and gossiping with other young girls, all of them with nipped-in waists, high-necked lace-collars, voluminous skirts and elegant, high-heeled, buttoned-down boots—*queu-de-Paris* outfits. My father knew instinctively who the charming laughster was. He introduced himself and joined in the animated conversation, all the while "devouring" my mother with his eyes. Moes was eighteen when they met, recently returned from Holland and from her "finishing touch" education.

4

They continued seeing each other and became romantically involved. They got married when my father became administrator of the plantation Branggah (which means tiger territory) in the Wlingi area. Truly, we have old-fashioned romance here! At the time of their wedding, my father was thirty-six and my mother was nineteen. So, he was almost twice as old as Moes, but they had a very happy marriage. Their wedding took place on 2 January 1902. You can find their wedding photo in Rob Nieuwenhuis' book, *Komen en Gaan*. January 2 is also my husband's and my wedding day as well as that of my brother.

My brother, Paul Otto Frans, nicknamed Pof, was born on 3 January 1903, and it became a running joke in our family to tease my mother in particular, for here she was with her so-called strict code of conduct, and yet, she herself was married on 2 January and bore a child only one day after! This always caused great hilarity, but Moes thought the joke only so-so.

Four years later, I was born on 1 October 1907. Four years after me, on 19 July 1911, my sister, Elsa Elisa Joanna, or "Tje," was born. At my birth in Wlingi, my mother was assisted by a mid-wife, while both my brother and my sister were born in a hospital in Blitar, where she was attended by a doctor.

My good parents also raised two nephews on my mother's side, Jan and Frans Geul; both of them had an Indonesian mother and had lost their father at an early age. Because I grew up with these cousins until they got married and started their own families, I always say that I have three brothers and one sister. For reasons unknown to me, Jan and Frans boarded with family friends in Malang; but they came home for every vacation and were then awaited with great anticipation and welcomed with open arms.

My father always called me *"Koffieboon,"* which means coffee-bean in Dutch, because I'm quite dark-skinned compared with my brother and sister. As far as skin color goes, I haven't aged well. But I always say, "Black is beautiful!"

My mother always called Elsa *"Schatje,"* which is Dutch for sweetheart, and I shortened that pet name quickly into "Atje." Even that being thought too long, it was further shortened into "Tje," pronounced "Chuh." And Elsa has kept that nickname until now, when she's already far past seventy; Tje it was and Tje it stayed. We Indies people are certainly weird, always inventing the oddest nicknames! But these nicknames sound so warm and sweet and so pleasantly homey. We didn't use nicknames out of laziness, but out of affection and friendship, or as an expression of goodwill. Outsiders find this genuinely Indies custom hard to understand. So, I think I've introduced just about all my relatives to you. I never knew my grandparents on my father's side, but I was on good terms with a younger brother of my father, *Oom* Wim Lanzing, who was a colonel in the army. Later, he had a house in Wassenaar, a suburb of The Hague, where I stayed a while in the 1920s. His wife, *Tante* Stien, a blonde-haired Indo woman, and their seven children (blondes all) were born in the Indies.

Now about myself. As you know now, I always was and am dark-skinned, and when I was a child, my curls and eyes were jet black. My relatives would tease me, saying that I hadn't washed my eyes thoroughly enough, and then, simpleton that I was, I would scrub and scrub my eyes with water and soap until they stung, all to no avail. Some adults can be very cruel.

My mother said that I started out as a tomboy in the cradle, for I was unruly even then, wild and difficult to control. Later, she used to say that I was just as adventurous as my father. I was born a tomboy and, even though I'm now in my eighties, I'm still somewhat of a tomboy.

TALUN, PAGAH, AND MY FATHER'S CATTLE FODDER MILL

My memories will now go all the way back to when I was about four years old. My father lost his position as an administrator at Branggah and moved to Talun with his family. Talun is located on the highway that leads from Kediri via Tulung-agung, Blitar, Garum, Talun to Wlingi.

At Talun, we lived in a house partially constructed of *gedek*, painted white with lime, and with an open front porch. Gedek is a kind of stiff, sturdy, plaited bamboo matting. It is often used in construction. Two vividly colored, porcelain bees hung on the wall of this porch, sporting lush growths of maidenhair and other ferns. I can still see them clearly. In addition, the porch was decorated with several pots, also painted white with lime, in which grew earth orchids, roses, and maidenhair ferns.

One incident from the Talun period stands out in my mind: my mother punishing my brother Pof, because he went into our chicken coop day after day for the fun of chasing the cackling chickens around. My brother's plaintive explanation entered history, "I don't want to go to the chicken coop, but my legs take me there!" *That* became *my* stock excuse whenever I had done something unexcusable once again.

Not long after, we moved from Talun to Pagah, higher up on the slope of Mount Kelut. Pagah was no more than a hamlet, with only about five Indo families. My father had bought a cattle fodder factory in Pagah from a Chinese by the name of Tan Sioe Bie. Quite a few adventures awaited me there.

The factory or mill in Pagah produced *gaplek* and *bungkil*, amongst other products. Gaplek is the name for dried cassava chips, bungkil are cakes pressed from the residue of peanut oil fabrication. I remember that peanuts were here and there visible on the surface of the thick, round bungkil cakes, which we children

7

would pick out and eat. The things children will eat! This cattle fodder was transported to the small station in Talun by a cart pulled by two oxen. From there, a cargo train would take it to its destination.

The mill also ground corn into flour. The yellowish powder would be deposited in large concrete tubs, where Indonesian women washed it until the flour had lost all color. Then the snow-white powder was dried, bagged and sent on its way. Once in a while, the bags of *Maizena* would be piled up for a couple of days in a shed, which invited us to scramble up on top until we could touch the roof of the shed. But my father didn't like us to do that, for it could be dangerous. Once in a while, the bags would slip away from under your foot, making you slip too, and you could get buried under a pile of bags.

About once a month or so, the cornstarch tubs were scrubbed and filled with clean water. We were then allowed to swim in them. Because there were hardly any other European children living nearby, we would invite the Javanese village youngsters to join us, and we would have lots of fun together.

The heart of the mill consisted of a machine with a giant flywheel, oiled with grease. That machine was made by Stokvis and Company. I remember that so well, because I used to hover around it all the time, curious as always to find out its workings. The Indonesian machinist, Sidin, and I were pals. He would patiently explain to me how things worked and why. It always smelled great in that machine room, of thick grease.

Outside the mill stood a large threshing machine, also made by Lindetevis Stokvis and Company. The Chinese would buy unhulled rice from the villagers and bring that to our mill for threshing. Then the milled rice was bagged and taken to its destination. The chaff was ground into *dedak* to be used as horse fodder.

If I'm not mistaken, molasses was used in the bungkil cakes and my father used to store the molasses outside, in a breezeway next to the mill. The Indonesian term for molasses is *tètès*. I simply couldn't resist tasting a mouthful of the stuff, to my own undoing, for it was unrefined molasses. Brrrr, it tasted truly horrible! Nevertheless, it's very nutritious for cattle.

To the left of the mill lay the drying-floors, used to dry unhulled rice and also kapok. A dozen or so kapok trees abundantly produced the green, oblong fruits that contain the kapok down. First, a group of women from the village would open the ripe, dry kapok fruit by hand, one by one, pull the downy kapok from the inner core and throw it, seeds and all, on a pile. The women wore scarfs over their heads and cloths over their noses, because the soft fluff would fill the air as soon as they started beating the pile with a stick with cross-bars attached in a form similar to a rake. They did this to separate the seeds from the down and to fluff up the kapok. This kapok was for our own use.

When the Javanese tailor came, he used the kapok to stuff our mattresses. They were wonderfully hard mattresses, on which you could sleep stretched out straight and healthy. Our *guling* or roll pillows (called "Dutch wives" by the English) were also stuffed with kapok. In the evening, everything was swept off the floors and stored in the sheds next to the drying-floors.

In an area sloping down to a nearby creek stood the houses of the village, built of gedek. Here, the mill laborers lived. The same creek separated our garden from the rice fields beyond.

Against one of the walls of the mill grew a riotous bed of tall tithonias, flowering with wild abandon. The large, orange flowers resembled sunflowers and had a delicious, bitter-sweet, herbal scent. We called them marigolds. We loved to play hide-and-seek under those shrubs by day. But at night, those bushes assumed all kinds of unearthly shapes in our young eyes, throwing shadows on the adjacent wall like so many shadow puppets. Then they turned into the *gendrowo* and *momok*, tree and forest demons and ghosts, which were very real to us children living on Java—apparitions from a dark and unknown world.

SCHOOL YEARS 1913-1920

By now, I was six years old and it had become time to go to school. I was driven in our own horse-cart, with a driver at the reins, to Wlingi, where the only elementary school of that whole area was located. Later, when I was a bit older, I held the reins myself—great stuff! My horse was a plongkuh, a horse with spotted skin and a white splotch on the forehead.

Going to school was an adventure in itself. I never shed a tear, in contrast to the other children, six boys, all accompanied by their mothers. In complete silence—yes, I was literally struck dumb with surprise—I watched my fellow schoolmates acting like sheep being led to slaughter. I wondered why they carried on like that. Finally, goodbyes were over and we went to our assigned classroom. There we were told where and how to sit: "with arms folded across your chest and sit still and no talking!" Now, this was a tall order for me; it took quite some doing before I had everything just right.

My mother had given me a new slate and a pencil box holding six slate pencils, the tips of which had been sharpened to the most beautiful point imaginable by our gardener. Because everything was still new to me, I could keep my attention focussed on what was going on around me; I kept my body, so used to sun and freedom, under control.

The first school year passed without problems. The second year was somewhat more turbulent, for I decided I'd been obedient long enough. So, to escape from the dull routine of 50 minus 2 plus 10 and all that, a lie was thought up easily enough. Holding up my finger with a painfully screwed-up face, I pretended I had to "go to the back," I really couldn't wait any longer. The Indies expression "to go to the back" means to go to the restroom. You were always allowed to go, for the teacher was much too afraid of "accidents." I would run as fast as I could to the service annex, which stood at least fifty meters away from our classrooms, throw my shoes in a corner, slip barefoot through the luntas hedge and onto the dirt path of the village, and run full speed down the slope to the river. Rivers have always held great attraction for children of every race.

I would undress, jump as naked as I was born in the cool, clear water between the river rocks and cavort with the *kerbau*, also refreshing themselves in the river. Naturally, I forgot the time. What is more fascinating than water, kerbau, sun, and blue sky, especially compared to hard school benches and arithmetic! Eventually, the school janitor would fetch me. Then all hell broke loose. I had to give my solemn word never to do this again and was sent home with extra homework as punishment. At home, my parents would pour scoldings over my guilty head and impose additional punishment; I would be grounded for a week, or something like that. Rotten luck!

Nevertheless, the river kept singing its siren song and I was drawn back to it time after time. I was endlessly creative in inventing yet a new excuse to escape from the dull classroom, with the result that I was retained in the third grade. That was a sad eye opener. I had never thought about negative consequences of my innocent crime spree. Having to redo the same grade with younger children filled me with shame and brought me to my senses. No matter how much and how often I longed for my river, I never ever had to be retained in a grade again.

My days would begin with breakfast at six in the morning. We had porridge, either oatmeal or rice porridge with a thick, red-brown syrup made from palm sugar. When I was little, I had a hard time swallowing the stuff—I would choke on it and even throw up—but now I love porridge. At that time, I would swear to myself that, if I ever became a "Mistress," I would never force my children to eat something they disliked; and I've kept my word.

So, I had to drive to school in our light, horse-drawn carriage with an empty stomach, but never fear . . . Our cook, named Koki, taking pity on me, would shove a penny in my hand. A penny was then still worth a great deal. I used it to buy delicious, piping hot, sticky rice or deep-fried cassava at a little eating house along the road. These snacks tasted delicious, not only because I far preferred them over oatmeal porridge, but also because Moes didn't like us to eat "from the street." Forbidden food tastes extra good. You can take my word on that.

Later, I held the reins myself and raced against boys from a family in Talun. Our carriage was a *dokar*, they drove a *bendy*,

11

another kind of horse-drawn carriage. I often lost, but I also won quite a few times.

Once my horse bolted and refused to obey anymore. The driver and I jumped from our runaway dokar. We got hurt a bit due to the hard surface of the road, luckily not too badly. The horse pulled the dokar up against a bridge, the poles broke, and he ran back to his stable. When the servants noticed our horse with his harness on entering his stall, they sounded the alarm. Moes was notified, and she in turn got my father. We also owned a bendy, which they took to look for us on the main road to Wlingi. Not long after they started out, they met the driver and me hobbling along the road, and we went home after the driver had gotten a thorough tongue-lashing for "allowing the young miss to hold the reins." As if he could help it that something scared the horse and made it bolt like that!

When my sister reached her sixth birthday in 1917, it was her turn to be subjected to the discipline of school. My sister and I were quite different from each other, on the inside as well as on the outside. She was fair, with brown eyes and brown, curly hair, and was very slim and small. She was calm and never got excited. Nevertheless, when necessary, she knew how to put her foot down. Now, take the opposite of those traits and you have me from head to toe: restless, in perpetual motion; disliking the indoors; always on the lookout for adventure in the outdoors, under the blue sky and amid the golden-hued rice fields, or prowling through the waving, grey-plumed sugarcane, which left my arms and legs covered with angry scratches.

I had better explain that, at home, my sister was used to speaking Javanese with everybody. She understood Dutch well enough, but she always answered in fluent Javanese. It tickled us. The reason for her speaking Javanese in preference to Dutch was that our playmates were Javanese children. My sister's special friend was Mentik, a little Javanese girl from the mill village. I played mostly with the Javanese village boys. My sister played indoors, with dolls and so on, and I outdoors, naturally, strolling around or engaging in all kinds of monkey tricks.

My mother took my little sister Elsa to school. As usual, she was quiet, until my mother left. Then she screeched in Javanese that she wanted to go home. I grabbed her hand and, talking soothingly to her in Javanese, led her to her classroom. Fortunately,

12

several of her classmates also spoke Javanese, and in that way the ice was soon broken and peace restored. This scene was repeated the next few days, but she finally adjusted and even started to answer my parents at home with a few words of Dutch.

I already told you a bit about school. I would take off shoes and socks as soon as I arrived in school. During recess, we played all kinds of wild games in the shade of the pink-flowered, leafy canopies of *waru* trees. Or we managed to sneak away from the schoolyard to buy snacks at a foodstand in the village nearby. Here, a woman sold the most delicious tasting *jemblem*—ground cassava, shaped into a ball around a chunk of palm sugar and deep-fried in coconut oil to a golden brown. Boy, was it good! And you could buy anything for a half-penny or a penny, or at most two-and-a-half cents. Food was cheap in the old Indies.

On the veranda behind the school, a woman sold *sumpil* every day. Sumpil is rice shaped into a roll and boiled; the roll of rice is then cut into thick slices and served in a twist of banana leaf, with a ladle of *sayor udang* on top. Sayor udang is a spicy vegetable curry with shrimp. Sumpil is incredibly tasty. The same vendor also sold *lupis*, which is also a roll, but made of sticky rice, sliced, and served with palm sugar syrup and fresh, grated coconut. It is out of this world!

Served on banana leaf, everything tasted different and definitely better, and that's absolutely not a figment of my imagination. A banana leaf exudes a certain scent, which, in contact with food, gives it that special flavor which the French call *bouquet*. Walk past a banana tree and you'll smell that special aroma. You may think, *Se non è vero, è ben trovato* (that is just a coincidence). But truly, the true truth I say (*sic*).

"This Indies girl, she ken words *yang paribasan*, still from school time this, is sometime she ken remember!" This is an example of *pechoh* or Indo-Dutch creole, a dialect spoken by many Indos, kept alive among Indos, and best understood by Indos. It never fails to evoke laughter, because of its inventiveness, humor, self-mockery, and so-called "corrections."

When we came home from school at around 1:30 in the afternoon, we would immediately sit down for our afternoon meal. My father, the totok, ate whatever was served. The only food he refused to eat was what he called "goat food," which included such

13

Javanese vegetable dishes as *pecil* or *gado-gado*. We had to take an afternoon nap after eating.

Three in the afternoon was the hour to seek out adventure. At four o'clock, tea, cocoa or coffee was served, along with homemade Javanese snacks, such as *kwee talem, kwee lumpur, kwee cina, bubur sumsum, kwee lapis, ondeh-ondeh*, and so many more, but usually no more than one sweet at a time. At 6 P.M., we were shooed into the bathroom. At 7 P.M., we had our evening meal, consisting of the usual *rijsttafel*. Now and then we would be served bread, or potatoes and vegetables, with soup and dessert. We children had to go to bed at eight o'clock.

My special duty was to fix my father a whiskey soda when he came home from the mill in the afternoon. Whiskey two fingers high in a glass, which I then filled up with chunks of ice and soda water, which would bubble up so prettily.

Once in a while he would relieve himself of gas with loud explosions—always in the privacy of the bedroom or toilet, of course—and if I happened to hear that, I used to say, "But Mannie (as we used to call him), that's really gross, you know!" To which his stock answer was, "Better into the wide world than into a narrow hole," the meaning of which escaped me.

Before I forget, my mother never said prayers with us, nor did she ever teach us a prayer. However, a lady visited our school once a week to teach the Catholic religion. My father was a Protestant freethinker, but my mother was a Catholic, so we were told to attend these Catholic catechism classes. These were exceedingly boring, because they were incomprehensible to a child of ten or eleven years old. When the lady arrived at the litany "Blessed is the fruit of Thine (sic) body," I asked what kind of fruit the Virgin Mary was carrying in her body, "for it could certainly have hurt a lot had it been a durian or a pineapple in her belly. Instead of explaining the matter to me, she called me blasphemous and threw me out. That ended my catechism lessons. What a relief! To me, these were a total waste of time which I could put to much better use.

I've not much more to tell about my elementary school years. School could never capture my undivided attention, so, between my sixth and twelfth year, it wasn't the most important thing in my life. I went through the usual routine: first learning to write with slate pencils on slates; then with pencils on lined paper; then with ink

14

special pens, used to learn the correct penmanship. Penmanship was one of the subjects I liked, for I got quite adept at it, writing the slanting script in a precise manner, here thin, there thick. I had a weird twist in my brain, for up through the third grade I found it impossible to write a normal number three. It was really strange. For I would write a three like this, ⅋ —a thin upright line with three tiny circles attached. The teacher, patiently showing me how to do it over and over again, finally let me do it my way for a while, hoping that I would catch on eventually. That went on for several months. One day, I was aimlessly noodling with pencil and paper when out of the blue my pencil drew two semi-circles, like this ろ , but much larger. Now I had my three and worked hard to give it the correct size and shape. I still wonder why that three was so difficult for me.

One day, I really went too far. I don't remember specifically what I'd done, but, whatever it was, the teacher gave me a vicious slap across my face, to the consternation of the class and my fury. Back home, I told my parents what had happened, and the next day they promptly complained in person to the principal. Not long after, that male teacher was transferred.

For the rest, my best friend, a Chinese girl named Oei Sian Tien, used to prompt me all the time in class. She sat next to me. Or I would peek at her work and thus get super grades, until I was found out. I had to move all the way to the back of the classroom, and nobody could sit next to me—I was all alone.

Our school had a mixture of races: Chinese, Arabs, totoks, East Indians, a couple of Indonesians, but the majority consisted of Indos. The Chinese always got the best grades in any subject.

My friend, Oei Sian Tien, and I kept in contact for quite a while. I called her Tien, pronounced "teen." She was a slender girl with slanting, jet black eyes and hair in a long, thick braid, which reached past her knees. As soon as this intelligent girl had finished the seventh grade, her parents married her to a much older man, picked out by them in the traditional way. Of course, Tien didn't want to get married at all. She was only fourteen years old and had such a bright mind. I found this child marriage deplorable. When I met her again afterwards, she had two children already, but otherwise she had remained the same Tien, my best friend. Would she still be alive now?

15

To be honest, I was really an average student in that elementary school in Wlingi, probably because it curtailed my freedom. I certainly wouldn't call school hell. But my childhood home and environment were a different matter altogether, for I lived in paradise.

MY MOTHER'S GARDEN IN PAGAH 1915-1920

Although I'd never heard of paradise at that time, my parents' garden was to me a Garden of Eden. I was eight years old when we moved to our house in Pagah. But even at that young age, I already had an eye for beauty. I may say that of myself, *ja*?

You entered our garden via a long, semicircular, gravel-covered driveway. A pink-flowering *trengguli* grew at the entrance. Next to the trengguli grew a so-called handkerchief tree with its fiery red bouquets of flowers. It derives its name from its tender, young, pale green to rose-mauve leaves which hang down at branch's end like elegantly folded handkerchiefs. It is a stunningly beautiful tree. Then followed a row of *jeruk keprok* (mandarin) on the border of a sizeable lawn. This lawn filled the half-moon defined by the driveway, and held flower beds filled with *soka*, canna, clerodendrum, roses, and other flowers.

On the other side of the gravel road was another lawn dotted with several flower beds. Here a gnome, a contented smile frozen on his stone face, waited for our daily chat, just between him and me. We would both give free rein to our fantasies and anything I dreamed up would have his blessing.

In the corner of this lawn were two *jambu aer* trees, Eugenia genus, one of which always sheltered a huge, gray beehive, from which hundreds of bees flew in and out, busily gathering nectar from the large variety of flowers in my mother's garden. When the hive had grown too large, it was burned out by our gardener with a large torch. I hated to see him do this. Within a month, however, the industrious bees would begin rebuilding their hive once again. The gardener gave the burned hive to his children, who would break it apart and consume the roasted, fat, bee larvae. Curious as I was about everything, I was eager to taste this treat; but once and never again!

Somewhat behind the jambu aer stood a *jeruk Bali* tree, a species of pommelo. Here hung the factory bell, which was used to

17

announce the various work periods: start, noon meal, and the end of the work day. The lunch period was called *laut* in Javanese. Our jeruk Bali produced huge, thick-skinned globular fruits with juicy, red meat that tasted refreshingly tart-sweet.

The gardener fashioned toy carts for us out of the thick, meaty jeruk Bali skin. We pulled these along at the end of a *biting*, the midrib of a palm leaflet. Indonesians are very handy and inventive; our servants were always good-natured and patient with us, the children of the *tuan besar*, the boss. Down from the jeruk Bali, you arrived at a row of banana trees and a gazebo overgrown with a blue-flowered petrea, happily intertwined with a mauve congea. In the twilight of this gazebo hung various special orchids, which demanded a dark and cool niche.

A *kantil* tree towered over all. Her spreading branches, fragrant with flowers and thick with leaves, sifted spots of sunlight over the gazebo, a kind of greenhouse sheltering hundreds of orchids in all stages of flower. Kantil is another name for the *campaka*, in the magnolia family.

The unusual, exotic scents which perfumed the still, sun-warmed air in this area, enchanted everyone who tarried there. Not to mention the extraordinary shapes and colors of the various orchids, epiphytes plucked from the trunks of forest giants, growing somewhere in the jungles of Brazil, among the tree ferns of Chile, or in our own ancient jungles on the slopes of the Kawi, or on Sumatra, Borneo, Amboina, or Celebes. My mother's orchid garden was a world apart—mysterious, beautiful, a feast for a painter's eye.

Further back grew a *belinju* tree, its red nuts ready for harvest, playing peek-a-boo among the dark green leaves. A belinju tree has fragile branches and cannot be climbed readily, so its nuts were picked by means of a special bamboo tool, called a *senggek* in Javanese. This was a length of slender bamboo fitted with a bamboo hook at one end. You used the hook to twirl the clusters of nuts loose. The harvested nuts were deposited on a round, flat, woven bamboo tray or in a woven bamboo basket. Usually, lots of immature nuts, catkins, and young leaves were harvested at the same time. These were set aside for *sayur lodeh*, a Javanese soup with lots of vegetables, and thickened with coconut milk.

Actually, you could add some of the ripe belinju nuts to the lodeh too. But for the most part, the ripe nuts were turned into crackers called *emping*. First the soft outer skin was peeled away, exposing the hard, leathery inner skin, which was also removed. Next the yellowish white nutmeat was beaten by hand into very thin disks. Then the soft, thin crackers were spread out in the sun to dry and harden. These emping belinju were served deep-fried in coconut oil as part of the rijsttafel or as a snack. On Java you had families who produced enormous quanties of emping belinju. I don't know whether these are now factory made, but I eat these chips often with my rice here in California. Unfortunately, the young leaves and catkins aren't available here. They would improve appreciably the taste of sayor lodeh and *sayor asem*, Javanese vegetable soups.

The belinju tree, and a *belimbing* tree across from it (which bears very sour fruits), shaded our deep well. Our well produced cool spring water, and it was very deep and dark. I was convinced Frau Holle, a German fairy tale figure, lived at the bottom of our well. To butter up that unwholesome presence, I would bend over the concrete rim from time to time and yell, "Frau Holle, Frau Holle, show me how you make it snow!" Invariably, her answer would echo back from the depths of the well. A child's imagination is marvelous, isn't it? I don't believe many parents understand how rich the fantasy world of a child is—a world that is very real to the child.

Down the slope towards the creek was our playhouse, with the chicken coop standing across from it. Even further downhill, was the horse stable for our two horses. One pulled our bendy and the other pulled our dokar. We didn't have riding horses.

Near the chicken coop grew a *kedondong*. Every year at a certain season, it would be crawling with red-stippled woolly caterpillars, hundreds of them, which would strip the tree bare. After the gardener had burned them out, the tree would leaf out again and bear dozens of kedongdongs. We used to press the fruits open between the door and the doorjamb to eat them.

Oh yes, near our playhouse grew papayas: the common one, with yellow meat, and another kind, with red meat. These papayas were not like the small ones you can buy here in California; they were big, and hung in great numbers from the tree's trunk. Two avocado trees grew nearby.

Behind the chicken coop and in a straight line from the outbuildings to our house was mother's vanilla orchard. You know, don't you, that the vanilla is an orchid? Lightly shaded by *peté cina* trees, also called *lamtoro*, it clambered up bamboo stakes. Vanilla has thick, leathery leaves and stems, and has pale, greenish flowers, which have to be pollinated by hand, for Java lacks the specific insect which pollinates it in its native land. Thus, once a week or more, I don't remember this clearly any more—my mother and I would move along the rows to transfer pollen from the stamens to the pistil with a match—so-called hand pollination. I found this job fun and interesting. You had to be patient, but, as young as I was, nine to eleven years old, I was so fond of flowers, that this was a labor of love to me.

Then you waited, full of expectation, to see whether it had taken. If pollination had been succesful, you could see the fruit slowly growing into long pods. When these turned yellow, they were ready for harvest. The harvested pods were carefully rinsed, dried off one by one, and spread out to dry on a flannel cloth in a glass case. Each bean was turned daily until it started to blacken. Then the beans were gently rubbed every day until, as if by magic, tiny, glistening crystals started to appear on the surface of the velvety black vanilla bean—it was ready for consumption. Another sure sign that it was ready for use was the intoxicating scent emanating from the beans. Then they were stored in glass apothecary jars, and, because Moes always had plenty of vanilla beans, many were given away and some of the harvest was sold.

As you see, my life was (and it still is) full of rich variation, unfettered, pleasant and instructive.

The peté cina trees shading the vanilla vines had many podded fruits. We would pick the pods before they were fully ripe, ripping them open and snacking on the small, green seeds. These seeds don't exactly smell like Chanel No.5—my parents even called them smelly—but they were nutritious and tasty. We ate the young pods in *nasi pecil*, a Javanese rice dish. Near the stable grew lush clumps of bamboo, which kept up a continuous conversation with the creek, over which they bent gracefully. We harvested young bamboo shoots from these clumps, for use as pickles or sayur lodeh.

A couple of meters in front of our front porch grew a huge gardenia, which produced a wealth of white flowers in endless succession. It always smelled heavenly. Nearby grew unruly shrubs of blue-flowered naughty boys and sweet girls intertwined with rose- and white-flowered vines, which we called bride's tears. It was a riot of colors, scents and shapes.

20

Oh yes, and in front of the pantry, between the pantry and the side veranda grew a mango tree. Under this mango stood my pigeon house, home to dozens of white and gray pigeons, as well as plump, round-breasted ones, which lorded it over the whole flock. Well, now I've been around the entire garden. Imagine how huge that garden was. Oh yes, I almost overlooked something. On the other side of the public road, my mother had built a park. It had a grassy knoll in the center bordered by merry cannas in hot yellow, red, rose and orange, and several beds filled with soka, roses, bride's tears, mimosa, and many other flowers. This pocket park was edged on one side by clumps of bamboo, on the second side by a row of about twenty coconut palms; a village path ran along the third side; and the fourth side was bordered by a lovely little creek. Various wild flowers grew along the creek's edge. Resembling Semiramis' hanging gardens, the wild flowers trembled on the moist banks, following the cadence of the water ripples.

On our rear veranda, village women would make oil from the ripe coconuts. The coconut meat was grated by hand, warm water was added, and then the moist, grated coconut was wrung out in a piece of cloth until the milk ran out. The women were given the pressed out, grated coconut to take home, but I don't remember what they did with it.

The coconut milk was poured into large pans, placed over a wood fire in a small charcoal stove, and boiled. The milk was stirred continuously, until a layer of oil floated on top. The oil was ladled into sieves, and the strained oil was bottled. That's how we made our own frying oil, which tasted very *gurih*. (It's impossible to do this term justice in Dutch or English. The closest you can get in English is "full-bodied.")

After practically all the oil had been boiled out of the coconut milk and had been poured off, a brown residue was left on the bottom of the pans. To us children, that residue was a delicious treat. It was called *blondo*. Our cook used to warn us not to eat it, for it would make us get worms. Ignoring her warnings, we would eat it with gusto. And as far as worms were concerned, we would indeed pass a roundworm or two once in a while, but it is debatable whether that resulted from eating blondo. My mother used to say that we got worms from walking around barefoot in all kinds of places unfit for bare feet.

OUR HOUSE IN PAGAH 1915-1920

Now I'll describe the house that stood in the center of this paradise, my beloved childhood home, where as a child my dreams came true. The details of this childhood home and its garden form part of the sharpest and most cherished memories of my happy, unfettered early years. They have been a strength to me throughout my entire life—from child to teenager, then as a young girl, a working young lady, a married woman, later on as a mother with children, even up till now. These happy memories are like a firm foundation which has withstood every event in my life without cracking or trembling. What an incredible treasure to have.

Our house looked like a white, stone building from the outside, but it consisted of whitewashed gedek walls on a concrete slab. We had concrete floors throughout the whole house—smooth, glossy and, what mattered most, cool. Here and there, my mother had scattered rugs.

You entered our house via a couple of steps leading to the open front veranda, which was wide, cool, and cozy, with rattan furniture and, everywhere you looked, plants in Chinese porcelain cache pots and displayed on brass racks. We had anthuriums, philodendrons, and lots of maidenhair ferns next to white-flowered *anggrek bulan* or moon orchids. In America, anggrek bulan is called *phalaenopsis* or moth orchid. The wall was decorated with the same porcelain bees we had in our old home, each holding a plant. To the side, another couple of steps led to the garden. This front veranda was used to receive visitors, and here we would drink our tea or coffee and read the paper and mail. Here too stood my father's special lazy chair, used for his afternoon nap, cooled by a delightful breeze which carried the scents of gardenia and arabian jasmine.

The first room of the house, the guest room, opened directly onto the front veranda with a glass door covered with flowered curtains pleated on a rod. This guest room contained an old-

22

fashioned, wide bed for two, complete with four pillows, two gulings and a white mosquito net, *klambu*, embroidered with angels or flowers. A klambu is a tentlike covering made of fine mosquito netting attached to a white cotton canopy. Completely surrounding the bed, it is designed to provide a mosquito-free environment while asleep. By day, the klambu was elegantly pulled up on either side of the bed and held back by means of silver klambu hooks in the shape of a pineapple or maybe a swan, sewn onto the end of a wide, white silk ribbon. This room was further furnished with a thin floor mat plaited of pandanus leaves, a set of chairs, a table and a wooden wardrobe, all to provide a guest with rest and comfort. The guest room had a second, double set of doors, a pair of glass doors, and an outside pair of wooden, louvered doors, painted brown, which opened onto yet another set of short stairs leading to the garden.

Entering the main house from the front veranda, you walked into a hallway, in which hung the old-fashioned telephone. To place a call, you had to take the horn off the hook, and then you promptly heard a voice, coming from some place in the great beyond, "Hello, south." The telephone office was apparently located somewhere in the south, and when you wanted to speak to somebody who happened to live in the south, you would say, "Yes, south 405," or something like that. At any rate, you first had to say "south" and then the number.

The doors to my parents' vast bedroom on one side and my father's office on the other side opened onto the dark entry hall. My father's office was simply furnished with desks, bookcases, chairs, a paper cutter, and an antediluvian typewriter, and opened with a glass door onto the other side of the garden, facing the public road.

In my parents' bedroom stood another one of those ample beds, similar to the one in the guest room, a wardrobe with a full-length mirror for Moes, a plain one for my father, and a commode for the night hours (the toilet in the service wing was much too far away). Such a commode consisted of a painted wooden box with a large hole in it, a chamber pot under the hole, and two smaller holes for the *cebok* bottles. Cebok bottles are bottles filled with water to cleanse oneself after using the toilet. We didn't have toilet paper. The commode had a lid on top and a multicolored cloth was thrown over it to camouflage it a bit. This commode was reserved for the females of the household. A big, blue-flowered chamber pot for my father stood next to it.

A pink-flowered washbasin stood on the dressing table, filled with fresh water in which petals of rose, campaka and *pacar jawa* floated. This table also held toothbrushes, toothpaste, and a water glass; towels hung from a wooden rack that stood next to the dressing table. An oval mirror hung on the wall as well as a colored, celluloid, funnel-shaped container, in which Moes deposited the loose hairs left in her comb after she had done her hair.

My curiosity aroused, I asked her why she collected her hair this way: "Why don't you simply discard them in the wastebasket, Moes?" She answered, "Oma taught us never to discard hair nonchalantly. For that would be an invitation to the devil and would bring bad luck to the family."

You remember, don't you, that I explained that Oma was a Javanese woman? Thus she had lots of superstitious beliefs. Anyway, any loose hair was scrupulously collected in that special container, later to be emptied in a paper bag and burned. Tje and I, the daughters of "venerable mother" followed this tradition for quite a while, not so much out of superstition but because it made sense from a practical and hygienic viewpoint. The Javanese servants who kept our house clean, never touched that container with hair, for they shared the same beliefs.

In addition, my parents' bedroom also contained a *sampiran*. That is a wooden stand, consisting of two upright boards connected by a third, wide board, on which my father's hats were stored. Several hooks were screwed in the bottom of the cross-board from which to hang clothes and kimonos presently in use. This stand was completely curtained off with cheerfully flowered, see-through fabric. Such a sampiran was very practical. Not only did it give a colorful note to the bedroom, it also did a good job of hiding the untidiness of clothes and shoes. Shoes and sandals were put on the bottom, hidden from prying eyes.

On top of the wardrobe lay a large, square, brass-trimmed, leather box. It contained my mother's hats. You know those nineteenth-century type hats decorated with ostrich feathers, flowers and whatnot, those intricacies with which European women of that era adorned their heads? My mother owned quite a few of them.

From this bedroom, tall doors led via a long and wide stairway to the garden, where the campaka tree and the orchid house stood.

And my parents' room also led into our bedroom, the one my sister and I shared.

Ours was a large room too, with two beds and two wardrobes. It was also our playroom. It had a window with wooden shutters, a door to the dining room, and a door to the outside breezeway. Our room was fairly empty, but it was airy and had lots of room. After dark, the only light was provided by a *lampu templek*, a small kerosene wall lamp, that threw a soft aureole of light on the white wall where it hung. Some time ago, I wrote a short story with the title "Lampu Templek," which Tjali Robinson, a well-known Indo writer and magazine publisher, included in his bundle, *Het Meisje Uit Indie*, or *The Girl From The Indies*.

Our dining room was also our family room. It was quite spacious, airy and full of light. To the side stood a long and wide dining table and six chairs. The wall shared with my bedroom was completely taken up by a huge sideboard. This sideboard consisted of various big and small cupboards that fitted together. These cupboards were decorated with woodcarvings and had small glass doors. There were lots of drawers, in which old-fashioned, heavy-weight silverware and damask table linen was kept.

In the center of the sideboard, stood a set of three crystal carafes. Silver labels engraved with the name of the particular liquor was attached with silver chains to each of the carafes. A tiny master key—that actually belonged in my mother's key basket—lay next to the liquor set on an embroidered, lace-edged doily. We called this set "Dr. Tantalus;" it must have meant torture for the thirsty had the key not been available.

Next to the liquor set stood two silver candelabra; its candles were lit only on special occasions. That sideboard was huge—it also had space to store magazines and books—but beautiful, and it lent an air of wealth and luxury to the whole room.

The concrete floor in that part of this combined dining-family room which served as a sitting area was covered with an Oriental carpet. In this sitting area, was a rattan chair set, leafy plants in brass pots, and a piano, often played by my mother. It was further furnished with white-painted rattan racks, filled with children's books and decorated with white doilies. On the floor next to my father's chair stood the so-called *trommel*.

The trommel was a wooden box, holding a selection of books and magazines, which was changed each week. I remember magazines such as *Panorama*, *Prins*, *De Lach*, *Life*, *De Gids*, and even—to satisfy my insatiable curiosity and passion for reading—*La Vie Parisienne*! At that time, we were taught French as early as the third grade, and I would use what little French I knew to figure out what was printed beneath photos of nude men and women. I didn't understand the half of it, but being exposed to nature the way I was, I surely could guess what it was all about. My parents never discovered that I was looking through that magazine on the sly. The curiosity of a child growing up, I tell you!

For the rest, I also learned "dirty facts" from my friends in school. My parents *did* find that out and took me aside for a heart-to-heart talk. That, and the warning of getting grounded, ended it.

However, my parents trusted me to rearrange the contents of the trommel each week, according to the list printed on the inside of the lid. After us, the trommel would go to other subscribers, and we would get a new one.

Of all the things in our family-dining room, I enjoyed the lamps most. We had two lamps hanging on the walls across from each other. These lamps were fed by gasoline under pressure. In the pantry, a small room you entered from the dining room, stood a gasoline tank connected to a kind of bicycle pump. On the top of the tank was a pressure gauge. When darkness began to fall, our houseboy pumped the tank until it reached a certain pressure. He would then carefully loosen a screw, also located on the top of the tank. A brush dipped in spirits was lighted with a match, giving a purple flame, and held above the chimney of the lamp while a valve on the side was turned open gently, causing the gas to buzz. After a few seconds, the flame would turn blue, a sign of things to come, and, floop, the light would spring to life. And what a light! So bright and cozy. As long as they were lit, you could hear the lamps buzz. Such a cozy, safe, mysterious sound. Those two lamps would light the room as if it were day. It was a light full of life, quite different from the reddish yellow, electric light we modern people have nowadays, which is dead, meaningless, but admittedly handy.

The pantry was a room filled with sinful temptation. Two cupboards stood here, their legs set in stone trays filled with water, to keep the ever-present ants away from the food. The back of these cupboards was covered with small-mesh wire netting to admit air.

The pantry had a window, in front of which stood a rack, consisting of a board with three holes resting on two uprights. The holes held *gendihs*, which are earthenware water pitchers, each with an opening at the top of the slender neck and a slim spout protruding from the belly. Water stayed nice and cool in these gendihs and tasted so good too. We children would often be in too much haste to use the glass standing ready nearby, and would drink straight from the spout. You had better learn early not to touch the spout with your mouth, but to hold the gendih at a slant and slightly above you and thus direct a thin stream of water in your mouth, in order to leave a clean spout for the next drinker. If someone did suck at the spout, we yelled, *"Ngocop*, you slob!"* and the spout would be scrubbed.

To return to the temptation I mentioned earlier, the pantry's cupboards always held an opened can of condensed milk in a saucer filled with water, you see. Often enough, in spite of the watery moat, we would still find ants drowned in the thick, yellowish white goo. Once in a while we would even discover a greedy *cicak*, a house lizard, in it, also dead, of course. We were only allowed to have this milk spread on a slice of bread or in a cup of cocoa; we were not allowed to sneak it from the can, quickly dipped out with a finger.

Through a door, you came out on a roofed, open porch, which Moes had set aside for her vanilla beans. Going down one step, you entered a three-meters wide and ten-meters long breezeway. To the left, you would pass the servants' rooms and come out at the carriage house, where the dokar and the bendy were kept, as well as the horses' harnesses and tools for house and garden.

Next to the carriage house was the room of our gardener and his wife and child. This child, Miran, was at that time an adorable, plump baby. When he started to stand up, his father made him a walking device—a length of bamboo for the upright, another length of thinner bamboo inserted lenghtwise in the hollow upright, and a short length of thin bamboo inserted crosswise in the second bamboo for the child to hold. He would shuffle along, drooling and roaring with laughter, causing the bamboos to turn around and around like a merry-go-round. Didn't I say earlier, Indonesians can always find a solution to a problem? They are quite inventive that way.

27

If you turned right, away from the breezeway that led to the house, you passed the guest room, the storeroom, and the huge kitchen where food was cooked on a wood fire. The kitchen had a porch in back with a rectangular concrete trough that was filled daily with fresh water by the gardener, specifically for use in the kitchen. In front of the kitchen was another kind of porch where the dishes and pots and pans were washed and left to dry on racks. The dirty dishwater was channeled to the creek, which took care of any refuse. That might be why the fish in the creek were so fat.

After the kitchen came the large, cool bathroom, which held two concrete troughs, one of which was smaller than the other. When we took a bath, we would use a dipper with a wooden handle fastened across the top to pour water from the large trough over our body. The smaller trough was used as a swimming pool by the children. Fresh vegetables, delivered from the mountains to our home twice a week, were set out on woven bamboo trays on the edge of the trough to keep cool.

In a corner stood our water purifier, a pear-shaped, fat-bellied, earthenware leaching pot with a wooden lid on top. The whole contraption was enclosed by a wooden box. Under this leaching pot, called a *gentong*, stood an open, earthenware basin to catch the water that dripped with a steady toong-toong from the gentong. The gentong would be refilled daily with fresh well water. The water leached from the gentong was transferred to the gendihs by means of a long-handled dipper, which hung on the side of the wooden box. The gendihs were then taken to the rack in the pantry described earlier. Thanks to this primitive technique, our drinking water was always pleasantly cool, not icy cold but cold enough, and was rid of all kinds of impurities as well.

Oh yes, the pantry also held a Berkefield filter, in which the purified water from the gentong was filtered for a second time. But I preferred the water from the gendihs with its special earthy taste.

Next to the bathroom was a lavatory of extraordinary dimensions. On top of a concrete platform, a wide board extended across a concrete-lined canal. This board had several openings, large enough to hold a person's behind. On either side stood racks with cebok bottles. From time to time, my father and I would sit there side by side and chat about any and all kinds of subjects. It was truly a marvelous place to have a discussion or a heart-to-heart talk. The "dirt" was washed away by the channel's water to the *kali* (river). What a weird sanitation system we had in those days.

The kitchen had a concrete platform containing four openings above a wood fire, over which cooking pots were set. The fire would lick with long flames around the bottoms of the pots. The firewood was bought on the *pasar* or native market. It was cut in the surrounding forests. From the smoke-darkened gedek walls of the kitchen hung pots, pans, Javanese-style long-handled ladles made of coconut shell, Javanese-style spatulas, and all that stuff. Looking back, it seems to me as if Koki could always be found in the kitchen preparing the most delicious food.

The storeroom was a place filled with strange smells, so peculiarly Indies. The things you found in there! Uncooked rice and potatoes; bags of raw *krupuk udang* (shrimp crackers); candied nutmeg peel and candied tamarind; packs of fresh *trasi* (Indonesian-style fermented shrimp paste); bunches of green *peteh* or stink bean; dried, salted fish and *ikan pedoh*, a small, whole, dried and salted fish; *dendeng celeng* (dried, salted slabs of wild boar meat), and sweet *dendeng sapi* (sweet, spiced and dried, thin, sheets of beef), all neatly wrapped in newspaper; thick rounds of brown palm sugar in tall glass jars; cane sugar in large tin cans; roasted coffee beans, also in tin cans; peppercorns; blocks of genuine sea salt; and, far removed from the rest to prevent contamination of the food with its penetrating smell, a can of kerosene. A hand pump attached to the can was used to pump kerosene via a funnel into bottles. This kerosene was reserved for use in the lampu templek. Then there were long rows of baskets filled with duck and chicken eggs, fresh as well as salted; sticky rice in see-through bags, both the black and the white kind; balls of yeast in earthenware jars; onions in cardboard boxes; in short, a little bit of everything.

Each morning, my mother would "do the storeroom." "Doing the storeroom," was the term used to describe the daily chore of getting things from the storeroom or giving them to the cook and other servants to use. This included the daily ration of raw rice, onions, sticky rice, eggs, kerosene, and so on. My mother would then make up the day's menu and give Koki fifty cents, telling her what to buy at the pasar. Koki would depart for the local market, carrying a basket on her back in a *slendang* (carrying scarf). We children looked forward to her return, for she knew how to juggle the shopping so that she always had a couple of pennies left over to buy us and herself some snacks. And she managed to surprise us every time, never failing to bring us something different than before. My mother insisted on getting the account squared to the last penny and Koki invariably knew how much she had paid for each single item, a half a cent for this and a half a cent for that, and so on, until the whole fifty cents had been accounted for. Sometimes, she would have a couple of pennies left over, which she always handed over to my mother without a murmur. Yes, my mother was no fool and knew how to stretch her household budget.

After this was done, my mother would go into the garden to check on her orchids, or she might go to the office to take care of my father's bookkeeping or to write some letters. When that was finished, she would sit down at her sewing machine to sew some dresses for us, or clothes for the little Miran, who was often allowed to crawl around on the floor of our house.

I forgot to explain that the whole house, including the guest room and the service wing, had ceilings made of plaited bamboo matting, gedek. Anywhere else, you could see the underside of the red roof tiles. At night, you could hear the mice or the *luwak*, romping about, *holderdebolder*, their feet drumming across the bamboo ceiling. You knew exactly when the luwak were around, for their musky scent would fill the whole house.

The whole roof of the house was covered with tiles, except for the front porch, which had a corrugated tin roof. It was so cozy when it rained: a soft rain sounded like a melancholy nocturne by Chopin; a hard rain sounded like Wagner's *Gotterdämmerung*, with lightning and thunder to accent the dämmerung aspect to full effect. I could listen to it for hours, even though I didn't know of the existence of Wagner or Chopin at that time, but when I think back, I now hear it this way. I would then sit on the steps, far enough out to get my legs spattered by the rain, between the blue china stands of the cache pots, which served as echo chambers. Time full of delights, time full of joy.

Once I saw a ball of lightning come clattering down right in front of me on the driveway. The fiery ball rolled on a little ways and then disappeared into nothing as if by magic. For a few seconds, I was paralyzed with surprise and terror. Then I jumped up and ran inside to tell my mother breathlessly what had happened. She was sitting calmly in a rocking chair, my sister safely cuddled in her arms.

30

Believe me, rain is a composer of joyful songs, mournful songs and delightful symphonies, in which something indefinably grand and majestic forms the leitmotiv. Later, much later, I came to understand that I was subconsciously searching for God and feeling His presence.

In the daytime, especially during the rainy season, you could hear the green-jacketed cicadas sing, glued to the trees. They loudly proclaimed to the world that they could smell rain coming—a veritable jungle concert!

Besides the rain's songs and the cicadas' songs, it was also fun to listen to the frog concerts; the frogs reserved their most beautiful symphonies for after dark. When the rice fields were flooded with water, they must have sheltered hundreds of frogs at a time, and every last one of these had his own distinctive voice. Every species, from the very small ones to the large *kodok bangkong*, had its own repertoire. Already snug in my bed, I loved to listen to them before falling asleep. Since leaving Indonesia this peculiar sound is one of the things I have always missed and longed for, no matter where I happen to be.

Deep in the night, when the whole household lay in a deep sleep, I often would be awakened by the passing of the *tukang keplek*. I could hear him coming from afar. Tukang keplek were security guards who walked the streets, carrying hollow lengths of bamboo, *ketongan*, on which they rapped loudly, from time to time calling out, "*Melek! Melek!*" which means, "Awake! Awake!" Whereupon our own guard, who slept on a mat on the steps to our front porch, would call out in return, "*Inggih!*" meaning, "yes I'm awake." I would fall asleep again, feeling completely safe and content.

Night sounds. I should not forget to tell you about the typical night sounds, to which you would listen when you couldn't catch sleep. Besides the familiar frog concert that I told you about, you could also hear crickets chirping, getting themselves ready for the annual duel of the sexes. This is such a cozy sound. We may also hear it in this country in summer. Here, I even have crickets in the house; they visit my bathroom every day. In the Indies, it could suddenly become very quiet and still; finally you would hear very soft and mysterious rustling noises accompanied by soft squeaking, followed by a "kuhduhbook!" sound, and you knew the flying foxes had found a ripe fruit, which they had dropped after nibbling at it.

31

I would listen: the sound of the kentong was repeated ten times and then died away in the distance. I had made it a habit to see how long I could still discern the lingering tones. It was such a comforting thought to know that all around you people were awake and guarding your safety.

Then, when the moon shone bright with a bluish green light, daubing the coconut palms and the ripening rice with a silvery sheen, the fireflies would appear as if by magic. It was a feast for the eye to see them move around in a cadence of fiery flashes, a *perpetuum mobile* consisting of hundreds of sparkling diamonds. It was a wondrous sight, peculiar to the Indonesian rice fields.

Even when it was pitch-dark in the evening, you would invariably hear some Indonesians walking along the road on their way to a *wayang* performance somewhere in a distant village. And you always knew when people were walking in the distance, for you would see a pinpoint of light moving back and forth. That light came from the burning tip of an *upet*, a twist of coconut fiber that keeps on glowing for a long time once it has been set on fire. It wasn't only used to light the way, but also to light your *kelobot*, which is an Indonesian cigarette made with dried cornhusks instead of paper. That pinpoint of light in the dark of the night formed an indelible part of my far-reaching fantasies.

The kentongan was also used to alert people to a solar or lunar eclipse, or rather, a dragon swallowing the sun or the moon. You would hear kentongan sounding frantically all around, the noisier the better, all to drive the dragon off. When we were outside, a servant would come and get us, "Hurry up, miss, or you'll be eaten by the dragon!" The hysterical tempo of the drumming and the increasing darkness made it very believable to us children.

MY PARENTS' SERVANTS

You always have to picture the houses and rooms in the Indies of that time as being quite spacious. Our *babu* or housemaid, Sanem, and our cook, who was always called "Koki" for as long as I knew her, slept in the servant's room. Koki is the Indonesian term for cook. To this day, I still don't know Koki's real name. I imagine she may have forgotten it herself.

Sanem, pronounced Sahnum, was the housemaid and took care of the bedrooms. Naturally, Koki bossed the kitchen. We also had a houseboy, who served our food and kept the other rooms of the house clean. The gardener took care of the garden, assisted by our driver after he had finished taking care of our horses and had polished the harnesses. All together, we had five servants. What a luxury! Many of our compatriots had as many servants or more, however. In California by contrast, I have to do everything myself, and everything is taken care of quite nicely, if I may say so myself.

Sanem was a pleasant, plump woman, who was always munching something. My father used to greet her in Dutch with the words, "Sanem, you old *bon-vivant*, are you eating something again!" teasing her a bit. And she would answer promptly, smiling shyly, "*Inggih 'ndoro,*" "Yes, sir," as if she understood him. Sanem never chewed *sirih* (the Indonesian term for betel nut), but Koki did. Mother forbade Koki to chew sirih when she was cooking, for she was afraid the chew would inadvertently end up in the soup.

Koki had another very bad habit, which was more or less condoned by the government at that time, because it brought in a tidy sum of money in extra tax; it was wrong, but that's the way it was. Koki was addicted to opium, which she could buy in limited amounts from an opium den, near the pasar in Talun. It was sold in tiny, square, flat, tin cans. During the afternoon hours, when everybody took a nap, she would lie down on her side on her platform bed of woven bamboo in the semi-darkness of the servants' room. On a small bedside table stood a smoking oil lamp, its flame

33

flickering spasmodically; in her hand, an opium pipe. An opium pipe is made from bamboo and ends in a round head with a tiny hole in it. She would push a tiny amount of opium into this hole and hold it over the flame, inhaling greedily. Then I would notice her eyes closing, rolling back in a half-dream, and she would lay there motionless. Enjoying what? Visions maybe, which the opium conjured up for her. Or did she feel physically refreshed after all those hours of labor in the kitchen? After a while, the scene would be repeated, and when the opium had been inhaled with a soft but sharp tick, she would fall again in her half-dream. The room always smelled strangely sweet. I'll never forget that smell.

Koki threw away her hard-earned money that way, while Sanem spent hers on food. You could see Koki getting more and more skinny, but she was a tough woman. She never failed to show up for work, was never sick, and she cooked like a dream. I'll tell you more about Koki and Sanem later on.

PETS

I really love animals and I used to bring home all kinds of sick animals, most of whom would die sooner or later in spite of loving care.

First we had a black, long-haired dog, a tenggerese or dog from the Tengger mountain region, named Moortje (Little Blackie). Unfortunately, Moortje was bitten by a rabid dog and had to be put to sleep. I grieved so deeply that I was unable to sleep for several nights in a row. Then we had two pointers, Lady and Lord, that were also bitten by a rabid dog, and a veterinarian had to put them to sleep too. Those were terrible experiences. In the old Indies, rabies was endemic. Only much later could you vaccinate dogs against this dreaded disease.

All of a sudden, we didn't have any dogs anymore, but we did have cats instead: Roo-Roo, an orange tom, and Witje or Whitey, a female. You get it, the cat population increased twice a year, but, after spoiling the kittens to our heart's content, we were always able to find them good homes. In the Indies, you were allowed to have as many pets as you wished and everyone loved animals over there.

The number of pigeons increased also and I suspect that the gardener made them into pigeon pie when I wasn't looking.

SOCIAL LIFE IN PAGAH

Along the road between Pagah and Talun lived several Indo families. The De La Combé family lived in a small valley planted with banana and cassava. The head of the household was an Indo, who worked as a field employee on the sugar mill "Kenongo." His wife was Javanese. His ancestors were reportedly related to French nobility. The same was said of the Chauvignie de Blot family, who lived farther down the road. Here too, the husband was an Indo and the wife was Javanese.

Then came a family in which both parents were Indo, with a slew of kids—ten to be exact—the Landegent family. Frieda, the middle daughter, who was my age, became my friend. She taught me how to play jacks. Near the station in Talun lived the Weynveldt family. The husband was an uncle of Dave Weynveldt, the well-known soccer player, who later married one of my nieces. Next to the Weynveldts lived the stationmaster, by the name of Padberg. He was an Indo and his wife was Javanese.

Catty-corner across the road from the latter lived the Crawford family. Husband and wife were both Indo and they only had boys. I still remember the father of the boys, a plump man, whose voice always sounded hoarse and whispery. Why? I've never been able to find out.

My parents kept in touch with friendly families by sending our house servant over with a message slate consisting of two slates fastened together with hinges, so that they could be closed like a book. On one side, Moes would write her message, and the addressee would write an answer on the other slate. Sometimes this exchange of messages would be accompanied by a gift of food. This gift usually took the form of some homemade delicacy, neatly arranged on a tray and covered with a crocheted, white doily. I liked the tradition of the message slates, but I liked the gifts of food even more.

36

The ladies would visit each other dressed in the most beautiful batik sarongs and dress kebayas of white voile, richly edged with the prettiest lace you can imagine. The costume was completed with a parasol held against the hot sun, dainty beaded sandals, and a beaded purse to hold the sparingly perfumed handkerchief. The most popular perfume of the day was genuine Eau de Cologne No. 4711, which has a refreshing citrus scent.

Perhaps even more than visits from friends, my parents loved parties. We would often be left home and Oma Maria would come over from Blitar to babysit. Well, we didn't mind that at all. Our sweet oma would sit next to us on the floor and tell us in her broken Dutch about her own childhood, or she would tell us Javanese folk tales while massaging our legs or our arms.

If my parents stayed away longer than usual, it meant that they had to take part in an amateur theater performance in a distant town once again. Wlingi, Blitar, and Kediri all had their own country club or *societeit*, "*soos*" for short, and they would travel there to share their acting talents with the public. Usually, both of my parents would have the leading roles.

In addition, they often had to go to audiences given by the local *regent*, a high-ranking Javanese official, the resident, or some other authority. That meant full dress. Father would be dressed in black tails and bow tie. Then, to get mother properly dressed was a ritual in itself.

A tiny waist was fashionable at the time, and to that end Moes needed me. She would put on her corset, fashioned of satin, whale-bone and, of course, lots of lace. The ribbons, used to tighten the corset, were in the back. I would take them in my hands as if they were reins, plant my feet against my mother's back, and, pulling with all my strength, I would tighten the corset until she had achieved the desired "wasp's waist." Just seeing this done, made me feel short of breath. This was exactly the kind of physical constraint that I hated with a passion. Once the corset had been tightened sufficiently, Moes would put on a pair of long-legged silk underpants, gathered at the bottom—for everything had to be closed tight, very tight—and decorated with lacy ruffles. Over that a long silk slip. And only then did she put on her dress.

I have to admit it looked adorable. By that time, crinolines were no longer in fashion. My mother's dress was still in one piece, however. It consisted of a voluminous, ankle-length skirt gathered to a bodice, which had a high-standing lace collar stiffened with whalebone, a jaunty ribbon knotted around the tiny waist, and in the back the famous or notorious bustle, which bounced merrily at the lowest point of my mother's back, in such a way that her behind was accented. The bustle was attached to the bodice in a fan shape.

The latest fashion of that time decreed the wearing of either long sleeves or arm-length gloves and elegant, high-heeled, gray dress boots with umpteen buttons, each of which had to be buttoned separately with a button hook. I despised those high-button boots. We children had to wear them too, either to school or when we went out. It's a terrible, terrible fashion!

But it's true, my mother looked quite elegant, fashionable, and attractive. She wore her brown hair in a bun, but, alas, it too was covered, with an enormous picture hat decorated with ostrich feathers or, even more chic and more expensive, a whole stuffed bird of paradise in all its dazzling plumage.

Sometimes we were allowed to accompany our parents to one of these events and then we would sit quietly on the side lines, looking on while my parents danced the Vienna waltz, the galop, or the lanciers. They were so elegant and so light on their feet, absolutely magnificent. My father, even though twice as old as my mother, could certainly hold his own and danced with fervor like a young god.

On those occasions, people had to write down in tiny ball books or dancing cards who had claimed a certain dance. The male dance partner would then come and claim his dance at the appointed time. That ball book hung elegantly from my mother's wrist and it was always filled to the last dance.

These were rich and elegant events. I very much enjoyed watching that colorful scene with all those beautiful dresses, the wide skirts fanning open and closed in a whirling dance, gracefully held partly up and aside with the little finger held high in such a way that you caught a glimpse of the long underpants. Oh yes, believe me, even then the women were naughty and coquettish. It was fun to have been an eyewitness to this era, right before we developed new ideas in dress.

I might as well tell you about the first bra to which I had to submit myself following the tradition of the Geul family. My breasts were hardly visible, so to speak, when I had to be fitted for my first bra. At that time, bras didn't look the way they do now, not by a long shot. It was called a *kutang* and was sewn by our Javanese seamstress from unbleached cotton. It reached from above the breast to near the navel and was closed by means of a row of buttons in front. It had all kinds of pleats and seams to achieve a pronounced bust shape. *Aduh, aduh!* I fought tooth and nail against this restriction of my physical freedom. It was very confining and I hated it, because it was such a change from what I had been used to. I despise these undergarments to this day.

Before we sat down at the table for our afternoon meal we washed our hands and took off our school clothes, changing into *hansop* or, as I did later, into a shirt-pant outfit. That was nothing more than a white cotton panty buttoned to a sleeveless shirt. It was delightfully airy.

CHILDHOOD PLAY

After school and on Sundays, I went around in bare feet and dressed in a hansop. This is a kind of sacklike romper or playsuit made in one piece, usually from striped cotton, with a big pocket on the belly.

Everybody took a nap between two and three o'clock in the afternoon. My parents slept, but I was much too restless to rest or nap. As soon as I thought my mother had fallen asleep, I tried to sneak out of the bedroom as quietly as possible. But Moes would hear me no matter how quiet I was and would call out, "Where are you going?" Without a moment's hesitation, I would answer, "I have to go to the bathroom." "Okay, but come back immediately." Once in a while, I really did have to go to the bathroom, but even then I would ignore that room and use the creek, which invariably played a major role in my plans. I risked getting my mother angry, but that was worth it to me.

At the creek, I would quickly run up the opposite slope until I reached the recently harvested rice fields, still covered with stubble. There a Javanese boy, my buddy Mingun, would already be waiting for me, holding a self-made kite, its glass-encrusted line wound around an empty milk tin. Not long after, we would be engaged in a hot kite fight high up in the air. Kites in all colors of the rainbow, with or without tail, were my dangerous opponents. I would fight my kite against those of up to six village boys at a time, all of whom also used homemade glass-encrusted lines with their kites. Sometimes I would win, sometimes lose; but every time a kite got cut off and fluttered away like a wounded bird, we would all run to retrieve it. The rule was that the one to catch it first could keep it, no matter who its original owner was. Often, I would return home with three or four kites over my shoulder. Here, my angry mother would be waiting for me.

Moes would paddle me across my behind with anything at hand, usually with her sandals; now, that didn't hurt too much. But

40

once in a while, she would get the *sapu lidi*—a bundle of midribs of coconut palm fronds used to smooth the bed—and that would hurt a bit more. However, when she took the rattan handle of the feather duster to my back end, I would yell my head off. Then I had to take a bath, change into a clean hansop, and write one hundred times on a slate that I shouldn't be disobedient.

I don't want to omit the bad things in my life's story, so here goes. My own bad acts consisted of saying "dirty" words and teaching them to others; lying so cleverly and so quickly that it made my mother's head swim; above all, I was terribly disobedient. The temptation posed by sky, light, water, and river was invariably stronger than the threat of my mother's feather duster.

As far as I can remember, my sister never received a beating, neither did my father ever beat me. So, it would appear that the main friction was between my mother and me, even though we did love each other. Actually, it was mainly my own doing; I simply found the great outdoors impossible to resist.

In those days, we had school on Saturdays too. On Sundays, I would often go for a walk by myself, crossing a second creek and venturing into the next kampong. Along the way, I would chat with anybody and everybody. All the villagers knew who I was, the young Miss Rita.

By the way, my name, Marguérite, means "pearl." This led my husband later to comment, "Granted, but a black pearl for sure." "Now, isn't that fortunate," I would shoot back, "black pearls are quite rare, much sought after and quite valuable." Had to have the last word, naturally. I was named after a very close Belgian friend of my mother, whom I met later in Holland.

Of course, I played with my sister too, whenever it suited my plans. We played "Mistress"—she was the mistress and I was the maid—or we played jacks, or *cina loleng*. Cina loleng or *klontong* were Chinese vendors who went door to door.

A klontong would come around once a month, alone or accompanied by a so-called *kornet* or help. He carried two huge bales of stuff hanging from a carrying pole. We addressed him with "Bah" (from the word *baba* as used in Malacca, now Malaysia) or simply "Klontong." Every household had its regular cina loleng. The one who came to our house in Pagah still wore a braid, intertwined with colorful ribbons, hanging down his back. He was a friendly fellow with a wide and almost toothless smile. The two or three remaining

41

teeth were black and glittered with gold. He spoke a broken kind of Malay that was hard to follow. The braid, at that time an unusual decoration on a man's head, fascinated me. Once, I boldly pulled on our baba's braid, a definite no-no. Moes immediately boxed my ear, even though our friend tried to smile my mischief away. Yes, I was naughty.

Moes and the baba were old adversaries as well as friends. They obviously enjoyed the game of haggling that was sure to follow the unpacking on the floor of our veranda of the shimmering Chinese silks, ribbons, crocheted doilies and tablecloths, and finely embroidered pillowcases. It was a kind of sport in which both sides would come out winners. Once a deal was made, Moes would often offer the cina loleng a bottle of soda pop. He would noisily gulp down the sweet liquid and resume his rounds.

These vendors would announce their presence by means of a small hand rattle tightly covered with leather. Twirling it around, the baba let fly two tiny cotton balls hanging on short strings. You could hear the dull rattle from afar. They wore sandals made of strips of rubber and often also socks that were once white but had turned black with dust on their endless walks. Wide, black satin pants hung limply from a cord knotted around their waists. On truly hot days, they would wear dirty singlets, otherwise a wide tunic with long sleeves. Many of these klontong covered their heads with black, embroidered caps.

We children would greet the arrival of these vendors with a little Dutch ditty: *"Klontong, klontong, hola hij, loop mijn huis toch niet voorbij. Wij willen graag wat van je kopen, waarom dan zo hard gelopen."* (Klontong, klontong, don't skip my house. We want to buy something from you, why do you walk so fast.) Or we would yell in Malay, *"China loleng, buntut-eh digoreng,"* a little nonsense rhyme that we thought very funny. A pun on his "tail" getting fried, it could refer to either his behind or his braid. These Chinese vendors were an integral part of our Indies life. So, my sister and I would play cina loleng, a carrying pole across our shoulder with two baskets hanging from it, filled with all kinds of stuff. We could sometimes prevail upon Moes to join our little game—that would be a high point.

When I wasn't playing in the fields or indoors with my little sister, I had quite another diversion. I happened to be crazy about trains too. When the cattle fodder I discussed earlier had to be

42

taken to the train, this was done by oxcart. I would then climb up into the driver's seat in front and drove the team of oxen. This is quite different from driving a horse. You hold the ropes in one hand—no leather reins, as with horses—a whip in the other, and by ticking the oxen on the left or the right side with the whip, simultaneously calling out "yah" or "yooh," you tell them in which direction you want them to go.

The station in Talun provided lots of adventures in itself. I have written a piece, called *"Het Stationnetje Van Mijn Leven,"* (The Station of my Life), which was published in *Tong-Tong*, at that time our one and only Indisch magazine. This particular station was just a plain, insignificant, little one, which the express train, shrilly whistling, would shoot past with a haughty air. But every slow train would take a leisurely stop there, taking in water and wood for the fire, as well as passengers, who had been waiting for its arrival since early morning, either standing around or lying down. Most of them were Indonesians, of course, but from time to time there would be a Chinese or an Arab among the passengers. They arrived in hordes, with their cackling chickens, their plaited pandanus boxes, their tin suitcases, their umbrellas, and whatnot.

Indonesians were only permitted to travel third-class, on hard benches. The second-class was reserved for the middle-class; here you had benches with open-weave rattan seats. The first-class, which had leather-covered chairs, was only for the wealthy. Yes, discrimination was rampant, believe me. As a child, you thought this was normal; you never questioned this system as you were used to it. Anyway, I disliked the first- and second-class. They were filled with boring and starchy people. Nothing ever happened there. That's why I sat with the Javanese whenever I travelled by slow train eastward to Wlingi or westward to Blitar, and shared their food, which was always homemade and tasty. I never asked to share, but an Indonesian is by nature polite and friendly and won't eat in front of you without offering you a bite. That's such a nice tradition, specifically Indonesian; lowborn or highborn, it makes no difference.

Often, I would go to the station's office, where I felt very much at home, and ask a hundred and one questions. For instance, I would ask about the Morse code machine being manipulated by an Indonesian. He delicately pressed a handle, producing various hieroglyphics on long sheets of paper, which automatically fell on the table or on the floor. It was an old-fashioned, primitive telegraph machine.

Once in a while, I was allowed to *jegret* a white or green ticket at the ticket window. You know what I mean, don't you, the sound you hear when a ticket is pushed into a machine with a slot in it—jegret! The machine neatly printed the date, hour and number of the train on that ticket. Europeans were issued white tickets and Indonesians green ones. Children travelled for half-price and were issued half a ticket.

Both slow trains and cargo trains stopped at that station and had to shunt, which meant that they had to switch tracks and hook up to a different locomotive. It was fascinating to watch the switchman picking up the hook from a wagon at the very last moment and coupling it to another wagon, assisted in his task by the locomotive, pushing the wagons together bumping and grinding. I would often hop on a train that was switching tracks. Those railroad cars would stay at the station for a while anyway, waiting for the next train.

We would find pieces of lead, fallen from mailbags, between the rails all the time. We placed these pieces of lead on the rails in the path of a switching train, and when the train had passed, the round pieces of lead would be flattened into long, razor-sharp strips. The kind of things a child will think of!

My passion for trains dates from that period. I played with trains until I was fifteen. The locomotive got my undivided attention when it took in water, puffing out clouds of steam. Water gushed from a high, iron scaffolding into the belly of the locomotive, while the engineer kept feeding the blazing fire. It always smelled so good there, of burning wood and grease. The silvery steel connecting rods that drove the giant flywheels were to me a wonder in themselves.

There! A train taking off. First it goes jubusss, then jass-jass, then the whistle blows. Now it's moving ever so slowly along the rails, gradually picking up speed, a chain of railroad cars dragging along behind, and finally the sound changes into a steady duhduhgluk-duhduhgluk.

Ah, the station of my life.

From time to time, all of us would take the train to school together, and then the conductor would be put in charge of us. When you hung out the window, you would invariably get a hot

44

cinder in your eye, and then the fat would be in the fire. But the conductor would get it out for you though.

Out of pure bravado, I would often hang over the edge of the balcony between two cars, a dangerous thing to do. I did it anyway, especially over yawning canyons or when the train thundered over a bridge across a river meandering deep down below. Then you would feel a special kind of terror-pleasure thrill, you know what I mean.

Of course, I also travelled by express train. That was a totally different experience, for then I was accompanied by my parents, or at least one of them. On a long trip, a gong was sounded at 1:00 P.M. as a sign that the dining car was open for lunch. I looked forward to this with great anticipation. The express train had an excellent cook. We would be shown to our table and my father would place the order. I always ordered the same: fried rice with steak and pickled beet. Delicious! A lot of people ordered the same dish.

Whenever Moes knew in advance that we would be passing through a tunnel, she would stick two hatpins in her hat instead of one. She said, "We could be robbed in the darkness of the tunnel, or attacked, and then I've my hatpin to defend us." My mother's defensive strategy interested me no end. I would open my eyes as wide as possible in the darkness, in order to miss nothing of the anticipated struggle. But, alas, nothing ever happened. We used to tease Moes mercilessly about this.

Back home, the evenings had their own charm. For then, in the evening, sitting in our family room, with the lamps buzzing so cozily, my mother would only have to start, "Once upon a time . . .," and we would tumble over each other like a pack of dogs in our haste to sit at her feet. She would have opened a book with fairy tales by the Brothers Grimm or by Hans Christian Andersen. We absorbed and digested the stories breathlessly, those incomparable fairy tales brought to life by my mother's skillful intonation. Those were magical hours. Completely content, we were ready to go to bed without protest. After we had kissed our father goodnight, mother would take us to bed to tuck us in, not so much to cover us with the ubiquitous striped army blanket, but rather to kill or chase away any mosquitos with a sapu lidi and then to tuck in the klambu under the mattress.

The days would seem to rush past in a dizzying chain of events which to us children seemed very important, events such as floating

45

down the river perched on a banana tree trunk, catching tiny fish. We threw the fish into our well, resulting in complaints by our parents that they felt slippery things slithering down their backs when taking a bath. Pails of water were drawn from the well by means of a pulley and, via bamboo channels, deposited in the *mandi* trough. That the fish would come along was to be expected. So much for that.

The public road near our house in Pagah was surfaced with pounded-down crushed rock. In the dry season, it was always covered with a thick layer of dust that would be thrown up into the air by every passing vehicle. So, the road had to be wetted down from time to time, to keep the dust under control. And that happened in a genuinely Indonesian manner, very matter of fact and logical. Along the road ran a small creek, which was then dammed up with rocks, banana and other tree trunks, until the water streamed over the road. But the water didn't reach the center of the road, so it was helped on its way using the hard leathery bracts of the coconut palm. This wasn't done by just one worker, but the whole kampong would gather to help. I too helped out, naturally, even if I was mainly spurred on by the desire to get myself wet once again.

When the road was dusty, we would look for tracks left by snakes crossing the road on their way to another rice field. Their zigzagging tracks would be clearly visible in the thick dust. We followed those to the point where they ended, sometimes finding the snake itself half-hidden in the grass and water of a rice field. We watched the beautiful snake from a respectful distance. Usually, it was a long, harmless, so-called *sawah* snake, which isn't poisonous or aggressive. Often found in rice fields, they are useful because they eat the field mice that eat the rice.

In a corner near the rice fields stood the guardhouse, a shed without walls that contained the kentongan, the hollowed-out tree trunk on which signals are beaten out with a wooden stick. By day, the kentongan was used to signal the noon hour, when the workers could rest and eat. After dark, the kentongan was beaten every hour. Otherwise, it was used to sound alarm. When there had been a burglary or a murder, it was beaten twice in a row with short pauses in between, like this: tong-tong, pause, tong-tong, pause, and this could go on for up to half an hour. When there was a fire, it was beaten continuously in rapid succession until the fire was extinguished.

Every day, a woman would show up in that guardhouse to sell food: steaming hot rice with fried tempé, fried or roasted salted and dried fish, and pecil, a vegetable dish. You could get a banana leaf cone full of food for two-and-a-half cents, and it would definitely fill your stomach. Workers who didn't go home to eat could always buy a meal here. Often, they would eat on credit, and it was mind-boggling to see the vendor keep track in her head of every last cent: who owed her and how much. When those that had eaten on credit suddenly lost their memory, it would often lead to words. But the vendor would stick to her guns and win, as was her due.

When it came time to plant out the rice, I liked to help. I did it mainly to stick my feet in the mud and feel the sticky goo bubble up between my toes. But I also thought planting the young sprouts was a lot of fun. The *tani* (farmers) showed me how to move the tender sprouts from the seed bed to the large rice field, and how to plant them out in long, straight rows. Holding the young plant between thumb and index finger, supported by the middle finger, you pushed the plant into the mud. Thus we worked, bent over for hours, under the blazing sun. Later, people often asked me how I can stand bent over so long. I would invariably answer, "It's because I helped to plant rice as a child, and also because the Dutch poet, Father Cats, once wrote, 'Those that bend, don't break.'" Actually, he referred to something quite different. But it might be true, my early training in the rice fields may have left me unusually limber.

Most of the women and men who helped plant the rice covered their heads with cone-shaped bamboo hats or with scarfs, for even the thick hair of the Indonesians doesn't offer enough protection against the sun. Of course, I didn't wear anything on my head, for that would be confining, right? My skin, dark to start with, got darker by the hour. I loved to hear the women sing naughty ditties, the meaning of which I learned much later. The melodies were lovely.

Somewhat farther out into the fields, the men would be plowing the recently harvested, stubbly rice fields. The plows were usually homemade, and were pulled by kerbau urged on by the crack of the long whip handled by the tani as if he were a dashing knight errant.

47

I used to love kerbau above all other animals. They were such magnificent animals. With their grey backs and sides shading into a soft-pink belly, their horns curving up as if always ready for attack or defense, genuine weapons, they were the image of strength and iron will. Blinking their moist, melancholy eyes continuously against the obstreperous flies—such a plague for man and beast—they would twitch their tails with bushy ends back and forth.

After a hard day's work, these buffalo would be driven to the river. Noisily blowing their noses, they lowered themselves into the water, and I would instantly jump on their backs. The little boys who were their handlers used grass plucked by the handful from the riverbank to brush them off—all the mud had to go. The back of a kerbau with its coarse, warm hair is so familiar to me. A kerbau would lie there, breathing deeply, dunking and drinking, its large, black, moist nose with its pink nostrils opening wide, the mouth with the large, yellow teeth steadily chewing whatever it had eaten that morning, before the day began. Usually its food consisted of corn leaves and stalks or young leaves of the sugarcane, or it might simply have been tender grass and, for dessert, a pailful of ground chaff mixed with water and molasses. They would lie for hours in the water, like gray river rocks. I and the village boys would play among them, petting them or diving from their backs into the water.

When the rice gleamed golden and ripe in the sun, it was time for harvest. Here too, I had to be right on top of everything. The women showed me how to handle the half-moon-shaped harvest knife, the *ani-ani*. This is a cross-shaped tool, in the cross-bar of which a razor-sharp, thin, iron knife is inserted. You have to manipulate this tool in a specific way to be able to cut off the ears of rice. If you don't do it correctly, the knife will slip down the stalk instead of cutting it through. After a few tries, I figured out how to do it and harvested rice as if my life depended upon it. It was a lot of fun.

The harvested ears were tied into sheaves and set aside, later to be transported by a carrying pole. In one corner of each rice field, a couple of sheaves were tied together and left untouched. These represented the rice "bride and bridegroom," which had to bring fertility to the next planting and blessings to the owner of the rice field. Next to the "bride and bridegroom" rested an open tray, folded of banana leaf, filled with fragrant flowers, a small basket, plaited of young, yellow palm fronds, filled with yellow-tinted,

48

cooked rice, and a small earthenware brazier filled with burning charcoal, from which fragrant whisps of burning *menyan* (Javanese incense) billowed up, enveloping everything in a mysterious veil of divine blessings.

PUBLIC HOLIDAYS

In the Indies, we observed all the usual Christian holidays and festivals, such as Easter and Christmas, as well as Dutch public holidays, *Sinterklaas* and Orange Day, among others. Besides those, we had other diversions such as amateur theatre and children's operettas. Once I took part in the children's operetta, "Cinderella." To nobody's surprise, I was picked to play one of the wicked stepsisters, a part I apparently played with gusto.

Most of the local Europeans would gather in the "soos" or club in Wlingi for Sinterklaas and Christmas. Sinterklaas Day was and is observed on the fifth of December. At one Sinterklaas party, a so-called Black Pete, one of Sinterklaas' traditional Moorish pages, pushed me yelling and screaming into a gunnysack—the accepted punishment for a naughty person—to the amusement of the public.

We also observed Sinterklaas at home, the way it was passed down through the ages, setting out our shoes, stuffed with grass, in the family room on the night of 4 December. For good measure, we left a banana nearby. The following morning, we would usually find a chocolate letter or a genuine marzipan by our empty shoes, left by the saintly bishop and his aides. To make Sinterklaas' visit as believable as possible, my parents would scatter grass here and there, make hoof prints and even leave some . . . horse dung. We would follow the tracks all the way to the outside, filled with wonder and tense anticipation—Sinterklaas had really, really been there with Black Pete! The evidence was overwhelming.

Once I found in my shoe—you guessed it—Black Pete's switch, one thin sapu lidih. What a nasty surprise! The note left next to the switch was read aloud by my parents: "You don't get a present this time. But perhaps, *if* you behave yourself today, you may perhaps, and very much perhaps, get a gift from Sinterklaas this evening." I felt like crying. But, it was true, I had been very naughty again. As a matter of fact, it wasn't even that hard for me to behave myself throughout that day and into the evening, I was

50

deeply impressed by the switch and the note. That evening, however, somebody banged on the door and the pfeffernusse flew through the air and in our faces, followed by a huge package shoved inside by invisible hands. Once I opened the gift, everything was nice and easy again. Those were wonderful feasts.

I kept believing steadfastly in the Saint for quite a while, that good, old fellow. I can't understand the fuss they make about it nowadays, saying that St. Nick, the Easter Bunny, and so on, don't exist, and that therefore our parents lied to us and we in turn lie to our children or, at the very least, keep them misinformed, and that this has a permanently destructive influence on a child's character. Do we, our parents or our children show signs of having been permanently scarred, and are we unable to tell the difference between reality and fantasy? Do any of us blame our parents for telling us fairy tales? To the contrary, we used to *live* those fairy tales, we *believed* that the good bishop existed, and the Easter Bunny. Gradually, in the course of growing up, those fairytales would lose their gloss. But did it ever occur to us to accuse our parents of lying to us? Modern day psychologists and child specialists think they know everything. No doubt there will always be sourpusses who'll do their best to spoil the fun. I myself, however, enjoy keeping alive the traditions of Christmas, Easter, and Sinterklaas. Up to this day, we can't help laughing when we think about all the ways in which we tried to stay clear of Black Pete.

Orange Day, the birthday of the queen of the Netherlands, then Wilhelmina, was very festive. First, the schoolchildren would sing an aubade dedicated to the queen. We were dressed all in white, with orange scarfs draped across our chests, and held small red-white-and-blue flags.

Then followed a parade featuring children in various costumes. My little sister would be a flower girl or something like that, seated on a pony led by our driver and holding a basket of flowers. Once, I asked my parents to transform my bike into a white airplane with orange flowers on the wings, and I put on orange goggles. Our gardener had to keep the whole mick-mack steady to keep me from toppling over due to the weight of the wings. But I felt on top of the world, and I won first prize for "Most Original." And that even though I had never seen an airplane except in pictures.

The Indies were then governed by a governor-general, who resided in Buitenzorg, now called Bogor. He was aided by such government officials as, in descending order, residents, assistant-residents, *controleurs*, regents, *jaksas*, and *lurahs*. The latter three ranks were reserved for Indonesians. The Indies was divided into residences, each with its capital city.

Once a year, the governor-general made an inspection trip following the main roads, but mostly keeping to the so-called Daendels road, originally built by Governor-General Daendels. When the official itinerary was set, the resident would send out an order which travelled down the ranks until it reached the village chief. He relayed to the people the message, that we had to show due respect for the highest representative of the Dutch establishment by contributing our fair share to the decoration of the main road.

These decorations were made by the local people from young, soft-yellow palm fronds and the spongy trunks of banana trees. On those occasions, the inborn artistry of the Javanese came into its full glory. The most beautiful arches, wreaths, and flowers decorated the houses along the street through which the "GG" (as we called him) would pass in his open limousine, with a golden umbrella held above his head and dressed in full regalia, a white costume trimmed with lots of gold.

The locals would line the road several rows deep, and when he finally arrived, a *gamelan*, the traditional Javanese percussion orchestra, would loudly play the well-known welcome song and the natives would yell, *"Horay, horay, Gendral e tekoh. Selamat datang, horay!"*, which means "Hurrah, hurrah, the general has arrived. Welcome, hurrah!"

It was quite an event. The gamelan would play on till deep in the night, providing the musical background to the wayang performances, which always drew hordes of spectators. The decorations would be left up until they were completely dried out.

"IVAN THE TERRIBLE"

My father had a friend, also a Limburger, who was born in Maastricht, the Netherlands. He was the notorious Stein van Callenfels, a professor in archaeology, who was nicknamed Ivan the Terrible. He was quite an unusual man.

He was slightly younger than my father, a giant of a man and as heavyset as my father. He had wavy hair down to his shoulders—shortened a bit in later years—a black mustache and a long, black beard. He had the kindest brown eyes behind eyeglasses. He used dentures, with which he used to amuse us by pushing them up with his tongue so that the teeth would protrude from his mouth. His only two negatives were that he drank beer by the case and smoked *"De Weduwe van Nelle,"* the Widow, a popular Dutch tobacco, as if it was going to be taken off the market.

Even though he was employed by the Dutch government as an archaeologist and thus had status, he didn't care a hoot about protocol. When his presence was required at a certain function, he never changed clothes, but arrived still wearing his work clothes, complete with greasy food spots and sprinkled with cigarette ashes. However, bowing to polite society, he did put on shoes for those events. Otherwise, he preferred to go barefoot. But no matter how he dressed, he was always the center of attention wherever he went. He was a good raconteur and generous with his money.

"Uncle" Stien, as all of us called him, Stien to close friends, sought out places where ancient statues lay buried or were overgrown by ancient forests, or wherever they'd been left behind, forgotten and alone. Then he would order up some water and wash the monuments. Gradually, inscriptions would become visible, which Uncle Stien read out loud. These inscriptions were written in Sanskrit, the ancient Hindu language. I learned some mighty interesting things from Uncle Stien in the course of the years. He certainly broadened my mind.

The Javanese called him *Raksasa*, which means giant, and even though he was indeed an impressive sight, what with his height, his long-legged stride, and his dark beard, no child was ever afraid of him. Children would go up to him, full of trust, and walk with him, hand in hand. Although he stayed single, he was very fond of children and attracted children of all races like a Pied Piper. I adored him.

Most ladies kept their distance, but my mother got along well with him. She didn't look at this giant's outside, but at his inside, his innate goodness expressed in his eyes. He was always welcome in our home. He would invariably arrive by car and would step out dressed in a striped men's sarong, called *plekat*, a *jas tutup*, or sometimes simply a striped pajama top, and with bare feet. Jas tutup is the name of the heavily starched, white outfit worn by Dutchmen in the Indies, but it may also be used to describe only the jacket, as it is here. Uncle Stien explained that he dressed in sarong and jas tutup because it was the most airy and the most comfortable to him.

He liked to visit us, if only to speak the Limburg dialect with his friend, my father, once again. He used to call my mother "Meerke" and my father "Jean," following Limburger custom. As I explained, Uncle Stien and my father were both originally from Limburg. God forbid you would call them Hollanders, for those were another kettle of fish entirely!

Uncle Stien always arrived with a huge, square case of beer and several packs of "The Widow." You always knew when Uncle Stien had paid us a visit, for wherever he went he left a trail of dozens of cigarette butts, smoked halfway, and empty beer bottles. In spite of that, I never saw Oom Stien drunk; he was invariably jovial and full of interesting stories concerning ancient history or his own adventures.

When we were little, we often persuaded him to tell us the story of "Tom Thumb." He had his own exciting way of telling it, and when he bellowed, "I smell humans!" we would start screaming and laughing and scattering in mock fear, with him running after us with giant steps. Often, he would crawl around the room on all fours with us on his big, broad back. Then he would roar like a tiger, setting the windows of the house rattling. We loved that. He knew how to make those stories come alive for us.

He would assure us that he was descended from German robber barons, who had a castle on the Rhine and robbed passing ships of their gold and everything else. Well, of course, I never doubted that for one second.

When we gave him a kiss, we would bury our face in his beard for a moment, because it smelled so nice of soap and cigarette smoke. He would always arrive unannounced, and then my mother had to order Koki to slaughter an extra chicken at the last minute, for that man could eat! We children were sure the giant in "Tom Thumb" ate just like Uncle Stien.

When I was around seventeen or eighteen years old, I often stayed with him at his house on the shores of Lake Ngebel near Madiun, Central Java. It was a wooden structure that offered a magnificent view of the beautiful lake. The house was filled with tables and glass cabinets containing stones, rocks and skulls. If you walked a little heavily on the wooden floor, everything would start to rattle, as if these artifacts wanted to telegraph a story from the past.

He had a maid and a houseboy. He would simply hand his whole monthly salary to the maid, who had to take out her own share and that of the houseboy, and use the rest to pay for the needs of the household, including beer, Dutch gin, and cigarettes. Oom Stien trusted his two servants completely, and, as far as I know, they never let him down. The maid, a wonderful cook, also took care of the meals. Uncle Stien had nothing to complain about.

He used to sit on the toilet with the door opened wide to the outside. To give notice of his presence there, a chair was set in front of the open door. Then, everyone knew, the Grand Seigneur occupied his throne. He left the door open in order to enjoy the view over the lake. Well of course, I had to see for myself how Uncle Stien sat there in all his glory. So I strolled past, threw him a sidewise glance, and didn't know how fast to run on, Uncle Stien roaring out hell and damnation after me.

He had a beautiful voice, warm and sonorous, and it carried far. I think his voice sounded just right to sing the *Kol Nidre*, a Jewish mourning chant. He could speak many native languages. Once I heard him talking with a regent, a high-ranking Javanese official, in high Javanese, a beautiful and refined language. Their conversation sounded almost like music to me. That's how I found

55

out that he was well-versed in the style that was spoken at the Javanese court.

Sometimes, I imagine that Moses looked just like him: tall, dignified and bearded. I own one of the books written about him, titled *Iwan de Verschrikkelijke* (Ivan the Terrible), and that one contains a lot of anecdotes of which I have no first hand knowledge.

He died in Ceylon (Sri Lanka), suffering with delirium tremens, and found there a lonely grave. Another version says he died of pneumonia. That such a brilliant man had to come to such a tragic end! He never had a real home. In his search for archaeological objects, he was forever going from place to place all over the world, where he was welcomed and honored by both low and mighty.

Yes, I feel privileged having known this exceptional man. I'll always treasure his friendship and memory.

OMA MARIA'S HOUSE IN BLITAR

To our great delight, we often got to stay at Oma's house in Blitar. Oma's house is worth describing in some detail. My grandparents, Opa and Oma Geul, had fifteen children, so naturally they had to have a large house built. Several of my uncles had already died by the time I was born, but the house, with all its rooms, still stood there like a rock.

When I was about eleven, my mother and two of her sisters were the only daughters left to Opa and Oma. The three Geul daughters were the first girls to ride a bike in public, dressed in long, lace-edged embroidered pants pulled tight around the ankles with laces. They wore straw hats, trimmed with a black ribbon and paper flowers. Their daring excursion caused a tremendous hubbub among the good people of Blitar. Of all things, they achieved this feat on those weird looking bicycles, those high ones, with a huge front wheel and a tiny rear wheel. Of course, I only saw this on photographs. When we children were born, all methods of transportation had changed again.

Admittedly huge, Opa and Oma Geul's house was nevertheless typical for the Indies of their era. A stone wall separated the front garden from the public road. The top of the wall undulated and the top of each "wave" terminated in a small platform. We would play on the wall, running down each section and then up again, resting a moment on each platform. There may have been as many as fifteen sections and as many platforms, for the garden was vast. There were two entries, designed in such a way that either of them led vehicles to a portico roofed over with corrugated tin, where the occupants could alight and go up a wide stairway to the spacious veranda.

In the front yard, eight *manggistan* trees marched down the wall. These regularly produced hundreds of toothsome fruits. Manggistan trees are beautiful, with leaves that are brownish red on top and green underneath, and fruits that are also brownish red

57

when ripe. The fruits have a little crown of sculpted sepals lying close against the leathery skin. When this crown has seven separate sepals, it means you are lucky. Seven sepals also meant the fruit held seven snow-white segments inside, each of them tasting wonderfully sweet. It's a beautiful and delicious fruit.

In the same area grew two very tall and shady *rukem* trees. Their fruit, rukem, purplish red and sweet, was also puckery. Then came a longish row of whitewashed pots on standards, holding earth orchids in all the colors of the rainbow; they were so pretty.

Finally, you had the front veranda, in the center of which stood a large, round table, covered with an oriental rug, and encircled by about seven open-weave rattan rocking chairs. To the left and right stood game tables, each with four chairs. In the center of the back wall hung a large painting of Opa, whose stern eyes seemed to dominate the area.

A wide double door opened onto a vast hall, which gave access to five bedrooms and an office. Two organs stood in this hall: a regular, table-sized organ stood against one wall, and the other was at least three meters wide by four meters high. In those days, houses in the Indies were often high-ceilinged, so even this large an organ could fit in easily. Opa had this organ made to order in Germany. In the back, a cube-shaped weight was attached with strong, steel cables to a pulley. When we wanted to hear the organ play, Kromo, Opa's house servant, pulled the weight up as far as it would go. Then he pressed a handle and the weight would slowly descend, turning the music roll in the organ.

The music rolls for the organ were stored in glass cabinets in what used to be Opa's office, the first room on the left on entering the hall. The title of the music was written in beautiful Gothic letters on the side of each roll. The rolls had hooks that moved past various steel teeth, which in their turn activated the musical instruments. The music consisted mainly of well-known operas, marches, and Strauss waltzes. The sound of this organ carried far and wide; it was truly awesome.

The hall was lit by a pressurized gasoline lamp and had a large, round table covered with a red-flowered oriental rug in the center. On the left was a small, carved, wooden table with an unexpurgated version of the *Thousand and One Nights* on top. It contained the most beautiful pictures, and was off limits to us children. Reason enough for me to take a peek or two. Well,

58

believe me, I had a naughty opa! And, as if Opa wanted to avert God's wrath, a similar table displayed the Bible, with the most marvelous colored engravings imaginable. This Bible was leather-bound with brass mountings, magnificent. I have no idea who inherited this Bible. I'm sorry I didn't.

After Opa's former office on the left followed two fully furnished guest rooms. To the right were two more guest rooms, and then came Oma's room, which was filled with various intriguing objects. Besides the large, white-sheeted bed, her room contained a large, carved, wooden wardrobe and dressing table. The ubiquitous commode stood demurely in a corner, and the sampiran took one entire wall. On Oma's dressing table stood a bowl filled with water in which flowers floated—*pacar* (shredded pandanus leaf), arabian jasmine, roses, campaka and *kemuning*—permeating the bedroom with a typically Javanese scent. When you opened the large wardrobe, a very special fragrance wafted out, of flowers and of the batik wax used to create the expensive *kains* of which Oma had an extensive collection. On the topmost shelf stood a long row of large glass jars filled with candied nutmeg peel and candied tamarind; pear-shaped candies, which were red on one side and yellow on the other; *angirian* (roasted, sweet rice-cakes); and the famous Indies candy, *gulali*, sticks of melt-in-your-mouth candy, striped in various colors.

Oma, a Javanese woman, had her own child-training system: she would dole out her sweets once a day and no more. She was strict, but loving and good. I remember her with great respect and affection. The lower shelves of her wardrobe were stacked with embroidered long-waisted bras, slendang (carrying scarfs), *kemben* and *udet*. Kemben are wide bands of unbleached cotton that a woman winds around her hips and belly. Udet are narrow, multi-colored, woven bands for daily wear, that are wound around the waist and keep the sarong up. Here too were Oma's slippers, those for daily wear as well as the black, embroidered, dressy ones. Hangers held Oma's plain, white kebaya for daily wear; fancy white kebaya, edged with lace, and a couple of beaded, black velvet kebaya for special occasions.

Oma's wardrobe meant something special to me, filled as it was with other-worldly scents, the most wondrously colored batiks, and the variety of objects. Everything was kept in rigid order, nothing was ever out of place. It looked neat and clean, and smelled good, just like Oma herself.

Now the rest of the house. The hall led to the back porch, which was also wide, large, and open. To one side stood Oma's carved, wooden sofa with open-weave rattan seat and back, a footstool nearby, and a spittoon a spitting distance away. Across from the sofa stood the narrow table where we children ate. To the right stood the large dining table for the adults. All the furniture in my grandparents' house was made of teak.

On the wall hung an old-fashioned clock with a gong sound, and several paintings, all dealing with the French Revolution. Opa must have been a fan of the French Revolution, for he named several of his sons after various generals of this conflict and after rulers of that period, such as Napoleon, Cambetta, Lodewijk or Louis, and Garibaldi, respectively shortened to Oom Nap, Oom Cam, Oom Lo or Lou-Lou and Oom Baldie.

Next to Oma's sofa stood a carved sideboard in which the tableware was stored, at least the daily cutlery. I don't know what it was made of, but it had always looked yellowish and full of nicks as far as I can remember. The pantry opened onto this back veranda and, like ours, it held a Berkefeldt water filter, a cupboard, a rack with gendihs, and a pantry table.

This back porch looked out over the enormous back yard with various fruit trees, such as *sawoh, jambu klutuk*, a red-skinned, long-haired *rambutan*, a red-skinned rambutan with short hairs, and another rambutan with yellow hairs. Among these fruit trees stood only one flowering shrub, the *srigaden*—a giant bouquet of snow white flowers with orange hearts—fragrant and lovely. The backyard held no other flowering plants except in a distant corner, next to the wall separating the Geul garden from that of the neighbors. Here, in a bog, a *gandasuli* showed off her stark-white, heavily scented flowers. Gandasuli is the white ginger lily. In the same bog grew so-called "pump rods," a rush-like plant that was used in Egypt to make paper. I only learned this later. The brown pump rods with their tall, slender, green stalks were preceded by whitish plumes. We would pick them for the vase once in a while. Not far from this corner stood the horse barn. Opa kept six horses, to pull his landau carriage.

In the garden left of the house grew *langsep* and *duku* trees, and a *juwet* or *jamblang* tree. This side was separated from the neighbors' yard by a lantana hedge. Our neighbor was a pharmacist who had two daughters, named Lala and Lolo, and, if I'm correct, two sons, the youngest of which I had fallen in love with. Imagine that, a romantic eleven year old!

Opa had built a system of ditches criss-crossing his whole garden, fed by a creek. We heard the soothing sound of flowing water the livelong day. The mother ditch was dammed up daily and would overflow to irrigate the greater part of the garden. The gardener would hand-water the rest of the plants.

To the left—facing the back yard—and one step down from the back veranda was a more or less T-shaped breezeway. On one side, this breezeway ended in a pavilion, where a front porch and bedroom were also furnished with a table and easy chairs.

When you turned to the right on the T-shaped breezeway, you passed another guest room and an exercise room. The exercise room was jam-packed with various old-fashioned exercise machines, designed to strengthen your body. These machines required some strength to use, so we used the exercise room to play out our fantasies instead. Besides machines, there were also some very large books stored in this room, illustrated books with stories, which we read with ardent interest. We learned later that these books were off limits to us, for, as soon as it was discovered we had been amusing ourselves with them, they were taken away and hidden in some secret place. So much for the exercise room. Next to the exercise room was a bathroom with toilet. Then came another restroom, and here this breezeway ended.

On the opposite side of the back porch of the main house was another step down and another breezeway, which took you past the dishwashing porch with its drying racks and washbasins and the smoke-blackened kitchen, where the most delectable dishes for the daily rijsttafel were prepared. A door next to the kitchen led to the carriage room, where Opa's landau and the horse harnesses were stored. Facing the kitchen and then turning left, you first passed a storage room and two more guest rooms and then you stepped into the backyard. Along the length of this breezeway hung cages filled with various kinds of birds, among which the chatty *beos*, crow-sized black birds with orange dewlaps and ears, attracted the most attention. Beos are quite fun, and the things they'll say! Well, the whole day long they heard the servants talking and the mistress of the house giving her orders. It's amazing how rapidly those birds learn to talk!

A second pavilion stood apart from the main house. It had its own yard within Opa and Oma's—in my child's eye immensely vast—garden, and was actually a house in itself, with a front porch, dining room, four bedrooms, and a breezeway which connected it to the kitchen, bathroom and toilet. Each one of the pavilion's beds could hold four sleepers easily. In front of this pavilion grew a tall *klengkeng*, which I always climbed when I stayed at Oma's house. The way in which its branches grew made them easy to reach and climb. I would nestle down in the very top of the tree, which would bend and sway dangerously in a heavy wind. From this vantage point, I could oversee the railroad and look out for the train's puffing arrival. Usually, I was by myself, but from time to time I would be joined there by cousins, also staying at Oma's, or my brothers, if they were on vacation.

Often, I would climb over the garden wall—against my mother's strict orders, naturally—to see my Indonesian aunt, Kasri. She was the *munci* of one of my mother's brothers, Uncle Cambetta, and the mother of his children. By that time, my uncle had died already, but he had provided well for Aunt Kasri, leaving her a brick house in the kampong as well as several rice fields. A munci is an Indonesian concubine. Kasri was beautiful: slender, with pale golden brown skin, black hair knotted into a heavy bun, lips that were always red, snow white teeth, and a lovely smile for everyone, but especially for us children. Later, we discovered those red lips indicated tuberculosis.

We children loved to visit her, not only because we accepted her as family, which indeed she was, but most of all because of the many delicacies stored in large glass jars, ready for the taking. She made them all herself. My favorite snack was *ampian*, peanut brittle made with soft palm sugar. But she would also have *ondeh-ondeh*, golf ball-sized, sesame studded, deep-fried rice dumplings, filled with sweet, black bean paste, *krupuk Palembang* (white, puffy crackers, as big as saucers), and other delicious snacks.

My mother felt a bit embarrassed by the fact that she had a Javanese mother and a Javanese so-called "sister-in-law." She didn't socialize much with the muncis, of which there were several. When she crossed paths with them, she would nod graciously, but we children were told to stay away from them. Later, much later,

62

when we children unabashedly acknowledged that we had Indonesian blood in our veins because of our Javanese oma, she came to see the error of her ways. She saw that she had been absolutely wrong in trying to deny her racial background. Because of the scarcity of European women in the Indies, many Indos and Europeans lived with Indonesian women. It was truly pitiful and unfair, however, that, when a European woman came along, the munci more often than not was pushed aside, the European woman was married with much fanfare and the children of the concubine were either sent to Holland or to boarding school.

I admire both: the munci, because of her loyalty, devotion, sense of service, and love for her children, whom she rarely or never was allowed to see anymore, as well as the European woman, because of her love, evidenced by her willingness to marry a man who already had children by a native woman. It was not easy for either woman and very painful. It always left scars.

But in our extended family, the children did visit their mother in the kampong. Some of my mother's brothers never married at all and stuck with their munci. Nevertheless, even these concubines were not allowed to sit down at the table for meals or be present at festivities, even though they slaved in the kitchen to prepare the most delectable dishes. That was a crazy situation, if you think about it, and so unfair.

As young as I was then, I think I already sided with the well-known ethical movement albeit subconsciously. Later, when I had reached adulthood, I sympathized to a certain extent with this philosophy. I liked to side with the underdog, if only to play the devil's advocate. No, just kidding. Actually, I have always meant it.

AT OMA MARIA'S

While everybody else in Oma's house was taking an afternoon nap, she would be doing her crochet work on the back veranda, sitting on her sofa with her feet resting on a footstool. She crocheted the most beautiful bedspreads and not one pattern resembled another; each finished piece was prettier than the last one. When I sat down beside her, she would tell me all kinds of myths and legends.

She would put her sirih box on her lap and pick out a sirih leaf with her small, capable hands, smear some lime on the leaf, and add a small chunk of *gambir*, an herbal ingredient that contributes a sweet aftertaste. Then she folded everything into a tight little roll and slipped this daintily into her mouth. She would chew it a couple of times. As soon as the red juice began to flow, she would pop a tobacco chew in one cheek and then would resume her crochet work or just sat there, talking, one cheek bulging with the sirih chew. From time to time, she would spit some red juice in the spittoon nearby. You could see that Oma really enjoyed this treat. After she had lost all her teeth, Oma would first bruise the sirih in a small, brass sirih mortar with an equally small pestle.

Oma only chewed sirih in the afternoon, and only when she was alone and there were no visitors to entertain. For she didn't think it looked right to chew sirih in front of a *belanda* (a European). Can you imagine! But this is just an example of the inborn tact and good manners of the Javanese.

She always kept within reach a long sapu lidih with the last fragment of leaf still attached, which she used to shoo off the chickens and geese that were forever venturing onto the veranda to peck at some fallen rice or breadcrumbs. They soiled the floor, of course, but the gardener would shower them with water, chasing them away and rinsing the messed floor at the same time.

My Indonesian "aunts" would often come over to talk with Oma. They would kneel down in front of her and would talk to her in high Javanese and, listening to what Oma had to say, would stay seated with their legs to one side and pulled up under their buttocks. For Oma was a lady of means, the wife of a wealthy belanda and the undisputed mistress of a mansion—you have to show proper respect. Usually they came to discuss money matters, for they received some financial support, which Oma would hand out to them. But at party time, they were expected to show up at the big house and help prepare the food.

On those days, Oma always cooked the main dish, be it fish, fowl or meat. Nobody else was permitted to cook it; this was her special job. I can still see Oma as she used to sit on a low stool in front of the kitchen, scrubbing a fish clean, taking out the innards, chopping off the fins, and slipping the fish in a big pot filled with clean water.

Oma was a little bossy, but she was fair. She had a cook by the name of *mbok* Gales; a housemaid, mbok Seyot; a house servant, Kromo; and two gardeners, whose names have slipped my mind. All these servants stayed with her for years; they were loyal, honest and pleasant, and did their jobs to perfection. Oma could neither read nor write, but she knew everything as if she had just read it in the paper, thanks to the *kabar angin* (the grapevine).

In the afternoon, neatly dressed women would visit and show Oma the newest kains and sarongs, in the hope she would buy some. And this hope was never in vain, for Oma was quite fond of beautiful clothes. I would often listen closely, while Oma looked over the wares with the eye of a true connoisseur, separating the printed or imitation batik from the genuine batik, appraising each piece and the various colors in minute detail. I always breathed in deeply, savoring the special scent that wafts from genuine batik. I still take a sniff of every kain and sarong, a habit left over from olden days. Anyway, we people from the Indies have to take a sniff of everything around us, that's just one of our Indies' traits.

Oma always bought the most beautiful batiks. Of course, these were also the most expensive. She would try to drive the price down, and most of the time she succeeded. When she was done shopping and had received her change, it was our turn to beg a two-and-a-half cent coin from her. We always got our way, because Oma was in a good mood and happy with her new, beautiful kain and with the many guilders she had been able to bid down. We would run to the public road, to buy some *dawet* (a drink), or *gempol* or *es gantung*, the latter of which is shaved ice in syrup with a hollow rice stalk for a straw. Or we might buy some fried nuts, such as *kacang kapri, kacang arab,* or cashews. Cashews are the monkey-face-shaped nut of the *jambu mente* tree.

Once in a while—I'm not sure how much time elapsed in between—a *rampok* event was presented to the public. This is the most cruel and heartbreaking sight I have ever witnessed in my life. A sturdy bamboo corral was erected on the *aloon-aloon,* the town square, and a tiger would be set loose in it. In those days, there were still many tigers in the wild. Opa was also an ardent tiger hunter. He hunted them for their claws or skin, or to please a particular kampong. Certain tigers could cause great losses among cattle. The skins would later be displayed on the wall or floor of the house. The claws were mounted in gold and worn as fobs on pocket watch chains by men, or as pendants hanging on gold chains by women. I inherited such a thing myself, but, happily, it has since disappeared.

Once in a while, a tiger would be caught alive in a trap and then it would be set loose in such a corral as described earlier. The kampong men would jab and poke that animal with their bamboo spears, sometimes keeping that up for hours before the tiger finally died. It would defend itself with its mighty claws and teeth as best it could. Once and only once did I watch this drama for five minutes. I ran home heartsick and in tears.

Quite another, in my eyes, quaint custom was the so-called promenade. I believe it was held in the city's park once a month. At such a promenade, municipal musicians dressed in neat white costumes played waltzes, polkas, marches and whatnot in a cute, old-fashioned gazebo situated on a low hillock. Ladies and gentlemen, all dressed to the nines, would then walk up and down the park's paths. Shaded by towering *waringin* trees, the ladies would slowly walk by, hanging on the arm of husband, fiancé or friend, swinging their hips to the rhythm of the music, coquettishly fanning themselves with a pretty, hand-painted fan held in their free hand. I, of course, thought it a ridiculous spectacle: flirtatious ladies graciously bowing their heads to passing couples, with their prim little mouths and their dainty manipulation of fans. We children thought it quite silly.

Nevertheless, we children were also dressed in our best outfits. And we would run around wildly, getting in the way of the stately walking grown-ups. Or we hung around the gazebo, staring open-mouthed at the musicians, captivated by the sounds of the various drums, clarinets, trumpets, and other instruments.

At the end of the promenade, the ladies would gather in groups to be introduced to each other. The gentlemen did the same. Then the gentlemen smoked cigars and the ladies nipped at their cup of coffee or even a tiny glass of liquor, everything with the utmost decorum. Later again, the gentlemen would be introduced to the ladies and the conversation would get loud and animated. By then, some of the ladies were clearly getting short of breath, because of their tight corsets, and quite a few would start feeling faint, necessitating the quick and liberal application of eau de cologne. This usually also signalled the end.

The only time I didn't dislike the promenade heartily was when I was allowed to put on my sailor's suit; it looked grand and, what's more, it allowed freedom of movement. It was much, much better than those beribboned and over fussy dresses I disliked with all my heart.

We always spent Old and New Year's at Oma's. Uncles and aunts would gather from everywhere, their children in tow. Several times a day Kromo would take the landau to the station to pick up the visiting relatives. Their luggage, consisting of various tins, suitcases, cardboard boxes, and woven bamboo baskets were all piled high on a cart and pulled home by Oma's gardener.

Oma would sit on the front veranda in her rocking chair, and every time she got up to greet her children and their offspring, the large bundle of keys hanging from her waistband would jangle loudly. Her waistband also secured her linen moneybag.

My uncle or aunt would ask Oma, "Ma, where did you put us this time?" and she would take them to their room and show them where they had to sleep. The assignment of rooms changed every year. And every year, I was curious to see where we would sleep

By 31 December, the house was filled to the rafters. Everybody would take a bath. Then, dressed in our best clothes, we sat down in the open front veranda. Uncles and cousins would be hard at work in the front yard, stringing up firecrackers from tree to tree. We got fireworks by the boxful from the *kapten* Chinese, the local boss, who was good friends with the Geul family. The boxes with strings of firecrackers and a roasted pig were always delivered promptly to Oma's house. It was always a whole pig, barbequed in a special way by the Chinese—their own unique recipe.

67

Finally, the fireworks were lit and the noise made it seem as if all hell had broken loose. There would be *mercon tambur* with their ear-deafening booms; *mercon rentengan* (strings of rapid-firing firecrackers); *mercon lombok empling* and more. That could go on for hours.

Once everything had been fired off, it was time for dinner, another wonderful event in itself. Oma had prepared the goose for the adults. We children were served chicken, because we didn't like goose, especially after we had seen how that poor goose was prepared for the table. It was grabbed, its beak was opened wide and vinegar was poured in. After a couple of hours, it was caught again, slaughtered, plucked, wrapped in papaya leaves, and buried in a hole in the ground. The day after, it was rubbed with spices and fried. I've never eaten goose, but anyway, after undergoing this elaborate ritual, that goose seemed to form the culinary highpoint of our New Year's Eve dinner.

After dinner, we all trooped back to the front veranda. There, we could hear a band of street musicians approaching in the distance. It consisted of three Indonesian musicians—a drummer, a flutist and a violinist—who serenaded us. Invariably, they would be wildly out of tune. Oma would dig in her moneybag and hand each of them a coin. They thanked her in high Javanese and would regale us with yet another number. They seemed to enjoy eternal life, for as long as I remember, they were present every year.

Then the clock would sound the midnight hour and we would clink glasses, filled with champagne by our trusted Kromo five minutes earlier. We children drank rose syrup. Everybody kissed everybody, tears were shed, hands were shaken, and more fireworks were set off.

Once that was done, we children would run to the servant's wing for what was to us the true high point of the evening: *satay ayam*! Two Madurese men would already be hard at work, turning hundreds of sticks of chicken satay over the hot coals in their earthenware brazier. Hundreds of steaming hot sticks of satay were piled high on large oval platters and, accompanied by *lontong* and *sambal-satay* sauce, carried to the gathered family. Lontong is rice boiled in banana leaf to a compact pudding, which is served sliced. We children hunkered down around the satay-cooks and ate our fill from tin plates.

The day after, the *spekkoek*, homemade of course, was served and it tasted as always—lip-smacking delicious. The literal translation of "spekkoek" is "bacon cake." It is a special kind of spice cake, very rich and flavorful, that is baked in dark (spiced) and light (vanilla) layers, resembling bacon, hence the name. Spekkoek used to be reserved for New Year's Eve.

I can still see tiny Oma sitting in the breezeway in front of the kitchen, the bowls with cake batter next to her, the *pan bakaran* already at the correct temperature. A pan bakaran was a large, round, legged oven, in which you baked this cake. I think it's called a dutch oven here. It was set over hot coals and the lid was covered with hot coals too. At the right time (Oma, an old hand at this, knew exactly when), the lid would be taken off, the layer inspected, the next paper-thin layer of batter poured on, and the lid replaced. That would go on and on until the correct number of layers was baked and the first spekkoek would be ready for eating.

With endless patience, Oma would bake several spekkoek at a time. The whole house would smell so delicious, of cardemom, cinnamon, cloves, and other spices. Our mouths would water in anticipation. Oma always used real butter in those spekkoek, naturally. Imported from Australia, it was called De Blauwe Driehoek (The Blue Triangle).

New Year's Eve at Oma's—we called it Old and New—meant to us a feast with special, delectable kinds of foods. In addition, it was such a joy to see your uncles and aunts once again, not to speak of your cousins, with whom you played all kinds of wild games. The feeling of family was quite strong among us.

If the visitors stayed longer than just a day or two, they would play cards in the evening—four tables with four adults each—and then they would play whist until the small hours of the night. We children would be in bed for hours already, and then I could often hear words like "spadille," "manille," "basta," "ponto," "king," "jack," "queen" followed by the sound of cards being slapped down on the table, and I knew that again somebody had won.

Then the first storm clouds appeared in the blue sky of my childhood: my grandpa on my mother's side, Opa Geul, left us forever; he had reached the end of his road. I don't remember anything about his funeral except that half the town of Blitar was present to say farewell to *tuan* Geul when he was taken to his last resting place with all the pomp and circumstance of a wealthy and locally prominent man. I remember that my father had a long talk with Oma, and I found out later that father had been appointed executor of Opa's will and thus had to take care of Oma, little Oma, who could neither read nor write.

I can still see myself standing in front of my Opa's burial vault. It wasn't pompous, but it was well-constructed of marble, covered with a corrugated tin roof and surrounded by a concrete platform. In the back wall of the gravesite were portraits and names of long-deceased uncles, aunts, nieces and nephews, with birthdate and date of death, as well as a bunch of dried flowers behind glass. One name stuck in my mind—Victorine—it was so beautiful. It belonged to a niece I never knew. She died at seventeen from tuberculosis. So young! It affected me deeply.

After staying with Oma for a few more days, we returned to Pagah-Talun, our home, still feeling kind of robbed.

Not long thereafter, in 1914, when I was seven and my brother, Pof, was eleven, my parents decided to send him to Holland, so that he could get a better education. In that era, most people who could afford it sent their children either to Holland or to another country in Europe.

We went by train to Surabaya, where we stayed at the home of one of my father's nieces for a couple of days. That's where I saw my very first modern water closet. You know, the kind we still use today. The only difference was, you had to pull a long chain instead of push a lever to wash the mess away. Naturally, I squatted with my bare feet on the seat, *jonkok* Indonesian style instead of sitting down as you are supposed to do. And there were no cebok bottles! *That* was the worst part. So, I yelled for my mother, "Moes! Moes!". She hurried to see what was up, thinking something bad had happened to me. She laughed at my distress, applied the famous piece of toilet paper, and, at my insistence, washed me off in the bathroom. Yes, we may have been little children, but we liked to keep our bodies clean.

Then the day, or rather the night, arrived that my brother would depart for Holland. In those days, Surabaya didn't have a harbor yet, so his ship—the *Jan Pieterszoon Coen*—lay for anchor outside. It was dusk when we were rowed to the ship in a small, wobbly boat. My brother's luggage was taken to the ship in another sloop. Then followed the heartbreaking farewell between my parents and their first-born, who was leaving for a distant and strange country.

After the third whistle, we were rowed back to land and there kept staring at the ship, that slowly turned around in order to leave. In the filmy night fog, I saw the ship's lights reflected as a solid line in the gentle waves until the ship disappeared from sight. We returned home feeling depressed.

And then it suddenly became even darker in and around us, for we heard—I don't remember how, for we had no television or radio—that war had broken out between Germany and England, and that the Germans had deployed sea mines everywhere, specifically throughout the area through which the *Jan Pieterszoon Coen* had to pass. Everybody in the household shared my parents' anxiety. It was very stressful. It seemed to us as if the sun had disappeared forever behind storm clouds filled with unknown dangers. Fortunately, the captain of the *Coen* got the ship safely in port in Amsterdam, from where Pof could continue his trip farther north, to the house of my father's brother in Groningen.

In World War I, Germany respected the neutrality of the Netherlands. Even so, food was scarce in the Netherlands, and during the period in which my brother was growing from a boy into a young man, he didn't get a great deal to eat. When Pof returned home after the war had ended, he was as thin as a beanpole. In the meantime, we, in the Indies, also had to make do with less rice, the import of which had apparently dropped off. I remember that we had to eat rice mixed with coarse ground corn for half a year or so. It was quite tasty.

Not only did we have to deal with Opa's death and the departure of my eldest brother for the Netherlands, we also had to deal with the sad loss of various animals, one after the other, as described in a previous chapter. Yes, the clouds had gathered thickly overhead.

SHALL WE DANCE?

In the magazines and books delivered to us weekly in the trommel, I also saw pictures of ballet dancers. Ballet attracted me, and gradually something in my soul demanded to be expressed in a special kind of physical movement. I rummaged in an old trunk filled with discarded curtains and yardage remnants and fished out a length of voile. Draping the voile around my body, I tried out steps, softly humming a melody, moving my arms and legs in various positions and swinging my hips. I invented my own dances, and, surprisingly, they were always slow and stately. I devoted hours to this exotic activity, that seemed so far out of reach.

One day, my mother happened to see me dancing among the banana trees, with slow movements and with such a serious expression on my face. She hastened to snap a picture of me dancing and henceforth unfailingly supported and applauded this unexpected side of me.

A great deal later, my sister also got caught up in ballet, and it was strange the way in which Tje, the serious sister, would create merry dances, while I, the tomboy, exposed my serious side in the service of Terpsichore. This was exceedingly curious. Later, we even appeared together in a couple of children's dance performances. Much later yet, I danced solo in a public performance and had a small dancing role as a female slave in the Russian ballet, *The Firebird*. But at that time, I "was still young and pretty, and lovely to behold . . . !"

Ballroom dancing on the other hand was very much in fashion in the Indies. And so, you guessed it, I was sent to a dance teacher in Blitar. Private lessons at that. One day my mother told me, "It's time you learned to dance. Every well-rounded person is expected to be able to dance and dance well. We've found this excellent teacher in Blitar who has consented to take you under his wing." I protested, "But Blitar is so far away! How can I get there and back in one day, that'll be impossible!" "That has been taken care of. You'll stay with Oma Maria for the weekend while you have the dance lessons. You'll sleep over Saturday night and come back Sunday afternoon."

So, after school was out one Saturday afternoon, I walked the fifteen-minute distance from our house in Pagah to the station in Talun and there hopped on the slow train for the thirty-minute ride to Blitar. There, it was another ten-minute walk to my grandmother's house. I loved staying with Oma, but the dance lessons were quite another matter.

It couldn't be helped, however. Late that afternoon, I walked the short distance from Oma's house to the local club, the Soos. I was eleven years old, decked out in gleaming patent leather shoes, white socks, big bow in my hair, and a straight up and down bébé dress with a square, hand-embroidered collar.

On the floor: a square in white chalk. The teacher was a middle-aged man with graying hair and mustache and . . . bowlegs. The first dance steps across the chalked square—the waltz. One-two-three, one-two-three, one-two-three. It didn't do anything for me whatsoever. I couldn't keep my eyes from the bowlegs and kept my body stiff. Well, after three lessons, that attempt at civilized behavior came to a merciful end.

Was I happy to be done with that crazy stuff! But my poor mother! As far as she was concerned, I was a lost cause. Come to think of it, she was truly to be pitied—so many of her attempts to mold me into a well-rounded young miss failed miserably. On the other hand, my father just smiled behind his mustache once again, keeping his thoughts to himself.

A couple of years after, we moved to the big city and the world of sophistication. Here, my brother, Pof, was hired by the largest local bank. I had turned fifteen, without having resumed dance lessons. The manager of Pof's bank gave a party at his house. Or should I say mansion? Pof had to go. He had no girlfriend at the time, so I was to come along, lucky me. I really didn't want to go. Here I was, still a tomboy at heart and a klutz on the dance floor, pressed into service for an evening of fun. The good part was that the seamstress had hurriedly sewn me a lovely black-and-white striped voile dress. I also got a new pair of black patent leather shoes. Thus, nicely dressed and with a big black bow in my hair, I accompanied Pof to the big house on Gubeng Boulevard in the fashionable section of town.

First I was introduced to our host and hostess. Then we were taken to another large room, already filled with around twenty or so teenagers of my own age and some a bit older. As we were introduced to them one by one, I would glance at them (feeling quite ill at ease) and say in a friendly tone of voice, "Hi!" They looked puzzled, so I knew right then and there I wasn't acting properly.

Next the gramophone was turned on. Everyone already had his or her own partner, except for a boy I'd never met before and myself. Neither one of us knew how to dance, neither one of us knew what to do. Nevertheless, he was kind and courteous enough to lead me to the dance floor. There we stumbled around a bit, stepping constantly on each other's toes.

For want of anything else to say, he blurted out, "We're dancing well together, aren't we?"

I said, "Oh, sure. It's obvious neither of us knows how to dance. Let's stop this and go eat."

We left the dance floor, all too happy to put this ordeal behind us, and spent the rest of the evening stuffing ourselves with delicacies from the well-assorted buffet.

To my great relief, I heard the toot of my father's Model T Ford in front at 11 o'clock. Safely home again, I told my mother, "That's once, but never ever again!" I meant it at the time, but I can happily say I changed my mind later and spent many, many merry evenings dancing the hours away. But that's another story.

RECUPERATING IN THE MOUNTAINS

I often used to stay on the plantations where old friends of my parents worked. I called all of them "Uncle" and "Aunt." That was the custom in our friendly Indies society. Many administrators were totoks who had married Indies girls, and some of these happened to be our nieces, in which case they were actually family. As I wrote earlier, my father was once a planter himself and I still consider myself a planter's daughter. I felt quite at home among coffee and rubber trees or—on another uncle's plantation—among cinchona, tea, cacao, sisal, or sugarcane. I knew many planters, administrators of widely scattered plantations, virtual lords over their domain in the mountains. It was heavenly to spend a vacation with such an uncle.

One day I came down with malaria. After a quinine cure, I had to recuperate in a cool climate and drink a glass of milk daily, fresh from the cow. You guessed it, I protested loud and clear. I ask you, what sensible Indies child likes to drink fresh cow's milk?

So, I was sent to a cool climate, to the plantation Kroewoek where "Aunt" Mali and "Uncle" Westendorp reigned. Neither of them was our relative. Aunt Mali was a Belgian woman, who was the housekeeper—and I mean, housekeeper, not concubine—of Uncle Westendorp. Her last name was Hageman. Even though Aunt Mali didn't seem to be popular among our relatives and among other high hats, she had stolen my little heart.

In the first place, she had a lot of animals. She owned at least fifteen tenggerese, who would emerge from their dens at the arrival of each visitor. These were long-haired dogs with a black tongue, and they were quite adorable. Aunt Mali had given all of them a name. As could be expected, this colony produced many pups each year, but Aunt Mali always found good homes for the new arrivals.

She also had a large enclosure built in the shade of a rubber tree, in which she kept orphaned and injured deer. Next to it stood a cage filled with monkeys, kept there for the same reasons. You

75

get it: to me, the animal lover, this was paradise. I helped Aunt Mali feed the animals and I was allowed to play with the dogs as much as I wanted. The grumpy dogs stayed away from me.

Aunt Mali took care of any young, orphaned monkeys herself. She nursed them with bottles of milk and they slept at night in her bed. When I was on vacation with her and was allowed to share her huge bed, I would often wake up when one of those little monkeys started playing with my hair. I would shove him as fast as I could under the blanket, where he would fall into a contented sleep again.

At this plantation, the climate was wonderfully chilly and the air was clear. I enjoyed every minute I spent there. Oh yes, I shouldn't forget to mention that Aunt Mali had a couple of cows too, dairy cows, which provided fresh milk to the area round about. So, I had to drink a full glass of fresh milk every evening. Aunt Mali stirred in a spoonful of thick rose syrup to make it more palatable to me. And then, just to please me, she would read me fairy tales by Grimm or Andersen.

I can still see myself sitting there, freshly bathed, in my sleep hansop on a footstool at her feet. She sat in an old-fashioned leather armchair under a lamp, which shone down on her and the book on her lap. The rest of the room, my uncle's office, was in darkness, and every story which featured a giant or a dragon had me secretly scanning the dark corners of the room. That always gave me such a wonderfully creepy feeling.

Actually, my uncle's office wasn't that cozy anyway, filled as it was with heavy, old-fashioned tables and chairs and with only one single lamp turned on in the evening. The tall bookcases were filled with a large assortment of illustrated Lord Lester and Buffalo Bill books. You could buy these books for a dime a piece in railroad stations or in the train. I read several of these books from cover to cover; they were riveting and filled with adventures.

So, paying close attention to Aunt Mali's reading, I sipped at my glass of milk, and by the time the tale drew to an end, I had finished my glass of milk too. Oh, how I hated that glass of milk, but Aunt Mali's stories helped to sweeten it.

THE SPANISH FLU EPIDEMIC OF 1918,
AND MUCH MORE

Not long after staying with Aunt Mali, the flu epidemic broke out, one which would ravage the whole world. This happened near the end of World War I. At that time, it was a new disease, and our doctor advised us to treat it by drinking a mixture of wine and orange juice, even us children.

In our family, everybody was deathly ill with it except for my slender little sister, who stayed completely untouched by it. She helped us as best she could, assisted by her friend, Mentik, the girl from the kampong, who also was unaffected by the influenza. Tje and Mentik would mix water, wine, and freshly pressed orange juice under the direction of my mother and bring this to our bedside. Fortunately, a nurse happened to live with us at the time. She looked after the kampong people, and also cooked for us.

This particular flu epidemic raged for one whole month. Many Javanese people succumbed to it and literally fell dead at the side of the road. It was a truly dreadful disease. Rumor had it that it was caused by the war, which was said to have poisoned the atmosphere, spreading disease over the whole world.

But the hot wine and orange juice mix served us well. I would immediately feel my legs get all weak and limp when I drank that wine, a kind of prickly-numb feeling, and I still get that same feeling whenever I drink even one drop of alcohol. I rarely drink the stuff.

In this period, we lost little Miran, our gardener's young son. His tiny body had no resistance against that strong flu strain. All of us felt the loss deeply, let alone his parents. My father and Moes paid for his funeral. I can still see the little boy lying on the open bier, covered with a sarong, draped with strings of flowers. His mother stayed home while his father, assisted by friends, carried the loved one, his little head shaded by an umbrella, to his last resting place. We felt as if we had lost a younger brother. Even then I

77

marveled at and admired the wholehearted surrender of the Javanese to Allah's will. After about a month, everyone could go to work or school again.

In the meantime, the mail brought books ordered by my father, which dealt with World War I which was still raging. These were all picture books with commentaries added below the illustrations. The only thing I remember about those is a picture of Death, you know the one, a skeleton holding a sickle over the earth, corpses piled at its feet with the names of the warring countries written on their bellies. And there was another picture: two men seated on one chamber pot, one of them fat, with "Germany" written across his buttocks, and the other was labeled "Turkey." Not understanding its full import, I found this picture hilarious.

The news we received from my brother in Holland stayed upbeat. Germany honored the neutral status of the Dutch and didn't harm them. Nevertheless, everybody went hungry.

After the eruption of Mount Kelut, and during and after the world war, life in the Indies went on as usual. The sugar industry was in its heyday. In those days, people described it as "the cork which kept the Indies afloat." The mountain products also produced more money than ever, the tobacco industry likewise. I've never seen this myself, but people have told me that men would light their cigar with Indies one-guilder bank notes. Be that as it may, people were wealthy and the streets were "covered with gold." In those days, there were people who bought a new car every year from among the latest models.

The very first car in which we made a short trip was a Spijker. This model had lots of brass on the outside. The gear handles were on the outside and were quite long. You needed a lot of force to push these handles forward or backward. The car had a running board on either side. The balloon claxon sported a brass tube that ended in an open mouthed snake at the front. We children delighted in pressing on the claxon, which produced a loud "dod-ded-dod-deeet." The car had a sailcloth roof, that could be folded to the back of the car like a harmonica. When it started to rain, all hands got busy to get the roof back up and then celluloid panes were secured to the sides by means of large metal fasteners. Then you sat safely inside without fear of getting soaked. We drove at a speed of around twenty-five kilometers an hour and thought that pretty fast.

Because this was the first car to which the local Javanese got exposed, wherever we passed, hordes of them used to run out of their houses to look at this new transportation, surprise, and sometimes fear, in their eyes. When darkness fell, we would stop at the side of the road. Those who sat on the back seat had to step out, for the carbide for the car lights was stored in a space under those seats. The front and rear lamps were screwed off, opened, and the carbide was put in its proper place. Water from the river was then poured on top of it and, as soon as it bubbled up really well, the lamp was closed again. A match was lit and held close to a small hole at the side and the bright yellow light would flare up. All the lamps were screwed onto the car and we could go our merry way again in the dark of the night, illuminated by the acetylene gas light.

Once in a while a tire would blow, but that was no problem. These tires were the so called *ban mati*. They weren't filled with air, but were solid canvas through and through. So, when we heard "gejeglog, gejeglog" and the steering wheel started to go awry, we knew one of the tires had blown (sic). Several handfuls of grass were plucked at the side of the road and stuffed into the tire to repair the hole, and then we resumed our trip. Later, the damage would be repaired at a garage. The car's wheels had wooden spokes, so the ride wasn't exactly noiseless, it creaked at regular intervals. Yes, that was the first car in which we drove along the Lord's highways. It was called the *kereta setan* or devil's cart by the natives.

We ourselves didn't own a car yet at that time, but we could rent one from Arie Heybroek, a fat Indo, who owned two cars for rent, as well as a workshop to service cars among other things. In our district, quite a few adventures revolved around those very first cars.

Another breathtaking spectacle was the first launching of a gas-powered balloon in Wlingi. It took to the air with a Frenchman in the basket. This Frenchman was a true adventurer, but new to ballooning. Rising high into the air, he disappeared from our sight. We heard later, that he had come down in a waringin tree in Blitar. The local people had quite a job getting him untangled from that tree and they took him straight to the hospital. Besides a score of bruises and scratches, he also suffered a broken arm. Jean *le Ballonier* never repeated that adventure! But later again, other balloon skippers came who were better at it.

79

Now I have told you just about everything that happened to me during my early years up until I turned thirteen, except for the great volcanic eruption of the Kelut.

THE KELUT ERUPTS 29 MAY 1919

One day, we were having our noon meal in our house in Pagah when the house and table began to shake, accompanied by loud rattling and rumbling. Our house servant burst through the door, yelling at the top of his voice, "Earthquake! Earthquake! Leave the house, quickly!" My father grabbed me, my mother snatched my sister, and we ran outside to the lawn as fast as we could. We saw the earth going up and down like the waves of the sea. I immediately got sick to my stomach, as did my mother. It had happened so fast, I was still holding my spoon.

This was the strongest earthquake I've ever experienced in my life. Its epicenter was in the middle of an ocean and every country on earth seems to have felt its impact. It was horrendous, and further news of the quake's effect was even worse.

Fortunately, our house remained intact because it was constructed of gedek and consequently flexed with the movement of the quake, the same as most kampong houses. Inside, we had to sweep up some whitewash that had come loose from the walls. But the mill with its brick walls showed huge cracks here and there.

When I look back, it seems to me that that quake lasted a very long time, at least the way I experienced it as an eleven-year-old child. And it was truly awesome, because it was so mysterious and so totally unexpected. It wasn't something you could see or hold in your hand. We did hear it coming from afar, however, a loud, drumming noise.

For a long, long time afterwards, I had difficulty falling asleep. I was afraid of another earthquake, an invisible enemy that shook the world like a rag. In that period, I often used to slip into my parents' bed and, safely between them, finally could fall asleep. Isn't it true how, in a child's mind, parents can always solve all their children's problems? Children believe that their parents can protect them, which they really often can't, for how can they protect against earthquakes or other natural disasters?

Anyway, safely ensconced between two gulings, I would fall asleep, soothed by the rhythm of my parents' calm breathing. From time to time, my little sister would join us too and there was always room enough for us all in that huge, wide, Indies bed that was even larger than a king-sized bed here, in America. We would all share one thin, striped, army blanket.

And then came 1919. I was eleven years old. I will never forget this episode, because it caused so much grief and loss of life. It was two o'clock in the morning. I was startled awake because of a strange, rumbling noise. It didn't come from the sky, it wasn't thunder or anything like that; it came from below in the earth. I kept listening to it and the earth growled louder and louder. Suddenly, somebody knocked on my parents' bedroom door. I recognized the voice of our machinist. He yelled for my father to get up quickly, for the mountain had gone berserk and that meant that *lahar* (hot mud) and lava would be coming down. Pagah lies at the foot of a mountain called Gunung Kelut. Mount Kelut had erupted. Our house lay smack dab in the center of the danger zone, where the lava could be expected to find its way downhill.

I jumped immediately out of bed and ran to my parents. They had already started to dress. My little sister slept on like a rock, but *I* was hysterical with fear. Tje was awakened and dressed. In the meantime, I also got dressed, and all of us gathered in the family room. The house servant, who had been awakened too, lit the lamps and all the servants joined us indoors, anxiously squatting down around us. As if instinctively invoking the protection of the tuan besar, the local mill kampong people gathered on our back veranda, squatting closely packed together, fearfully awaiting the turn of events.

The earth kept on growling ominously. Suddenly, with an ear splitting explosion, a pillar of fire rose up, clearly visible to all, spreading a fiery fan of smoke wide and far. Then ash began to rain down, together with small gravel that clattered down on our roof. Within the blink of an eye, everything was covered with a blanket of ash as if it were a gray death-shroud. Tree branches groaned and shattered under the weight, birds came flying into our family room and alighted all over, chirping shrilly in fear and panic.

My father ordered a couple of men from the cowering, huddled crowd to come forward, told them to put on a hat and cover their mouth and nose with a moist cloth, and sent them up on the roof to sweep away the thick layer of ash. Volcanic ash is quite heavy, and our roof could cave in under the rapidly intensifying rain of ash.

We could hear loud noises in the distance, but they were different from the growling of the mountain; that was now decreasing in volume, even though she was still shooting small explosions of fire and lava into the air—a magnificent, albeit fearsome, sight. Much later, when I saw pictures of the mushroom cloud accompanying the detonation of the atom bomb, I recognized the same phenomenon I had seen years before, over the Kelut volcano.

By that time it was around five o'clock in the morning, and it was still pitch black. The anxiously chirping birds, feathers standing on end, were still sitting on the window ledges, the piano, the paintings and many other spots—a heartbreaking sight.

My mother had calmly made us some cocoa, but I couldn't drink it, because my stomach had shrunk into a tight ball with fear and uncertainty about what would happen next. She explained to us what was happening, and also that we might be in danger.

Half-weeping, I said, "I don't want to die. I don't want to die. Let's leave and run. Let's go where it's safe!"

Moes answered quietly, "We can't make a run for it, child, for we don't know where the lava's going to go. It's better to stay here and wait until we know more. And should the lava come here, you don't have to be afraid; it will grab you, and before you know it you'll be dead and safe in God's arms."

Can you imagine how I felt and what I thought at that moment? Fear grabbed me by the throat and we huddled against Moes, while our father sent his machinist to measure the height of the water in our river. If it was rising, this meant the lahar was seeking its way down along our river and we were in immediate danger. I can still see the machinist, seated on a large, flat rock with an oil lamp nearby, a measuring stick in his hands, while the rain of ash changed him into a snowman, or rather, an ashman. Each time he answered, "No," to my father's anxious query, "Is the water rising?" I would heave a sigh of relief, as did the kampong people huddled together on our porch.

All of a sudden we heard loud voices and we saw ten or so men, covered from head to toe by their sarong and holding flaming torches, entering our yard. Excitedly, they told my father that the lahar had arrived. It had come roaring down the mountain a little farther on, sweeping away their cattle, their wives, their children, and their houses. My father tried to calm them down and told them to await sunrise, when we could see what to do.

It was a night, or rather a morning, of darkness and horror, of fear and of not knowing what would happen next, while the lahar roared on in the distance, creating havoc in the course of its rolling, devouring force, while we waited and waited for it to come to us, to smother us in its fiery embrace. I admired my parents' serenity and their trust in the Highest Power, whose name is God. My own fear and lively imagination created the most hellish possibilities in my mind's eye, and I began to panic more and more. My little sister didn't understand what was going on and had fallen asleep again on the sofa in the family room.

The steady rustle of the rain of ash and the rattle of the gravel on our roof made everything even more foreboding, and our feeling of despair increased, even reaching out like a ghostly presence from where we sat to the men, women, and children on our veranda. Some of them began to pray to Allah and the softly spoken *hamin* (so be it) expressed their complete trust in Him.

It was two o'clock in the afternoon, when twilight finally broke through and the sun tried to peek through the clouds of ash. Around three o'clock, the sun overcame the darkness, the ash stopped falling, and my father went out with the men to see what had happened. Of course, I went along too. On our way to the place of horrors, more Indos and Javanese joined up with us and together we set out for our goal, pointed in the right direction by people who had already been there. We could smell the sulfur mixed with various other smells, and we knew we were approaching the area where the lahar had taken its deathly route. And then we saw.

Where once fertile sawahs had been and friendly little kampong houses, now I saw nothing but gray, smoking-hot lahar, spread like a death-shroud over all, wide and far. Huge, dolmen-like, gray boulders had been swept up with the stream and were now lying all over the place. The lahar had stopped flowing and it was already beginning to harden. To give you an idea of the height of the mud in that area, I'll tell you that, from where I later stood on top of the lahar bed, I could easily pick coconuts from a palm, which now stuck out only one meter above the surface.

The bridge over the railroad had been destroyed and now lay some distance away like a crumpled shrimp cracker draped over uprooted trees. Everything but everything had been swept away. It was a wasteland, with only here and there some coconut palms sticking their crown up above the mud.

We could hear people moaning; a heartbreaking lowing of cows or kerbau—it was terribly desolate and utterly hopeless. Where would we begin to help? What could we do? What must we do? We felt like crying. Thoroughly discouraged, we went back home.

Not long after, soldiers arrived, ordered up from Malang by the government. They immediately set to work, digging out the road with pick and shovel and removing the mud from the area where once kampongs stood. Soon enough they found human bodies, burned to the bone by the boiling-hot mud, unrecognizable. Dozens of animals were dug out of the muck. The stench was well-nigh unbearable. Some people were found with only their head sticking out of the mud, driven raving mad because of what they had gone through in that hellish night, because of their pain, that incredible, fiery pain.

Medical doctors and nurses did what they could. One nurse stayed with us. Our old home in Talun that was standing empty, became a temporary clinic. Here, the frightfully burned survivors were taken, nursed back to health and fed—men, women, and little children. I saw them—it was nightmarish. The doctors managed to keep many of them alive, but many of them died in spite of loving care. A sickening stench of death hung over our village. Everyone did what he could to bring some relief to the survivors and to those who had lost all they had.

I looked up at my Gunung Kelut, at whose foot I was born and raised, and I saw that my volcano had calmed down again after her lusty debauchery of the night before. She was still puffing some smoke. The smooth shape of her flanks had changed; a deep canyon had been gouged out of the outer wall by the force of the lahar.

You have to understand that the lahar of the Kelut or other Indonesian volcanoes is different from the lava streams of Etna's or many other mountains. You can walk alongside a stream of Etna's lava and photograph it at leisure; it flows forward at five kilometers per hour. In contrast, the Kelut sent her burning innards downhill at a speed of five-hundred kilometers an hour or thereabouts, towards the sea. That's what is so dangerous about the lahars in Indonesia—they roar down the mountain, but you have no idea which path they'll follow. There is no escape; their speed is greater than that of any transportation on earth, let alone that of your two legs.

My mother's decision to stay was quite sensible. For when daylight finally arrived, we discovered that we were in a two river area, right between two streams of lahar. God had looked after us and I am still alive to tell you about a gigantic, natural catastrophe, the eruption of a volcano after an eighteen-year silent sleep, treacherously spitting out her innards in the course of a nightmare. This was the Gunung Kelut, the Broom, at whose foot we lived and loved.

The eruption had changed the river Semut into a wild, roaring, muddy river filled with hot water, rendering it impassable. Semut is Javanese for "ant," and this river had the name Semut because it had a wide bed but carried very little water. To the east of us, rivers and creek beds had been changed into mudflows, still steaming-hot in spots. There, it was uncannily quiet now; there, death ruled over fields of mud, stretching as far as you could see, now solidified and silent, horrifyingly silent. The sun, sending down its bright rays again, showed in cruel detail the wasteland of boulders and mud which covered hundreds of people, animals and plants—forever lost, forever swallowed up by the hell of fire and heat. The mud reached so high that I could easily climb around on roofs where houses used to stand. It really was too much for me to grasp.

At that time, it dawned on Moes what my oma might have experienced in Blitar, the city of sorrows, which had already been visited by Kelut's lahars twice in the past. Blitar lay directly in the course of the lahar flow, and thus it would have suffered a third visit. We went to Oma as fast as we could. Coolies carried us across rivers filled with fast-flowing, muddy, warm water to the road that led to Blitar, where a car waited. This was the day after the eruption.

At the entrance to the city, the odor of the lahar and of decaying bodies assailed us. We left the car to continue towards Oma's house on foot. The city's leaders had already put all their manpower to work clearing the main roads, removing the mud and piling it up along the side. Wherever we went, telltale marks left on houses and trees showed us how high the lahar flow had reached.

Arriving at Oma's house, we were relieved to find it still gloriously upright. A part of the pavilion had been swept away, however. A meter-thick layer of mud covered floors and garden. My quick-acting oma had already set coolies to work. They were removing the mud from where it had invaded the halls up to the front door, piling it up in the backyard. Chairs and tables, all partly burned, lay scattered throughout the house. Even furniture from other households had come to rest there.

Then Oma told us her story, quietly, with wholehearted surrender to the Highest Force. Don't forget, this was the third time the Kelut had paid her a visit, not a friendly one, but one with brute force. But every time, Oma had been spared from harm.

She too had been alerted by servants of the approaching lahar, and the fiery "atom bomb" plume and explosion had been seen and heard by one and all. Led by Our Father, Oma had walked to her rocking chair in the front veranda where her loyal servants had gathered. She had closed the front door and waited.

Suddenly, she'd heard a loud claxon and saw a car jam-packed with people, friends of her, who yelled loudly, "Mrs. Geul, Mrs. Geul, come here and get in! We're fleeing to safer grounds."

But Oma Maria had answered, "No, you go ahead. If I have to go, I'd rather go here, in my house. You go on. May God protect you."

Hardly had she said that when she heard a dull thumping against the front door behind her and a wild thundering noise on either side of the house. The lahar had come and was flowing with incredible speed onwards, towards the road, where the two flows united like the strong arms of the giant Raksasa, picked up the car with fleeing people and smacked it down in a wild tumble of death and destruction, Oma looking on from her rocking chair in speechless horror. That car filled with Oma's friends has never been found. Obeying God's voice, Oma was spared and lived many years after. All of us were so thankful to find Oma alive.

Several of her chickens and ducks had found refuge on a bamboo platform bed that had come floating past. The lahar never got past the front door of Oma's house. Not a drop seeped through to the wide front veranda where she sat, awaiting in resignation the fate God had allotted her.

Even though in my memory it seems to have taken only a short time, it must have taken quite a while, of course, before everything was scrubbed clean and had returned to normal. Everybody helped everybody else. Here too, soldiers came from cities that had escaped damage to help the city of Blitar. The city jail was completely demolished and most of the prisoners had escaped. It was quite unsafe in that period, not only in town, but everywhere; people had easy access to damaged houses, where they always managed to find something they could use. During evil times, people's good as well as bad traits are spotlighted. It's true, however, that most of the looters were driven by hunger.

One of Oma's acquaintances was found very high in his flooded house, pressed up against the window grille right below the roof of the house—that's how high the lahar had come. He was still alive and, after intensive care, he lived several years longer, with a scarred face and a limp as reminders of the catastrophe. In this particular Kelut eruption, about five thousand lives were lost.

Another anecdote concerns a physician, his wife and two children. When the lahar arrived, the doctor was away on one of his rounds and his wife fled the house, taking one of the children with her, saying, "*This* is my husband's favorite," with the thought of saving him. She left the other child behind in its cradle. But the lahar overtook her and snatched the child from her arms, burying it for eternity under the mud. She herself was saved and lived on, with a limp in her leg and a guilty conscience. The other child floated around the room in its cradle. It cried and a nurse, who happened to also live in that house, found it and began to sing to it to keep it quiet. Neighbors later said that hearing her sing like that in that dark night filled with wild and fiery horrors made their hair stand on end.

Horrible things happened in May 1919, when the Kelut erupted. This event is forever imprinted on my mind. It is burned into the memory and soul of an eleven-year-old child. Later, when I was eighteen and in high school, we were assigned an essay of our own choice for our final grade in Dutch. It seems I described this catastrophe so well, I was asked to read it aloud to my classmates. At the bottom, my teacher had drawn a huge, red eight—that day, I received the highest grade in Dutch. Even now, writing this down, I can see and feel every detail as clearly as if I were there again. It's hard to believe that once I truly experienced this.

Still, I can't help feeling affection for her, my Gunung Kelut, who is not a cone-shaped volcano at all, but rather a grand lady with a haughty air, a sinuous shape, and deeply carved wrinkles. Close to the top, her slopes used to be covered with ancient forests populated with tigers and monkeys. Days before the actual catastrophe, these wild animals left the mountain and sought refuge in the kampongs and towns downhill, and nobody could make head nor tail of this sudden migration. But *they* knew what was coming. They came down into the various coffee and rubber plantations, and then went progressively downhill until they reached the sugar plantations, the rice fields, the coconut palms, down, down, down.

SURABAYA 1920-1925

Then the dam burst—we had to leave our paradise, because we children were to attend the HBS, a prestigious Dutch high school. We were moving to Surabaya, a port city, which was a veritable metropolis compared to Pagah. I was to attend the seventh grade at the elementary school there, in preparation for the HBS. By then, World War I had come to an end and my parents decided that it was time to resume living together under one roof, like a true family. So, my brother Pof returned home from Holland.

In fact, my dear parents sacrificed everything they had achieved, and moved to the big city in order to give us the best education possible. It must have been an extremely hard decision to make, both for my father, who had to sell his beloved cattle fodder mill, as well as for my mother, who loved her garden so. This period must have been indescribably painful for her. But my parents always did everything they could to provide us with an excellent education.

So, it was up to Surabaya, the city which offered access to a variety of schools, and which was nicer and friendlier than Batavia (now Jakarta) into the bargain. But before we left Pagah, I had to listen to a long speech by my mother, which came down to: "We're moving to a big city and your free and uncivilized way of life will no longer be possible there. You are a young lady now. You have to learn to act like one and may absolutely no longer wear hansops or climb trees any longer!"

I was struck speechless. A big hand got hold of my heart and squeezed it. I ran to my room, snatched my favorite hansop, and stuffed it deep down at the bottom of my already overflowing tin suitcase. I still feel near to tears, reliving these good-byes: good-bye to freedom; good-bye to my animals; good-bye to my friends, the kampong boys; good-bye to the huge garden with its trees, shrubs and orchids.

My father had been hired as director of the *Landbouw Fonds* (an agricultural institute) in Surabaya and was also employed as inspector of houses. He had travelled to Surabaya a couple of times and found us a house there: No. 72 Slamet Street, Ketabang. This house was a great shock to us when we first saw it. Sure, it was brand-new, having been finished only a short time before, and it smelled of fresh paint, but compared to our former Eden this house seemed fit only for Lilliputians. And the garden, oh my, that garden was completely bare and oh so tiny! Just the sight of our new home made me feel terribly upset and close to tears.

The electricity hadn't been connected yet, but the day after we arrived we already had to go to our new schools. I still see my mother putting brown paper covers on our schoolbooks by the light of a Stormking lantern. She also sewed a cotton cloth cover for our large atlas. My mother was like a rock. Nevertheless, she must have felt deep pain and grief over the loss of her orchids and her grand old house. We children, or at least I, were sunk in our own sorrow.

The new house had three interconnected bedrooms. My sister and I shared the front room, my parents occupied the center room, and my brother Pof and two cousins shared the last room. We were indeed one big family again, united under one roof. Later on, a younger cousin, Eddie Geul, joined our family, and he was assigned to the back room. When another bedroom was added, it was given to one of the other boys. Eddie was the son of my uncle, Ed Geul. As I remember it, Eddie came to stay with us in order to finish his education in Surabaya. He probably attended a technical school. Eddie left when he had graduated from this school.

Our new house had a nice living room—we called it a sitting room—that opened onto the dining room. Our living room also opened onto a front porch, which was later enclosed with leaded-glass windows, at which time a small portico with a tin roof was added on to it, from which you stepped into the front yard. There was a small backyard, with an enclosed well for the servants' use, and a complete servants' and utilities wing, consisting of a storeroom, a kitchen, a bathroom, a separate restroom, and a maid's room. There was an area set aside for washing and line drying our clothes, and in front of the kitchen was the usual space for washing the dishes, pots, and pans.

On either side of the house was a breezeway. The one on the left was later fenced off, because we soon got a dog, a fox terrier by the name of Scoutje (Little Boy Scout). It wasn't long before our yard was planted with flowers and various other plants. A waru tree was planted in the front yard. It grew fast and provided nice shade.

We had been in Surabaya for a week and I had put on my beloved, blue-striped hansop once again and climbed a telephone pole. But my mother discovered me there all too soon and ordered me to come down. "Take off your hansop right now and change into a housedress! And bring me that hansop right away!" The hansop was thrown into the fire. This was truly the end of my happy childhood and the start of my life in the big city.

My brother, Pof, went to the new HBS not far from our house. My other two "brothers," Jan and Frans (they were actually my cousins), were in the same grade at the technical school all the way in Sawahan. I went to the seventh grade, and my little sister was in the third grade at the elementary school on Simpang. We used our bikes to get around, except when it rained, when a dokar was hired. And thus, bit by painful bit, I got used to life in the city.

I loved having my brothers around all the time. As I explained earlier, when we lived in Pagah, I saw my brothers mainly during their vacations. Strangely enough, I don't remember much of what they then used to do. Once in a while, we used to play together in the rice fields, flying kites, or we stole sugarcane together, or used catapults to bring down mangos. Now, however, with all of us older and living together under one roof in Surabaya, we interacted a great deal more.

At mealtimes, the seven of us would be seated around the long dinner table, and later, when Eddie Geul joined us, there were eight of us. It was always a time of animated talk, for everybody had to share his or her experiences at school and my parents listened closely. It was a very noisy table.

I forgot to explain that Sanem, our maid, and Koki, our cook, came with us to Surabaya. The food tasted as delicious as ever. I remember something very odd. We would always have potatoes and vegetables after we had finished with the rijsttafel. That was our own custom. My father, the totok, helped himself generously from the rijsttafel dishes, only to join all of us right after when the European-style course was served. It's doubtful, therefore, that we had this strange custom simply to please him. I admit, it was quaint. In spite of this, none of us was fat.

We had another food custom: about once a month we would be served potatoes boiled in the skin, which we peeled ourselves at the table and ate with butter. We knew that dish would invariably be followed by curried rice: a thick ring of rice served on a large platter, and, in the center, meat cooked in East Indian-style curry sauce. We thought it tasted delicious and different from the usual fare. Shrimp crackers were served as a side dish. We never got tired of eating fried tempé and gado-gado, a special Javanese salad with peanut sauce, day after day, and to this day I am not tired of it yet.

And so we grew up together in that house on Slamet Street in Surabaya, the whole family together once again. Then came a change in my life signalled by a change in the shape of my body. It happened when I was thirteen years old. One day, I felt a painful ring around my breasts, which had begun to swell. I asked my mother about it, and she answered, "Oh, all girls experience that when they grow up. The pain will go away eventually." Well, that much was okay as far as I was concerned.

Not long after, we went to stay at Oma Maria's in Blitar. Several of my young cousins were also spending their vacation there. One day we children were playing outside in the yard when one of my cousins yelled, "Rietepiet, you sat on a sirih chew! Look, your pants are red all over!" And that ushered in a new phase in my growth, one about which I was totally ignorant.

I ran inside, changed into new pants, buttoning them to my shirt, and ran outside again to resume play. But my cousins yelled again, "Are you sure you changed your pants? Look, your pants are red all over again. You just came outside, where did you sit on a sirih chew?"

Frustrated, I ran to my mother to ask her where I could have hurt myself making me bleed like that. For I had discovered already that I hadn't sat on a sirih chew, I was bleeding. She hadn't prepared me for the monthly menstruation. People didn't do that in the old days, it was taboo to talk about things below the navel.

Moes wasn't sure how to explain this phenomenon to me but she took me to the bathroom. There she used practically the same words she had used when I'd felt those rings around my breasts, "This is a sign, child, that you're growing up. You're becoming a young lady. Every girl of your age gets that every month." Can you picture me, shocked and protesting unhappily at this unwelcome news?

She went on, "And then you have to wear this cloth, to prevent staining your panties and *nobody* is supposed to see it. This is a secret of older girls. When menstruating, you're not allowed to swim or ride horses. You have to sit around quietly. No more hansops, as I told you before, only dresses, like a nice girl. You also have to change these cloths often and wash them out yourself by hand before handing them to the wash maid."

I was beside myself with indignation and anger at this sudden limitation of my freedom of action. And this only increased when Moes told me, that I definitely had to start wearing a long-waisted bra to support my breasts and prevent them from losing shape. Never before had I felt so deeply unhappy. I told my mother then and there, and with the utmost firmness I could muster, that I absolutely refused to wear those things and that the bleeding just had to stop and that I refused to have that happen every month. The rebel from head to toe.

Moes explained hesitantly that it couldn't be helped; that was how girls were made and I was growing up to be a woman. Disbelieving, I listened to her, questioning the truth of her words. In my heart, I suspected her of being the cause of this limitation of my freedom. Can you imagine that? A rebellious nature can lead you far astray indeed! But Mother Nature helped my mother by sending me pain in the loins and making me feel tired all over, causing me to be sleepy and move slower.

It took months before I was reconciled to this natural, physical, freedom-robbing change in my life. Later, my father would laugh heartily at my sense of personal rights and freedom, but that didn't help me at all. My father had a way of saying nonsense in a funny way, just to get me smiling again, like, "Grietje, can you still polish the spoons?" To this day, I've no idea what he meant by that, but my smile would return and my anger would be gone. After a while, I adjusted and allowed life to take its appointed course.

We had lots of friends and acquaintances. My parents had their regular card playing evenings, no longer whist but bridge by now. The piano had also been moved to Surabaya and we continued our custom of singing the hot new songs of the day together. The whole family joined the Boy and Girl Scouts and I slowly rose through the ranks from Scout to group leader of the "Red" Girl Scout troop, so called because we wore red ties. My brothers belonged to the "Black" troop. Soon we had joint campfires and joint Scouting trips.

A Scout troop consisted of four patrols, and each patrol counted at least ten members, the patrol leader included. Every patrol had a name. A troop was usually known by the color of its neck cloths or by a certain number. Thus, amongst others, Surabaya had the Red Girl Scouts and the Black Boy Scouts, as well as the Cub Scouts, whose members were under twelve years old. Later on, we also had the Chinese and Arab Scouts, each with their own color, but I've forgotten which they were.

Many of the Scout meetings took place at our home. My parents became honorary members of the Scouts. At one of our gatherings, Moes was officially given the name "Meerke" and my father was named "Father" of all the Scouts represented by our troops, encompassing all the non-denominational Scouts, including the Arab, the Chinese, and the Javanese troops. It was one big family, united by the Scout oath. Everything was very nice and idealistic, and done in the spirit of friendship.

Here follow the names, in alphabetical order, that I still remember from those wonderful Scout years: Anna Antonius, nicknamed Poetertje (from the Javanese *puter*, to turn), because she could never sit still; John Couwenberg, whom I would meet again in California, but that would happen much, much later; Darmadji, also Tjangah, because he was as tall and thin as a pole; Dien van Domburg Scipio, nicknamed Planchette, because she was extremely thin and flat-chested; Annie, Do and Broer van der Eyck; our cousin Wim Geul; our cousins and "adopted" brothers, Frans and Jan Geul; Boyke Haccou; Scout-master Haccou; Jan and Fientje Hehuwat, who could sing so beautifully; Richard Jansen; my sister and myself, Els and Rita Lanzing; my brother, Paul Lanzing, also called Pof; Evie Meyer, nicknamed Poes (Puss), because one of her eyes was brown and the other blueish; Helga Olsen, who had a Danish back-ground; Wim van Oorschot; Noortje Persijn; Suze Oudemans; Lotje and Jack Provoost; Nel von Schaick, also called Sheiki; Hoppie Siedenburg; Beth van Spreeuw; our leader, Mrs. De Uil; and Frans, Carlos and An van Lawick; An became my sister-in-law when she married my brother Paul.

Eventually, my parents were given official awards for their services to Scouting. My father got the "Golden Swastika" (the nice kind), while Moes received the "Golden Lily." My father's swastika had the arms going counter clockwise and had a French lily in the center. I think it has something to do with the idea of the trinity. You can find the same idea in the Scout salute, in which you touch the side of your head with three fingers. Also, the Scout Promise consists of three parts. We Scouts would always give each other a left-handed handshake wherever we happened to be in the world.

We used tents on our camping trips, or, in the rainy season, we might use empty factory storehouses or empty employee houses on coffee plantations, chartering trainwagons or trucks to get there. If the camping area happened to be nearby, we would walk there or take the bike, loaded down with our backpacks, tents, and what have you. We held many contests amongst ourselves. What a life! And my parents unfailingly took part in everything.

When we had a birthday in the family, we would learn little skits. Then the dining room was changed into a theatre: a table-cloth was hung to separate the "stage" from the living room, where the audience was seated and where Moes played the piano. We had so many cozy, wonderful days there, spent in true friendship and innocent fun, and with such a rich mixture of races in our circle of friends. We pulled so many crazy stunts; you wonder in whose brain they originated.

In the meantime, we all moved to the next higher grade. I went from the seventh grade to the Girls HBS, the so-called Genteng School. After three years there I took the teacher's course, from which I didn't graduate. Actually, I never wanted to become a teacher, but a nurse. I wanted to take care of sick people, but I never realized that desire.

As I explained, Frans and Jan attended the technical school. As soon as they had graduated after four years, they were hired as machinists by the KPM, a ship company. My cousin Jan had to give his job up soon after, because he suffered from seasickness. He was then hired by the BPM oil company and was sent to New Guinea (now Irian Jaya). Later, Jan was put in charge of drilling for oil in the jungles of Sumatra, the huge island northwest of Java. He soon married an Indonesian woman, with whom he had two daughters. One of these was born blind. She is now a resident of an institute for the blind in Holland. Jan's other daughter had a good head and was very pretty. At a young age, she married an employee of the BPM in Serawak, North Borneo. Her husband later rose to the top in his company over there in Borneo. I don't know what his exact title was. They have a beautiful house in the Netherlands. After Jan's first wife died, he married an Indo woman, a widow with three children. Together, they produced eight children, all of whom became solid citizens and live in the Netherlands.

Frans stayed with the KPM and was eventually promoted to chief machinist. He married an Indo woman and they had four children together, three girls and one boy. These children also became solid citizens and also live in the Netherlands, except for one daughter who lives here, in America.

My brother, Paul or Pof, and the Indies Baroness, An van Lawick, not only knew each other from the Scouts, but were also in the same class of the five-year HBS. They got married after both of them had graduated from this prep school. They have three daughters, all of whom live in the Netherlands. My brother was a chemist at the Gending sugar mill in Probolinggo.

As a young lady, I had many male friends with whom I went dancing or saw movies. Another diversion was offered by a newly started theater and art association in our city. Because it offered excellent programs, our family joined immediately. We attended classical concerts, the Russian ballet, and well-performed plays.

I myself once danced in one of their dance performances. I floated around in a rose-colored tutu with flowers in my hair, executing high jumps the whole way through. People liked my efforts quite well. Later on, I had to dance as a slave in the Russian ballet called *The Firebird*. I loved classical dance dearly.

As I look back on that period in Surabaya, I notice how much fun and pleasure filled our life then. We had all kinds of things to do. For a girl, it was truly an idyllic life of romance and moonlight, dance parties, and house parties. We would party at home, go to a dancing, or go to the Simpang country club, which was only open to the upper class. Hans Nepveu, my future brother-in-law, got me admitted to the Simpang Club. He was an air force officer. Actually, now that I look back on it, that was a lot of phony baloney, for it meant that you could only become a member of that club if you happened to wear a uniform or had lots of money.

ON THE PLANTATIONS

I was lucky enough to be able to spend most of my vacations on plantations managed by uncles or cousins. These relatives, even the cousins among them, were all much older than I. They were administrators of plantations in the mountains or managed sugar plantations in the flat lands.

I especially loved to spend my vacation at the plantation Soember Agoeng, managed by Nico Celosse, who was married to one of my first cousins, Do Geul. She was the daughter of Uncle Frans and Aunt Marie Geul. I addressed Do by her name. Her husband was a great deal older than I, however, which is why I called him "Uncle" Niek. Do and Niek Celosse had two children by the name of Niek and Marla. Niek much later had a tragic end—he was in the underground in the Netherlands during World War II and was caught and executed by the Germans.

Soember Agoeng's location was exceptionally beautiful. The administrator's house was built on the slope of Mt. Smeru. A long driveway brought you to the wide steps leading to the front veranda of this huge house. The floor was concrete, and the walls were constructed of double-decked gedek painted brown. The interior was simple, but nevertheless comfortable and cozy, with a lot of nice paintings and rattan furniture. There was an old-fashioned gramophone with horn and a dog-listening-to-His-Master's-Voice emblem, complete with lots of opera records. There was also a player piano with an extensive collection of music rolls, most of them containing classical music. The spacious and airy sitting room had a magnificent view of Mt. Smeru.

Standing on a slope, the front of the house was rather high off the ground, but the back was level with the lovely garden, which flowed in a riot of colors and shapes down the incline until it reached the mill compound.

The dining room was enclosed with glass on three sides and had a tiny tower on top, in which hung a bell that was rung thrice a day: early in the morning, it called the laborers to work; at noon, it announced the lunch hour; and at four o'clock in the afternoon, it called the workers to the mill to have their harvest measured. Several steps down and at the end of a long breezeway, you came to a two-room pavilion. Its bathroom and restroom were across from it. Past this pavilion was the vast kitchen and the storeroom. Somewhere on the grounds were the horse stables and the garage for the cars and trucks.

Seen from the distance, this house, its spacious verandas encircling it on all sides, rather resembled a small castle. It was flanked by silver oaks on one side and casuarina trees on the other. In the back was a small vegetable garden, in which I was allowed to dig up fat, pale asparagus, and—as far as I remember—pick tomatoes, cabbage, and lettuce. I spent most of my vacations here, in Soember Agoeng. I would ride horses, take long walks, play with the dogs (two great danes) and the six cats, and feed the ducks and chickens. It was a truly wondrous place.

Soember Agoeng was a so-called mixed plantation. The highest level, where it was also the coldest, was planted in chincona. Yes, I did taste the chincona bark. Of course! Don't you have to try everything at least once? Brrrrr, it was bitter, bitter, bitter. But at least, now I know what chincona is and where quinine comes from.

Somewhat lower down the slope grew tea shrubs. And even lower came the coffee trees. There were different kinds of coffee. The coffee was interplanted with shade trees—lamtoro in this case—and so-called cocaine shrubs. The latter had yellow leaves and small, fiery red fruits that resembled *letek* peppers, quite lovely to see. Now that I think about it, it's strange that I never thought to ask why those cocaine shrubs had been planted. I always assumed they were intended for green manure. I never wondered if they were indeed used to produce cocaine, or whether they were planted for the laborers to use. I do remember vividly that my uncle told me to stay away from them because they were poisonous.

Even farther down the slope, at the lowest level, grew rubber trees, which would change color in the dry season. It stands to reason that the mill grounds had to be vast in order to accommodate such a mixed plantation. Each division had a separate work area and its own employees.

When the freshly picked tea tips were turned over and over in slowly revolving drums under a blast of heated air (a process called rolling, fermenting, and roasting), you could smell the tea from a great distance. The most flavorsome and also the most expensive tea was called orange pekoe. The tea was sent off in crates that were made at Soember Agoeng.

The baled leaves were brought in by men and women and sent from the highest levels down to the mill by means of a cable transport system. Naturally, after a time some of the more intrepid among the workers used this cable to speed themselves down the steep slope and across a yawning ravine. One day, the cable got stuck and the men were left hanging right over that ravine. With a great deal of trouble and all manner of tricks, they were finally dragged to safety. That put a definite end to that fun right there. They had been scared off for all time.

I enjoyed walking through the rubber plantation. It was interesting to see the trees being tapped with a sharp knife, after which a small cup was carefully attached at the lower end of the cut to catch the latex dripping from the fresh wound. First, the worker would scrape off the thin crust of hardened latex and deposit this in a special pail. Then the new cut would be made, and white latex would start flowing down and into the cup. After a while, the full cups would be emptied in pails. The workers would then go to the mill, two pails filled with fresh latex carried on a pole across the shoulder, and a pail filled with crusts in one hand, to get measured.

Here, the liquid would be measured in a large tin tub, which in turn would be emptied into a huge concrete tank. Some kind of acid would be added to the liquid in the tank, after which the mixture would be stirred with large wooden paddles to bring about uniform coagulation. The thickened mass would then be transferred to rectangular containers to solidify. The resulting blocks of latex were rolled out into very thin sheets, which were hung out on large racks in a smokehouse. Whew! That gave off a truly obnoxious stench. Eventually, the smoked sheets were neatly folded, crated, and sent on their way.

I especially loved Soember Agoeng when the coffee flowered, the sweet scent spreading far and wide over hill and vale. The pure white flowers thickly covering the spreading branches resembled nothing so much as freshly fallen snow. An indescribably beautiful sight, all those blossoming coffee trees, like so many brides dressed in their pristine white. Then I would wander around for hours among the coffee, breathing in the perfumed air, not to return home until noon, the great danes constantly at my side.

I participated in the coffee harvest once. Coffee doesn't ripen all at the same time; red, that is ripe, berries are intermixed with green ones. Of course, I didn't have the skill to quickly pick the ripe berries from the fat clusters and I gave up after an hour. For the life of me, I can't understand how those women can keep on picking berries from the row assigned to them by the leadman, up and down the slope, for hours on end. I took my harvest to be weighed and got paid . . . five cents. A princely sum indeed. Well, you could argue that at that time a nickel got you at least ten times what you can get for it today; probably far more than that. At any rate, I took my hard-earned money to the local eating house, where I greedily wolfed down two portions of nasi pecil, complete with tempé and fried salted fish.

The coffee harvest was carried down the slope to the mill in gunnysacks and baskets. There were both men and women pickers. If the harvest took place in an isolated area, it was brought in on horseback. The coffee berries were then measured in a large tin which had increments engraved on the side. Each worker got paid according to what he or she brought in that day. I thought they were paid poorly. Few of them managed to earn as much as 100 cents a day. Most of the pickers earned no more than thirty to fifty cents for a whole day of harvesting coffee.

After the day's harvest was measured, the berries were transferred to large concrete tubs to be rinsed. Perforated baskets on a moving belt—called a Jacob's ladder—dipped the berries from the rinse water and transported the dripping load to other machines to be peeled. The peeled coffee would finally be spread out to dry in huge barns. When dry, the berries were fed into another conveyor to be sorted. Here, women would open a small door at the side, catch a certain amount of berries on a woven bamboo basket, and pick out any that looked odd or worm-eaten. The sorted coffee would finally be put up in bags and stored until transport.

The best coffee was the so-called *luwak* coffee. These were berries which had been picked out from the droppings of luwak, which feasted on the ripe berries. Luwak were said to only eat the ripest and best berries, and, during the process of digestion, the

101

berries also got peeled. What could be better indeed. I assure you that those luwak berries were cleaned with great care before use. My uncle and aunt only drank the best quality tea and coffee, naturally.

Early each morning, the *pesuratan* (plantation mailman) would arrive with his little pony to ask my aunt for instructions. He would take care of the mail as well as any shopping that had to be done in Dampit, a hamlet that lay in the center of the mountain plantations on the Smeru. Dampit was the central transport hub for these plantations and also had the only large store in that area. The mailman would keep the business and personal mail in a special leather pouch, which hung around his neck. His pony had two baskets strapped to its back to hold the shopping. This man had to store the whole shopping list in his head, just like our cook used to do, and, again just like Koki, his memory never failed him. An astounding knack for memorizing!

Very early in the morning, the mailman would go down the mountain, walking next to his pony along the rough dirt road to Dampit. By late afternoon he would return, and we would gather around to see if he had any mail for us and to see what he'd bought in the Dampit store. Yes, that mailman had an important role at Soember Agoeng. My aunt and I would always be present if only to offer his pony some sugar or a banana. She was just as fond of animals as I am.

In this life story I refer to her as "aunt," even though she was really a first cousin and I actually called her by name. Her husband was the same age as my mother, however, and, as I said before, I used to call him "uncle" because of that great gap in age between us. The opposite could also happen, where you called an uncle or aunt by name because they were your age. You encountered either situation quite often in the Indies, where, say, a three-year-old toddler could already be an uncle or aunt, while first cousins could greatly differ in age.

When I stayed at Soember Agoeng, we would often drive up to Malang by way of Dampit. It was only an hour's car-drive if the weather was good. We would see a movie or pay a visit to the Malang country club, which would often have something going on to entertain the planters, who loved to party and, above all, to drink. Those parties were always a lot of fun, and when the annual bonuses had been paid, Bacchus was king. Then people would appraise the latest-model cars with an expert eye, and buy them or order them on the spot. Everybody would brag about his wealth to everybody else. Or people would bowl. A servant set up the pins and rolled back the ball after every turn. And there were great billiards tournaments.

At that time of the year, the Indonesians would get their own entertainment on the town square, the aloon-aloon. They could climb a tall palm trunk greased with soap, in the top of which was a little bag holding twenty-five silver guilders. That was quite a prize in those days. They also could participate in bag and foot races, soccer games, and other contests. They, too, would have a merry old time.

We would also visit the Malang club on more serious occasions, however, such as for theatre performances, concerts, and the like. For instance, during one of my vacations at Soember Agoeng, sometime in July or August 1935, I forget exactly when, we received an invitation to hear the well-known head of the Dutch National Socialist Party (in Dutch, the *NSB*). This man, Anton Mussert, was scheduled to give a public speech. A totok, he was touring the Indies, visiting all kinds of towns, both large and small, ostensibly to get acquainted with the people in our archipelago. We had read and heard of his views and were on the whole warmly receptive to them. So, we drove that day to the club house, which we found packed to the rafters with planters, business men, retired people; you name it, they were there. I even ran into my own father and mother there, who had come over from Batu where they lived at the time.

We listened with great enthusiasm and open ears, vigorously applauding from time to time when Mussert said something that pleased us, laughing and yelling our support. Whenever he referred to our queen—at that time Queen Wilhelmina—or the House of Orange, he did so with apparent love and respect. We got the impression that the various social changes he envisioned for the Netherlands and the Indies would have the prior approval of the queen. Everybody felt satisfied with his presentation and reacted eagerly. When he had finished his talk, he asked us to bring the NSB-salute while calling out, "Long live the queen!" We lingered afterwards, discussing this good and noble man, who had just given us a glimpse of an appealing future.

Not long after, World War II broke out. Then we found out that our little Anton was in fact another Quisling (a notorious Nazi collaborator). It seemed Mussert had sold out our country and people to the Germans; he had given them information about the lay of the land and about people in the Dutch underground. We felt tricked, and were dismayed to discover that the man we had given our trust, was in fact a turncoat who had, by hook and by crook, induced us to become members of the NSB. Faster than I can recount this, most membership cards were burned or torn up. Various meetings were held in which Mussert was denounced openly. Our illusions had evaporated overnight. We stayed loyal to our queen, who managed to escape to London. It was a harrowing episode for us.

Some people in the Indies stayed in the NSB, but they never betrayed our country. It never occurred to them to become traitors or to befriend the Japanese, even though they remained free during the occupation. After the war, we heard or read in the paper that Mussert and his close associate, Blokzijl, had been executed in the woods around Waalwijk, the Netherlands.

To return to my visits to various plantations in East Java, my uncle, Ed Geul, another of my mother's brothers, managed a coffee and rubber plantation, called Blawan, on the Ijen plateau. Uncle Ed or Edie (spelled with one "d") was also called Uncle Baldie after one of his other first names. His wife was Madurese and had a little convenience store for the Madurese plantation workers on the back veranda of their house. They had no access to the usual native markets because of their isolated location. In contrast to Soember Agoeng, where the workers spoke Javanese, here they spoke Madurese, which I didn't speak or understand. My aunt taught me a dozen or so Madurese terms, that's all.

Their house was built off the ground on posts and had wooden walls and floors. Uncle Ed kept a pet deer, which he got as a nurseling. It would traipse through the whole house without ever soiling anything. Early in the morning you could hear it coming, trip, trip, trip on the wooden floor. Then it would push the bedroom door open and, poking its moist, black nose between the klambu curtains, nudge you awake, looking at you sweetly with its lovely, gleaming black eyes. It was so sweet and would follow you around wherever you went. All the guests spoiled it terribly.

When we stayed at Uncle Ed's, we would often ride to the Kawah Ijen, a turquoise-colored, sulfurous mountain lake. We would ride our horses through a forest of casuarina trees, softly whispering in the wind, and across *alang-alang* fields, where the grass grew waist-high. At that time, black panthers called *macan kumbang* still haunted these grassy fields. From time to time, the administrator's grounds or one of the kampongs nearby would be visited by a panther snatching a goat or even a calf.

It's strange, but I have only the vaguest memories of this plantation even though I stayed there quite often. As I remember it, Blawan was quite isolated. To get there and back you either had to take a *tanduk* or ride a horse from the nearest railroad station in Bondowoso. I used to be picked up at a certain spot somewhere, and then was carried by tanduk to Uncle Edie's house. A tanduk is a kind of chair with two long bamboo poles attached to each side. It was carried by four coolies. Along the way, the bearers would change places from time to time, to give one shoulder some rest. A weird contraption actually. I would be confined to that thing for a couple of hours, for it was quite a distance to Uncle Ed's plantation.

The first time I was carried along in that way, it made me very seasick. The men had to stop and put the tanduk down to allow me to get rid of the contents of my troubled stomach. They brought me some cold, fresh water from a little brook murmuring along the side of the footpath we were following, to refresh myself and rinse my mouth. They took good care of me.

I remember leaving Blawan on horseback, hanging half-asleep in the saddle in the deep of the night, headed home in unearthly darkness, a Madurese with a flaming torch walking next to my horse. Sometimes, we could see the red gleam of a tiger's eyes watching us from the shadows. Tigers feared the fiery torches. We would be alerted to their presence because our horses would start to snort and rear. It always terrified me when this happened, but the men guarding us would make a lot of noise and the tiger would slink away. I would be deeply relieved when finally the dawn broke through, making the world around us visible once again. The air among those trees used to be spine-tingling cold. But the sun playing peek-a-boo behind the leaves turned the forest into a lovely picture. It would become noticeably warmer the lower we got. Even though it was exhausting, every trip up or down to Blawan was an adventure in itself.

Somewhat lower down the same Ijen plateau lay the plantation Pantjoer Anggrek, managed by another brother of my mother, Uncle Frans Geul. Uncle Frans was first married to Aunt Marie, a nice woman with whom he had two children, Jan and Do. My niece Do was the wife of Nico Celosse, the administrator of Soember Agoeng, the plantation I described earlier.

After his divorce from Aunt Marie, Uncle Frans married Emmie van Ligten, a warm, vivacious, and hospitable Indo woman I called Moes van Ligten. She was a good organizer and an able amateur actress. They had no children. Their house was built on a hill, surrounded by an extensive, sloping flower garden. Uncle Frans and Moes van Ligten enjoyed people, so their house was always filled to the rafters with guests. Their house with its many spacious rooms could hold many guests. Being lower down the plateau, Pantjoer Anggrek was easily reached by car or truck.

Mealtimes, with everybody seated at the long dining table, were invariably relaxed and fun. The food was exceptionally tasty. Moes van Ligten didn't cook herself, but she had taught her cook all kinds of nifty tricks, resulting in a surpassingly good rijsttafel.

Once a year, she would invite about fifty needy children to be her guests at Pantjoer Anggrek. They would be housed in empty employee houses but would be served food cooked in the kitchen of the big house. The men and women who were in charge of these children would pick up the food at mealtime. Usually, these children would stay for a month. You could see them blossom, body and soul, putting some flesh on their bones and becoming more animated, the sun and fresh air painting a blush on their cheeks.

The Scouts, which our family belonged to, also stayed here once a year. Usually, both the Girl and Boy Scout troops would gather there at the same time, arriving by truck. In the evening, we would light a campfire on the vast front lawn and then we showed off our artistic side. My elegant, fine-boned sister, for instance, once did a "fairy dance" among the trees and flowers, flitting in and out of the moonlight, the fire casting flickering shadows. Her white, gossamer gown fell in loose folds around her limbs, conveying an impression of feathery lightness with every move to the music from a gramophone. It was like a scene from a fairy tale. Everyone was captivated by it.

I too would act out my love for Terpsichore, doing my own version of an Indian dance to the rhythmic beat of drums. I imagined myself to be Winnetou—the heroic Indian warrior depicted in the spine-tingling westerns of Karl May—the eagle feathers of my war bonnet standing straight up on my head, the long ends trailing down my back. Wearing a skin-tight leotard and moccasins, and brandishing a tomahawk, I would be off. That dance was me from head to toe, wild, woolly and full of passion, but also filled with dignity and pride—Winnetou was a proud man.

The guests who came to stay at my uncle's house came from various races and ethnic groups, but everybody got along with everybody else. There were Arabs, Chinese, totoks, Indos, Amboinese, Javanese, and each one of us had a special talent or something unique to share. The Amboinese among us excelled in song, having such beautiful voices. They were often asked to perform. There, in the moonlight among the pine trees, their songs with their peculiar hint of melancholy would sound more melodious than ever.

Those were delightfully carefree days, in which we learned from each other in a spirit of genuine friendship. We lost touch in the course of the years, due to various migrations, deaths, marriages, and simply because we grew up and away from each other. Once in a while, I'll wonder what happened to those of us who are still alive. It's odd, having spent so many years together sharing tears and joy how we have become strangers to each other. We used to have such a strong bond, and we used to enjoy each other's company so much, and it happened so naturally, without any strain or undue pressure. I find it a great loss no longer to have these kinds of friendships. As my husband used to say, "Sudah! As long as the skin is that of a child of God."

Napoleon Geul, yet another of my mother's brothers—we called him Uncle Nap—managed a rubber, coffee, and cacao plantation called Bajoe Lor in East Java, in the region which we called the *Oosthoek* or Eastern Corner. Here, too, I used to arrive and leave by tanduk. Uncle Nap used to ride his horse to the nearest town—I forget its name—to reach the outer world. He is depicted on the title page of *Komen en Gaan* (Coming and Going) by Rob Nieuwenhuis. In that book, he's described as being the administrator of a tobacco plantation. I think this is wrong, but I'm not sure of this. He too had a Madurese wife. They had one daughter, Coba, who was a great deal older than I, which is why I called her "Aunt" Coba. I have forgotten the name of my Madurese aunt.

Uncle Nap's house was also built on posts. In the space under the house were a lot of cages with various animals. Here I saw my first kangaroo. It had a pouch, so it was a "she." She hopped around in a large enclosure in my uncle's garden and was quite docile. She too was spoiled by everyone around. But I think she must have been lonesome, being by herself.

Here I saw my first cacao trees. They were beautiful, with yellowish green leaves and fruits that grew close against the light-colored bark. Green when young, the fruits turned red when ready for harvest. The fruits were cut open to free the ivory colored seeds, which tasted sweet. Those seeds were ground into cacao powder at the mill, but I don't remember how it was done.

SOJOURN IN SWITZERLAND 1926-1927

When I turned nineteen, I was sent to Europe for the "finishing touch." I was going to be turned into a real lady, whether or not I wanted this. I had been the group leader of Surabaya's Girl Scouts Red Patrol. They all showed up to give me a proper send-off when I left for Europe on the *Karnak*, a German freighter with passenger accomodations.

Aunt Do, my mother's sister, chaperoned me. Her name Do was short for Lodojo, a kampong near Blitar, where she was born and for which she was named. She hated that name, if only because it reminded her that her mother was Javanese. She never mentioned Oma Maria, except in passing. She was married to a German, Fritz Hanfland, who was the administrator of a coffee and rubber plantation in Lok Tabat in Borneo. Their son Fritz, whom we called Bub, was a student somewhere near Munich, in Bavaria.

Their daughter, Marga, was on the boat with us. My destination was the farm of the De Vries family in Onex, five kilometers from Geneva, Switzerland, where I would board. Nel van Dam, a neighbor and my best friend, was going too. Both of us had to learn to speak foreign languages.

A freighter is kind of fun. We stopped at places regular mailboats didn't go near, such as Athens, Greece, where I had a magnificent view of the city from between the pillars of the Acropolis. You had the same temperature there as in the Indies, so it was nice and warm. I looked up in awe at those pillars, arches, and temples, still standing there. It touches something inside, when you feel yourself surrounded by the same atmosphere you know from the Bible, even though so many centuries have passed. We had fun trying to pay with *drachmas* for our delicious Greek food, which was unfamiliar but tasty.

Before Greece, we had stopped at Ceylon (Sri Lanka), Port Said, and Suez. Later on we also visited Gibraltar before finally disembarking in Marseilles. Here, the icy-cold mistral kept us away

109

from deck and we could see our arrival in Europe only through the windows of the dining room. Even our warm overcoats weren't heavy enough to protect us against the cold.

Busses took us to our hotel, where we showed how ignorant we really were as far as toilets were concerned. That's to say, my friend, Nel, and I did. We had noticed a violin-shaped, white porcelain bowl in the middle of the bathroom. My friend had "to go" urgently and we didn't know any better than that she relieve herself in that bowl, with all its unhappy consequences. The bedroom lost its sweet fresh-air smell, and we couldn't figure out how to get rid of the stool, for we couldn't find anything with which to flush it away. We found a clothes hanger somewhere and started the unpleasant process of cutting up that thing into small pieces, so that we could get rid of it. At that moment, Aunt Do entered the room and immediately said, "Heavens! What a horrible stench! What have you two done?"

When we told her what had happened, she burst out laughing and said, "That's just what I came to tell you. That's not a toilet, that's a *bidet*, to cleanse yourself after using the toilet. The toilet is over there, across from our room. You wipe yourself off with toilet paper and then you use the bidet to cleanse yourself."

Of course, we joined Aunt Do in laughing at our ignorance. Who of us had ever seen a bidet, or read about it and knew what it looked like! It pleased us to know that the French were hygienic as far as that went, but what a roundabout way of doing it. I prefer the cebok bottle. Anyway, we had learned something new again. We freshened the air in the room by spraying eau de cologne everywhere. *Aduh*, really, here we were, rustics abroad.

We only stayed one day in that hotel in Marseilles and then travelled by train to Switzerland, destination Geneva, where the family with which we were going to stay already awaited our arrival. We could see the Swiss Alps all around us and also the Lake of Geneva, or Lac Leman as the locals call it, lying like a blue gem among the forests sprinkled with colorful villages.

At the station, we had a warm and cordial reunion with the De Vries family, who had spent a long time in the Indies. He was a totok who had married a Swiss woman. They had two children: a boy, whom they had lost, and a girl of our own age, whom I knew from the Girl Scouts; she spoke Dutch and French fluently, like her

110

father. Mrs. De Vries spoke Dutch only haltingly, but understood it quite well and would fill in any gaps with French.

We drove to Onex sur Salève, where Mr. De Vries had bought a large farm, past friendly villages and farms, and wonderful forests. The De Vries farm was a long, barn-like wooden dwelling with lots of windows and a couple of doors to the outside. "Uncle" Jacques de Vries had changed the "barn" into a kind of villa with a real barn built on, in which he kept rabbits and all his tools. The house was painted a cheerful pure white and soft red, which looked fresh and different. A gated short entryway led to the front door, which opened onto a nice hall containing chests of drawers, and a hat and coat stand. One door led to the large, old-fashioned kitchen, where the large, iron oven was fed with wood. The walls were lined with gleamingly polished copper and iron pots and pans. It was warm and cozy there. Another door opened onto our rectangular, narrow study room.

The hall opened immediately onto a huge sitting-dining room, which ran the whole length of the house, and was totally furnished in Indies style: cloths woven in Sumba hung on the wall, flanked by magnificent leather wayang puppets in various dance positions. Sarongs were used as table cloths. Rattan easy chairs had been placed on the oriental rugs in the sitting area of the room. A huge dining table stood on the far side flanked by sideboards left and right. From this part of the house, wooden stairs led upstairs (let me call that the *lotèng*), where all the guest rooms and bedrooms were located, all of them large, airy, and high-ceilinged. First came the bedroom of the sisters of Mrs. De Vries, who took care of all the household duties; then followed the bedroom of Mr. and Mrs. De Vries; then a large guest room; a smaller one came next, in which stayed a niece, there to recuperate from tuberculosis; and then came our huge room, which was shared by Lous, the De Vries daughter, my friend Nel, and myself. Each of us had her own wide bed, night table, and wardrobe. With its large windows, the room was delightfully airy.

The same corridor on which the bedrooms opened left and right also contained a bathroom and toilet. Downstairs, near the kitchen, was a second toilet. So, we never were in each other's way. To my great surprise and relief, I discovered that each toilet held a rack with three cebok bottles each. It was a truly delightful house.

In the front yard grew the most beautiful, huge roses. Along the front fence stood flowering chestnut trees, three on each side of the gate. Then, farther down the front yard, there were plum and nut trees, cherries, flowers, and greenery—a delight to the eye. The Swiss flag flew from the top of the house in our honor.

And then the backyard! This consisted of a vast, square lawn that sloped down towards a creek. That whole square was bordered by 150 fruit trees: apples, pears, plums, apricots, cherries, a veritable fruit paradise. Uncle and Aunt De Vries, as we called them later, had transformed the incredibly large piece of land into an Eden filled with flowers and fruits.

After staying there a couple of months the glory had faded somewhat, for even though we paid a goodly sum of money for room and board, the care Nel and I received was only so-so. We got in contact with Dany, another Indies girl we knew from home. She boarded in another little town bordering the Lake of Geneva. I can't remember the name of that town. Saying nothing, we took the trolley to visit her, to see if there might be room for us in the household where she was boarding. I can still see us walking that day, in our thick winter coats, holding an umbrella over our heads, while the rain clattered down on us in a heavy downpour. We walked along, feeling cold, miserable, and homesick in that strange town, which then looked so somber and depressing, until we reached Dany. But there was no room for us there, not even in the near future.

When we came home again, a nasty surprise awaited us. Lous, the De Vries daughter, had taken up the unpleasant habit of snuffling through our mail, because our repeatedly coming home late from school the last few weeks had made her suspicious. She had read in our letters that we wanted to leave. Uncle De Vries called us over to question us, with Lous at his side.

First of all, we took Lous to task for reading our mail. Her defense was that the letters had been lying around in the open and she had by chance read the words, "We want to go away from here." Now, that was a great big lie, for those letters had been in their envelopes. Anyway, that was out of the way.

Then followed Uncle De Vries' questioning. He said, "I'm not angry at you two. But I do feel hurt. Why didn't you talk this out with us?" Nel and I then shared all our grievances with him and he could see our side of it. He asked us to give them another chance, for he definitely wanted to cooperate with us.

So, the whole problem had been solved in a friendly and wonderful way, and all of a sudden the whole atmosphere changed, and from that time on we were able to live in harmony together. We had a marvelously delightful stay with them afterward. It was pretty, and exactly my cup of tea there—a rural environment with trees to climb, fruit trees at that. You could take nice walks in the neighborhood, and then there was that deliciously fresh air you breathed the whole long day.

We took the trolley every day to the *École de Correspondence*, the business school where Nel and I studied shorthand, typewriting, and conversational French. I stood out from the crowd, of course, what with my brown skin, hair, and eyes, let alone my heavy accent and the fractured French I spoke.

One day while I was typing, I heard somebody say, "It's snowing." It had been cold and dark throughout the day. "Oh," I said, *"Neige t-il?"* I had jumped up and run out the door before the teacher could call me back, leaving my classmates staring after me in surprise and bewilderment. I ran down the stairs, out the front door, and jumped into the snow-white world. I turned my face heavenwards to catch the snowflakes; I danced around like a dervish in all that white substance, and was in ecstasy over the metamorphosis of my surroundings into a picture-pretty world. The branches of the trees bowed down under the sweet load; voices seemed to come as from afar, the white blanket of snow smothering all sounds. I forgot my école completely and just stood there, enjoying a miraculous, natural phenomenon—snow.

Suddenly, I was shaken out of my dream by a hand being placed on my shoulder. One of the students had been ordered to haul me back to my typewriter. From what she said, I concluded that the teacher wasn't mad at me and that she had immediately understood that it was the first time for me to see snow. There was a lot of understanding in that corner. On my return to the classroom, I begged her pardon in my halting schoolgirl-French, adding that it was the first time for me to see snow. Yes, she had come to that conclusion already, but now duty called again.

Naturally, everyone stared at me when I sat down again at my desk, my hair and cheeks wet, and the last remnants of snow still clinging to my woolen sweater; they melted all too soon in the

113

heated room. But they all smiled at me with kind understanding—this child from the tropics had seen snow. To write pages and pages home about! I'd lost my concentration completely, and I would look every so often at the window, where snow was piling up on the ledge. The first snow. I'll never forget the impression it made on me. It has stayed with me as if it happened yesterday. It's indescribably beautiful to see the world in a white bridal gown, with tall and slender pine trees providing glimpses of green here and there. And when the sun broke through, the Alps surrounded us like so many white grenadiers. Magnificent! I drank it all in.

We either walked or took the trolley daily, to school and back. The environment was truly breathtakingly beautiful. Near Geneva, the Rhône and the Arve flowed together into a large, white-fuming river, densely forested on either side.

On my frequent walks, I quickly became friends with the children of Onex, from whom I actually learned most of my French. They would follow me everywhere I went, and finally the lord of the manor, Uncle Jacques, invited them to play in the garden on specific days. The children would ask me all kinds of questions: who I was, where I came from, and what I was doing there in Onex. It was so cute.

I finally remember the names of all the people that lived at that time in *Campagne au Port*, as Uncle Jacques de Vries had named his house. His wife was Aunt Lous, she and her daughter had the same name. Then there was the niece on his side who was staying there a while to get over a bout of tuberculosis; her name was Christina.

Two sisters of Aunt Lous lived there also, Aunt Rose and Aunt Cecile, you may say as maids. They were both at a rather advanced age already and had poor postures as well as plain faces. But they had the kindest eyes and their character was excellent too, sweet, kind, and patient. Both of them wore dentures that clappered as they talked. Aunt Rose was tall and spare, Aunt Cecile was plump and walked with a limp. Neither of them had ever been married and they had found a safe haven, room and board with their brother-in-law, Uncle Jacques, who also provided them with some pocket money. Out of gratitude, these two women worked from early morning until late at night. Uncle Jacques would tell them, "You don't have to work so hard," but they did it anyway. They were so grateful. They wanted to make themselves useful and

114

couldn't sit still. It's true, however, you could often find Aunt Cecile resting in the sitting room, her poor feet up on a footstool and a piece of knitting or mending in her busy hands. I was quite fond of these two "aunts" and I also felt great compassion for them.

Aunt Rose was usually to be found in the kitchen, so that's where you could find me, too. She was an excellent cook of simple but delicious and nutritious peasant fare. I added several kilos to my weight immediately. Everything tasted so different and tasty. Once a week she washed the clothes for the whole household by hand, on an old-fashioned washboard and with a mangle. Her large hard working hands would be red after all the scrubbing. Usually, Christine would help her fold and iron. The bathroom couldn't be used for bathing then. On washdays, our evening meal consisted of soup with bread.

Evenings, when all our tasks had been finished, we would all sit together in the Indies sitting room, and then Aunt Rose and Aunt Cecile would listen with interest to our stories about the Indies. Such sweet, good people. They were in awe of Uncle Jacques, who could bark at them in a nasty way when they had made some mistake. Poor dears, they really tried to please him so much. He wasn't mean to them; to the contrary, he would often tease them and, as I said earlier, they received a stipend and also had free room and board. Of course, their services were invaluable. They would do anything for even one kind word or act, and they tried to show how much they cared for me by doing me little favors under the table, but I didn't want them to do that, because they had enough to do as it was. This household had a character of its own. Uncle Jacques at first tried to put us under his thumb too, but discovered quickly we weren't easily cowed.

Two of Aunt Lous' brothers came to visit almost every Sunday, and they would stay for dinner. Those were *Oncle* August and *Oncle* Gerard, two hard-working watchmakers, well-known in Geneva, who made the most delicate watches as well as the largest of cuckoo clocks. Gerard was slender and quiet. August was fat and merry. We interacted mostly with Oncle August. He was fun to be around, was always in a good humor, and knew a lot about the environment. We made a trek with him up the Salève mountain in winter, when it was blanketed with snow. We rested somewhere along the way and ate Swiss buns with Swiss whole-milk cheese, enjoying the wide white expanse of hills, mountains, valleys, and farms. We went on many wonderful treks with Oncle August and laughed a lot and had a lot of fun with him.

From time to time, Christine's father would come over from Holland, to visit his daughter, and his brother, Jacques. Often, friends from the Indies would visit the family and extra food was prepared immediately. Everyone had to stay and share the meal; it didn't matter how many extra mouths there were. Then Aunt Rose would really shine, for there would always be plenty of food and everything would taste good.

One day, a family came to visit. They were Indies through and through and in Europe for the first time. It was winter and very cold. They weren't dressed adequately at all. The grandmother of this family wore tennis shoes and only a thin coat over her summery dress. While riding the trolley, she became incontinent and let it all flow out. The Swiss conductor looked on with interest and with a kind smile on his face, listening to the Indo-jargon of the brown-skinned old lady, which to him must have sounded like gibberish, "Oh dear, yeah sir, don't be angry yeah, but so cold yeah. No WC here. Like a horse yeah, just let it flow. I'll clean up later." Under the curious stares of the snickering passengers, we hastened to take her off the patiently waiting trolley. Safely home, we borrowed some clothes for her from Aunt Rose. Bathed and dressed in clean clothes, the old lady warmed herself at the blazing hearth. It was truly pitiful. Why in the world would these Indos venture into Europe in the heart of winter so totally unprepared? Uncle Jacques went shopping with them later and helped them pick out the right shoes, winter coats, and whatnot. They had money enough.

I must admit I was just as stupid, however, when I danced in the snow in tennis shoes and then had to stumble back into the kitchen, my toes frozen. Good, sweet Aunt Rose brought me back to life, setting me down close to the wood fire next to the steaming pots and pans.

Mornings we would get a hearty breakfast, with heavy, round, solid Swiss loaves of bread, and cheese, jam, coffee, milk, or cocoa to go with it. Lunch was the same fare, and then at four in the afternoon, there would be fresh-baked bread, home-made jams, coffee or tea. We had our evening meal at eight o'clock, and it consisted of potatoes, meat, and vegetables, with soup as a first course. We seemed to be eating the whole day long and we always had an appetite. In summer, we ate a lot of fresh salads with

116

homemade dressings, varying from day to day. Everything tasted delicious.

Aunt Rose would often send me to the border of the large lawn in back to pick *dent-de-lion* with my gloves on, looking especially for young leaves. Dent-de-lion, or lion's tooth, is called dandelion here in America. It's basterdized, of course, for most Americans don't speak foreign languages, or speak them badly. These low-growing herbs had tiny thorns, which would get stuck in your fingers and itch painfully, hence the gloves. It was eaten as a salad, and, freshly picked from the garden where it grew wild; it was truly delectable. It's actually a fast-spreading weed that nobody welcomes in his garden. But when they show off their yellow flowers, it's a delightful sight—a veritable blanket of merry yellow faces.

We would often play croquet on the backyard lawn, or we played children's games, like *"Twee emmertjes water halen"* (Fetch two pails of water), a Dutch nursery song, or blindman's bluff, and other games. Everybody would join in and we had great fun, all the while breathing in cold, fresh, pure air.

When it was time to pick fruit, I was promptly present. I would gobble up two or three pears, one after the other, before I finally climbed the tree to pick pears. Plums were shaken off the tree. Apples and pears were picked. In this Swiss grape country, you would expect Uncle Jaques to have a large arbor overgrown with vines heavy with grapes somewhere in the garden, and he did. We couldn't eat all the fruit ourselves. Much was canned, but most of it was given away in the village—loads of the various kinds of fruit.

Switzerland was a safe country. Burglary or theft was unheard of. Newspapers lay in front of the shop in a rack; you picked one out and deposited the money in a receptacle nearby. We would often walk to the concert building in Geneva and went back home in the dark through the forest, a nice walk home. It took about an hour and was wonderful. Lake Geneva looked so inviting, one day I just had to take a nice swim in its cold, blue water.

We also went to the *Fètes des Fleurs* in Neuchatel, a flower parade. You could buy hyacinths along the road, to throw at the decorated carts or at each other. What a waste actually. These flowers would be in full bloom around that time of the year, blanketing the hills around Lake Neuchatel. You would stroll around after the parade, walk through the lush grass up into the hills among cud-chewing, fat cows with huge bells hanging from their necks, bells which would echo back and forth in the valleys. And everywhere you looked, flowers, flowers, flowers: blue gentians, yellow hyacinths, pink alpine roses, and whatnot—the famous, sweet smelling, Swiss alpine meadows. We would also hear the Swiss yodel. That sounded so sweet, and would be echoed tenfold.

Yes, Switzerland was and is beautiful, especially the fresh, pure air you breathe.

We made trips to the *mer de glace*, the glacier of the Mont Blanc, in Chamonix, France. That's beautiful too: the blue ice that flowed like a river from the Mont Blanc till near Chamonix. I walked on it, cautiously peering into the deep chasms in the ice, viewing in the distance the Mont Blanc itself, the white mountain, with its eternal snow on the cone-shaped top.

After I graduated from business school and had received my certificate in typing and French shorthand—both of which I've long forgotten—we said farewell to the De Vries family and travelled by train to Germany, destination Munich. There, Aunt Do and my German uncle, Fritz Hanfland, who had arrived from Borneo in the meantime, already awaited us.

UP IN MUNICH, DOWN IN ENGLAND
1927-1928

A rented car took us to the Friedrichstrasse, to the *Familienheim für junge Damen,* a boardinghouse for young ladies. Frau Krauss reigned here supreme. She was a tall, Bavarian woman who welcomed us with kindly warmth. She led us immediately to our room. (This time "us" means my niece, Marga, the daughter of Aunt Do and Uncle Fritz, and myself. Nel, my friend, went on alone to London where I would join her later.)

Our room was large and airy with a huge double-hung window. The latter consists of one window on the outside and one window on the inside, both of heavy glass. It was made that way with an eye on winter; it kept the heat in. In addition, you tightly closed the draperies in the evening. Our room also contained a washbasin, complete with mirror and cabinets, as well as a marble, coal-burning hearth. There were some easy chairs, should we want to be by ourselves, but we were also welcome to use the large, cozily furnished, general room.

Two doors opened onto this general room. One led to a hall, which gave access to to our bedroom and the kitchen, the other led to a long corridor, on which other bedrooms opened. Two German-Swiss girls shared one huge bedroom; another room was occupied by an Italian countess; in the third room slept a Hungarian girl. The bathroom and the toilet we all shared opened onto that corridor.

Because I was the only one to take a daily cold water bath, I wasn't in anybody's way and could use the bathroom whenever I wished during the week. The others washed themselves in their rooms. Every Saturday, however, baths were taken in the one bathtub by rotation after one of the housekeepers filled the tub with warm water. I never used that tub. I have never used a tub anywhere. I either take a shower or pour water over me the way we used to do in the Indies.

I don't remember anymore when it was washday; then the bathtub would overflow with dirty clothes. At that time, they still didn't have washing machines or dryers. I'm talking here about the years 1927-1928. I don't know when the washer and dryer were invented.

Soon enough, I had adjusted myself to the new environment and my fellow boarders. I became especially fond of Frau Dr. Krauss, whom I soon called Frau Mutti. I also adopted the German custom to add, *"Grüsse dich Gott,"* or *"Behüte dich Gott,"* every time I wished Frau Mutti good morning or good evening. You had to follow this greeting with a curtsy, the well-known sinking through the knees, while you bowed elegantly over the hand of the one you were greeting and blew it a kiss. The song *"Ich küsse Ihre Hand, Madame,"* was at that time very popular. This was fun and I tried to do everything as elegantly and naturally as possible.

Munich, one of the oldest cities in Europe, with its wide streets and beautiful parks, is magnificent. It's the most beautiful city I have ever seen. It offered many cultural diversions: operas, operettes, theatrical performances, art. You name it and you'll find it in Munich, a city of which I retain many happy, sweet, and fun memories.

The months I spent in Munich were very special indeed. The Bavarians were nice and cheerful people, whose costume consisted of dirty-looking, well-worn, chamois leather shorts, a short-sleeved shirt embroidered in bright colors, and a hat decorated with a "chamois feather." A chamois is a kind of mountain goat, so that chamois feather was just a little joke. Everywhere you went, but specifically on the paths in the mountains, they would greet you with, "Grüsse dich Gott!" That's such a lovely greeting; it makes you feel warm.

Here too, I had to attend school every day, to learn typing, shorthand, and German. Evenings were spent doing homework, after which we would look each other up or visit Frau Krauss in her private parlor. Frau Doktor Krauss—that's the way she always introduced herself—was the widow of one Doktor Krauss. In Germany, the custom is for the widow to take the title of the dead husband. She was a well-educated woman herself, was always busy, and was always very interested in what we were doing. I soon

120

became her pet, and I was Ilse's and Inge's pet too. Ilse and Inge were Frau Krause's daughters. Ilse taught dance and gymnastics, classes I joined as a matter of course. They were held in a large room, right across from the boardinghouse. It was easy to reach; you only had to cross the street.

Frau Krauss had two female servants, who cooked, washed, and cleaned the rooms. They also brought us our breakfast and evening meal on trays in our rooms. We never knew in advance what we would be served, except on Sundays, when we were always offered a dish I didn't care for, some kind of cut-up crepes with some kind of sauce; I don't remember exactly what. I would ask the cook, *"Heute wieder kaputte Pfannkuchen?"* ("Cut-up pancakes again today?"). From then on, that became the name of that particular dish. And then there was a dish which I loved: boiled meat, boiled cabbage, potatoes, a spoonful of horseradish, and a spoonful of jam, all neatly arranged on the plate. I have forgotten what it was called originally, but I called that dish *"Zungenstreichelung,"* or tongue caress. Well, they thought that was cute, and it was, "Rita, *heute wieder Zungenstreichelung."* Then I would lick my lips to show them I approved wholeheartedly.

One day, it started to snow, and it was very cold again—fourteen degrees below zero. Everything was frozen hard, and I stayed cozily home, with the hearth going full blast, and dressed in all the woolen clothes I owned. I just didn't seem able to get warm. Nevertheless, I went outside to look for a minute and immediately sank up to my hips in the snow. Right away back to my warm room, where frost flowers were starting to form on the windowpane. Wondrous frost flowers, the most beautiful shapes imaginable traced in ice on your window. Again, a divine wonder. Such superfine crystals, taking the shape of stars, crosses, ferns, flowers, whatever. I could watch that process for hours.

Frau Mutti was always thinking up ways to make our stay with her even more enjoyable. A month before the event, she'd told us that she was going to give a masked ball at her home at such and such a time. Every one of us was given permission to invite a boyfriend. I quickly wrote home, "Quickly send me the *serimpi* dance costume." It was an authentic, Javanese court dance costume my parents had bought for me. They sent it up by return mail. Soon enough, I received notice that a package had arrived for me at a certain location, but I had to pay import tax first. I went there and explained to them that this was the way I dressed in the Indies, and that it was, in fact, my court costume. When they saw me, this brown-skinned, dark-haired girl, they believed me without question and I didn't have to pay import duties. One day, when we were sitting together having a cozy chat, I shared this incident with Frau Mutti and the other girls, and from then on I was "the Javanese princess," which flattered my ego no end. At the age I was then, young people are often all too easily taken in by compliments and flattery, and I was no exception.

Anyway, the day of the masked ball arrived and everybody was present, all of us wearing masks. Every girl was accompanied by a boyfriend, also disguised as clowns or lion tamers or Arabs—all the costumes were different. Marga and I didn't have boyfriends yet, so we invited her brother, my cousin Bub. At midnight, we took off our masks. Throughout the evening, everybody had thrown curious glances at me—the lady with the brown arms, wearing a sarong and golden headdress—but nobody could place me as coming from the Indies. As soon as we had taken off our masks, people crowded around me, asking me what I represented and where I came from. That was lots of fun.

After the *démasqué*, I didn't have any complaints about a lack of dance partners. One young man in particular, handsome and fair-haired, seemed very attracted to me. His name was Günther Gerloff. Günther repeatedly asked me to dance. The others hardly got a chance. It became a wonderful, merry party that went on until two o'clock in the morning.

Frau Kraus' masked ball was not the only time I succesfully displayed my serimpi costume. I wore it once again at a so-called *Künstlerfest*, at which all kinds of artists were represented: sculptors, painters, pianists, dancers, composers, you name it. On this occasion, I also danced the "serimpi," albeit the way I had taught this classical dance to myself. Afterwards, I was literally mobbed by those artists. An Egyptian wanted to use me as a model for a sculpture; another man wanted to paint me; and a third wanted to teach me dance.

The result was that a portrait of me in serimpi costume was hung in a collection of paintings, called the Pinacotheca, in Munich. It was painted by the brother of Frau Doktor Kraus, one Hans something or other. The following year, when Tje stayed in Munich for *her* "finishing touch"—which she didn't need—she saw my likeness hanging there. Taken by surprise, she pointed it out to anybody who seemed the least bit interested, exclaiming, "That's my sister!" and regaling them with stories. Later, that painting was offered to us for the sum of five hundred marks, but at that time none of us had the money for it. I have no idea what Hitler did with my painting; that's still an unsolved mystery.

But I have to return to the scene of my early social escapades again. At some of the teas Frau Krauss gave occasionally, I met yet another young man, tall and dark-haired, a child of the "chosen people." Wolfgang wasn't handsome, but was nevertheless very attractive, polite and well-mannered. He was broadly educated, and could sing beautifully. He had a baritone. After we had met at those teas, he came to visit more often. Once he took me on a horse-drawn sleigh ride through the Englische Garten, a large park not far from our boardinghouse. I loved it. Naturally, Wolfgang found it necessary to warm my cold, Indies' hands under the thick horse blanket, and I didn't protest. It was so romantic, driving through that silent, white forest in a sleigh drawn by a black horse, the bells on his harness tinkling loudly as he ran. And Wolfgang kept singing and looking at me adoringly. Some time later, he took me to his home, where his parents greeted me warmly. They were sweet, old-fashioned Jews. I immediately felt at home with them.

Wolfgang taught me to understand and appreciate Wagner's operas. I saw almost all of Wagner's great operas and loved them all. He told me later, "I watched you more than the opera. You are such a foreign element in my life. I enjoyed watching your delight in Wagner's art. I've seen and heard these operas many times before, but I've never met a girl like you." Imagine that!

The problem was, I didn't return Wolfgang's love. I felt sad for him. He was such a sweet fellow, so well-mannered and polite, but I just couldn't fake what I didn't feel. Finally, I told him honestly, but as tactfully as I could, that I loved him as a friend, but nothing more. He looked at me with such hurt and pain on his face. I still feel a stab through my heart to have had to hurt him so much. He left and never showed himself again. Later, much, much later, I heard that he'd died in the Holocaust.

In the meantime, Günther, the blond young man from the masked ball, had also looked me up, to take me for walks or just to talk. In Munich, Mardi Gras, the riotous feast day before Lent, is called *Fasching*. It always falls close to Easter and in the middle of winter, in January or February. People dress up in all kinds of costumes and the whole city participates. On that day, you can enter any café and join the party going on there, and after several hours you might continue the party in the street.

Your breath blows out like steam, your feet dance through the snow, while a round-faced moon smiles good-naturedly down from a starlit sky on the wild Fasching world. That scene was new to me and I hopped around with gusto, Günther, the blond young man at my side, protecting his lady as if he were a dragon.

I was dressed in a so-called devil's costume: a red, tight-fitting dress with red cape and horned cap, and a tail that swept around provocatively whenever I moved. We swept into a large student hall where a noisy party was going on. Soon, Günther was taken from me by other costumed girls, and I was taken in arm by gentlemen I'd never seen before. During Fasching, you were expected to flirt a lot and drink a lot of hard liquor, sin it up before you had to fast. That "flirting" consisted of kissing everybody you met, preferably on the lips. However, romantic as I was, I had promised myself that I would save my lips for the man I love, and that I wouldn't present them to everyone who came around. So when these young men stormed towards me and wanted to hug and kiss me, I snapped at them and dealt them a few well-placed but gentle slaps, causing them to stare at me in surprise. They had to get to the bottom of this, and several of them edged up to me, peppering me with questions, patting my brown hands and cheeks and asking me if the color was natural, wondering where I came from. We ended up having a very interesting conversation; the ice was broken and they understood, "This lady doesn't want to be kissed," and I had a lot of fun after that. But, exactly because I acted different from the other ladies, they crowded around me to see what kind of strange bird I was. In the meantime, Günther stuck close to me, saying repeatedly, "She's in my company." From this moment on, he was very possessive and acted very much in love. And I . . . ? I too!

Günther was a law student. He was fair-skinned, blond-haired, and blue-eyed, and had a slender, athletic body. Soon he declared me his love, and we became an item, seen together at various outings and house parties. When the time neared that I was scheduled to leave for England to learn English, Günther had a vacation, and he wanted to introduce me to his parents.

124

But before this happened, Günther and I went on a fourteen-day ski trip in the Austrian Alps. He taught me to ski and I was a fast learner, not an expert by far, but good enough for a two-week ski trip. We stayed in a wooden mountain cabin that also served as a café, where the fire burned bright in the open hearth day and night. There were bedrooms galore, as there were toilets and washbasins, and we could order our daily meals from that café—it couldn't have been more comfortable.

The sun shone bright and hot, and because of the reflection off the snow most skiers got sunburned and had to wear sunglasses and rub themselves with sunburn lotion. It got so hot on the ski slopes, that I started to ski in a swimsuit, but, oh goodness, when we rested in the shade of the pine trees, we would shiver from the cold. Naturally, we had a wonderful time there together, and we were more in love than ever. Everything was romantic and beautiful. Günther skied very well, of course. You could clearly see he had done that before. I think skiing is the most beautiful sport in the world—to glide at top speed over the snow while the pine trees flit past like so many ghosts, and then there is the pure air, the hot sun, the blue sky. And Günther's presence made everything even more exciting for me.

Evenings, we would all gather around the hearth and laugh and talk with the other skiers, and then we would go to bed early. I want to make it clear to all old, head-shaking grandmas, mothers, aunts and who else, that we had separate rooms, very nice and proper. Mornings, we would get up at dawn, and watch the sun rise over the high mountains with a cup of hot coffee in our hands. Then followed a hearty breakfast and gone we were for the day. Before the vacationers went their separate ways, we would call out to each other, *Ski-Heil und Hals- und Beinbruch*! (Something like, "Have fun skiing and break your neck and legs.") You greeted everyone that way. It was one large fellowship, everybody was always in a good mood, and the skiing provided the common link. It was truly wonderful.

Then I said farewell to Munich and left for the Polish border, for Landsbergen an der Warthe, where Günther's father was *Oberburgemeister*, mayor; he might have been a dishwasher for all I cared. His father stood waiting for us, a dark, large man with brown hair and eyes. He received me cordially, and gave me such a hearty handshake with his large hands, mine were almost shaken off. He included me totally in the animated conversation with his son while we drove in his car to their house, which looked quite impressive. It looked like a small, old castle, constructed of brownish yellow brick, with various cupolas and façades and a weathervane on top. An iron fence encircled a small front yard planted with all kinds of flowers and shrubs.

We shed our overcoats and overshoes in the lighted hall, Günther courteously assisting me, at which time he squeezed my arms encouragingly. With his father in the lead, and Günther's arm around me, we trooped into the large family room. A young girl, who turned out to be Günther's sister, ran with fair hair flying and outstretched arms first towards her father and then towards her brother. She stopped in mute surprise when she noticed me, then hugged me too, with a warm *Seien Sie willkommen!* or "Welcome!"

On the brocade-covered sofa, I noticed a lady dressed in blue, with platina hair and the largest violet-blue eyes I've ever seen—a tiny woman, like Dresden porcelain. With a gentle smile and outstretched arms she bid me welcome and gave me a warm hug. Then it was Günther's turn, and I noticed immediately the close likeness between mother and son, and felt the special relationship that existed between them.

They were full of interest, wanting to know from where, what, and how I was. Among these fair heads with their white skin, I stuck out for sure. The conversation went smoothly and I felt quite at ease, in spite of the abundance of material wealth and luxury around me.

The whole house was furnished rococo-style, but it wasn't stiff or somber, for Frau Gerloff had lightened it up here and there with a nice color or shape. At mealtime, we were served by a maid wearing a white lace apron and a starched, white lace cap. Everything was quite elegant, yet not stiff at all but relaxed and cheerful.

I was given a large guest room and soon the rumor spread that Günther had brought home a Javanese princess. Innocently, I took walks with Günther along forested streets. Everybody seemed to have taken to the streets and they all seemed to know Günther, and while greeting him, they ogled me. Günther walked at my side, as proud as a peacock with seven tails, amused by the curiosity of the people.

Günther's sister was called Inge, and he also had a younger brother, called Walter. I was soon on good terms with the whole family. All of them were nice and kind to me. I got along especially well with Günther's sister and brother, who confided to me later that there was a girl in Landsbergen, who had been Günther's first love interest. I was introduced to her later; she was a sweet, handsome girl, also a blonde, of course. I wanted to get out of the way immediately, but Günther swore to me it was she who had been in love with him; he had never been in love with her. A tricky situation, for sure! I hoped she wouldn't hate me because of this rivalry, and that never happened, fortunately. We got along famously.

One day, a tea was given, or something like that, and Günther presented me to the higher circle of Landsbergen. I did the rounds, chatting with all these wealthy people in their beautiful clothes. Most of them acted in a normal fashion and were kind, but there were some who looked down their nose at me and gave me a listless, limp handshake. I burned with desire to stick out my tongue at them, but Günther, who kept an eye on me, would step in and lead me to another group of people. All in all, it was a succesful tea, and the curiosity of the people had been satisfied.

Landsbergen isn't that small, but the rumors spread like wildfire anyway. Everybody knew the mayor and the mayor knew everybody. One evening, there was a concert, a gala performance, so everyone had to be dressed to the nines. Günther insisted on personally inspecting my collection of dresses, picking out a taffeta evening gown. Its main color was hot pink, with nuances of green, red and blue flaming over the surface of the gown at every move. I think it was called *changeant* taffeta, taffeta that changes color. It was a simple design but it looked very rich, and it gave my brown skin an extra glow. At that time, I still had long hair, which I wore in a chignon on my neck. My only jewelry consisted of a single strand of pearls. The whole family complimented me on my looks, and Günther gave me an extra long kiss and a bouquet of red roses. Moments before, he had knelt down before me, taken my ankles in his hands and murmured that he had never seen such slender ankles, at which he kissed my foot. Now, was that romantic or not? I burned with love for him. He was from head to toe a gentleman, sweet and patient.

Wrapped in a shawl of the same color as my gown, I drove in a car to the concert building, where a box seat had been reserved for the mayor's family. Günther, his sister, and brother sat in the front row, with me next to Günther, of course. We'd hardly taken our seats, when opera glasses were trained on us from all sides. Such a dark thing next to all that platinum blond and white skin must have been quite a sight for these people, who had never seen an Indo girl before. Of course, the flashy color of my gown among all that black, brown, rose and white also set me apart. In the Europe of that period, it was quite an daring color—you didn't wear something like that. At any rate, I finally got bored with all this unwonted attention (but I've to admit, it also tickled me pink). So, I rolled a program into a tube and stared back at them through this, to the great amusement of the family, who noticed how people turned away one by one and put down their opera glasses—and that was the end of it.

Naturally, during the intermission, everybody wanted to meet the mayor in the salon next to our balcony and to get a close-up view of "the Indies wonder." Never in my life did I curtsey so often and did I say so many times, *"Wie geht es Ihnen"*, (How are you). But they found out that the foreign girl was quite a normal person and worthy of Günther, the much sought after bachelor. Neither Günther nor I cared one bit one way or the other—we loved each other and the world smiled at us.

But then we had to say farewell. I had to go to England on orders from home, to perfect my English. Of course, leaving was heartbreakingly difficult, and with lead in my shoes and a heart heavy with grief, I said farewell to Günther and his family. The train took me straight to Hook of Holland, where the weather didn't help my depression—it rained and the wind blew cold and hard. I stepped onto the boat to Dover straight away. It wobbled badly in the wind. I promptly got seasick again, of course, and stayed sick for the eight-hour crossing.

Shivering with cold, nausea, and grief, I took the train to Victoria Station in London, where my friend, Nel, awaited me. The subway, an underground train, took us to Swiss Cottage, a suburb of London, where our boardinghouse was. There I would board with a nice English family, who made me feel welcome. Nel and I shared a room.

In this boardinghouse, I was reunited with the Hungarian girl I knew from Munich, and there was yet another boarder, a young German. All of us were in London to learn English. Soon, we became pals, went out together, explored the city, took the double-

128

decker trolleybus together to the heart of London, where the expensive shops were—Bond Street, Trafalgar Square. We also took the "tube," a train even deeper underground than the subway, which sped through its tunnels like an arrow and took us in a minimum of time to our destination. The tube didn't stop everywhere as the subway did. This way, we were, in the blink of an eye, in Kew Gardens, the famous, and truly beautiful, public gardens in Kew, another London suburb. I find it really hard to describe the trees, the flowering shrubs, the flowers. First of all, there is the expansiveness of the grounds, then there is the variety of flowers, orchids, and hothouse plants. Kew Gardens looks the way I imagine paradise to be. Of course, you need months to see the whole park. I went there on my own several times, but even then I have seen, at most, one-third of the park. There was a huge laboratory, where people mixed seeds, prepared cuttings, and did research on bacteria. There was also a grapevine, that was reputed to be one hundred years old and which still bore fruit. It was very knotty and bent like an old man, and its vines spread out over an area of at least twenty meters. It was gigantic and one of the wonders of the world. In California, I saw it again on television and its vitality surprised me, for by that time it must have been 150 years old or more.

While in London, I also experienced its notorious fog. It is yellow and hangs like a veil before your nose, so that you literally can't see a hand in front of you. You would carefully shuffle step by step along the street and still bump into people every other moment. The mumbling of "Beg your pardon" would fill the air. London fog would make you feel short of breath too, because the world around you became so limited while the moist blanket of yellow fog enveloped you on all sides. During such a fog, many accidents happened—even though traffic was usually brought to a standstill—and also a lot of crime. Most of all it was a heyday for pickpockets. You would hear people screaming "Hold the thief!" all the time.

A month after arriving in London, I received a letter from Günther. He wrote that he was breaking off our relationship, because he still had to finish his law studies. And then the truth came: his mother refused to let him leave for the distant country of his sweetheart. His father had immediately offered Günther three thousand marks, to cover the cost of the trip and his stay in the

Indies with me. But his mother had persuaded him against it. It wasn't that she didn't care for me, but without her son, her life wouldn't be the same. My love-filled, romantic heaven exploded like a pricked balloon. I was inconsolable.

I sought distraction by going out a lot, especially to famous museums, to the Crystal Palace, and to the changing of the Guard in front of Buckingham Palace. I also took boat trips on the Thames and went to listen to the soapbox orators in Hyde Park. It was in that period I saw my first "talky," with the beautiful "Old Man River" sung by Paul Robeson, a deep baritone. The songs he sang in that movie became popular all over the world. It was a beautiful, moving picture, which played in theatres worldwide. It was wonderful to actually hear the voices of the glamorous stars. The movie was sold out for months.

In the meantime, I had my hair bobbed short, and had started wearing the latest fashion: skirt and blouse. When it was time to go on to The Hague, I had calmed down a little. Here I stayed with my father's brother, Uncle Wim Lanzing and his family, in Wassenaar, a suburb near The Hague. He could have been my father's twin, except that my father was much taller. Their house was named *De Instuif*, the open door, and it was indeed always crammed with relatives.

Uncle Wim and Aunt Stien—a blonde Indies woman—were hospitable, warm-hearted people. Theirs was a large, old-fashioned house, with the bedrooms on the second floor, and the sitting-dining room and the kitchen on the first floor. It had a nice garden, in which all kinds of plants grew happily together.

There I spent the last months of my European adventure, already getting a whiff of home. Then the whole cake had been eaten and I went back home with the *Jan Pieterszoon Coen*, to the Indies, to my dear parents, who had made great sacrifices for me, so that I could get a finishing touch worthy of the Lanzings-Geuls.

A year later, I received word that Günther had died in a motorcycle accident. In his shirt pocket they found my picture, which, according to his mother, he always kept with him. His mother stayed for a year in a hospital because of a mental breakdown. She wrote me a letter afterwards with deep feelings of guilt, "If I'd only let him go with you, he would still be here with us," she grieved. I quickly sent her a letter in return, telling her not to think or feel that way, for I believed that "Man chooses, but God

130

disposes." Who knows what might have happened to him in the Indies which was so foreign to him. So came my romantic fairy tale to an end. In the words of Von Scheffel in *Trümpeter vom Sächingen*, *"Behütte dich Gott, es war zu schon gewesen, es hat nicht sollen sein"* (Go with God, it was too much to hope for, it's not to be).

BACK FROM EUROPE 1929-1935

On my return to the Indies, I was picked up by my father in Batavia. With a wide grin behind his gray mustache he told me, "What a relief! You haven't changed a bit!" But my mother, who waited for me at the station in Surabaya, said, "Is this what I sent you to Europe for?" I couldn't help laughing up my sleeve.

I moved back into my parents' home. Soon after, I was hired by the Dutch oil company, *Bataviasche Petroleum Maatschappij* (BPM). People often jokingly referred to this company as *Banyak Perempuan Manis*, which means "many pretty women" in Indonesian, a pun on its acronym. Indeed, many pretty girls worked there, so this was an apt nickname. I worked there over five years and had a good time. The workday lasted from eight in the morning until four in the afternoon. After work, my friends and I would do sports, mainly a form of basketball, but also tennis or rowing on the Kali Mas, a branch of the Brantas River, or athletics. We would also attend soccer games. There was always plenty to do.

I resumed my duties as group leader of the Red Girl Scout Troop, but I had earned the Scout Leader Badge in Holland and was now promoted to Scout leader for real. While in England, I took an official Scouting course and there I met Lady Baden-Powell, the wife of Lord Baden-Powell, who started the worldwide Boy and Girl Scout movement.

One of the highlights of my girlhood in Surabaya came after I had returned from Europe. It has to do with dance, but, in contrast to my earlier experiences, this one was utterly delightful. One of Surabaya's best-known personalities was one Mother Van der Steen. She was already quite old when, by popular request, she decided to give a last performance of the play *De Pariah van Glodok* (The Pariah of Glodok), a well-known Indies drama. Through the grapevine, she had heard I had done a version of the famous, classical Javanese court dance, the serimpi, once before. So, to gild the lily, Mother Van der Steen decided to surprise the audience with a serimpi dance performed by me. She happened to be very good friends with the Javanese court, and asked a relative of the Sultan of Yogyakarta to provide the necessary classical training. For I was self-taught, by studying a book on serimpi—written by one Dr. Wormser, I think—in which that dance was depicted in extensive detail, accompanied by the necessary explanations.

So, one day, I was introduced to a prince who was to train me in Mother Van der Steen's big house on the corner of Genteng Kali. As a start, he asked me to dance the serimpi my way. Strange but true, I had learned to dance it to a slow-paced tango, because I didn't have access to gamelan music. Trembling with excitement, I danced for the prince, but without music, surprising him with my skillful performance. When I had finished, he said, "Well, Miss Lanzing, you have to do that again, but now to gamelan music. That's something else again." And, true, it was quite different indeed. It was more demanding, because of the tempo, the degree of modesty, the dignity, and the perfectionism with which the various dance patterns and the hand and finger movements had to be executed. But, oh, I felt in seventh heaven! I have always loved the gamelan anyway—its tones, so deep and yet so light, floating in the air like the scent of flowers on the night wind.

That day, we studied until we were soaking wet with sweat. Finally, the prince said with satisfaction, "You're pretty good for a European girl." I answered, "That's because I've never felt European, and also because I was born and raised here and have Javanese ancestors on top of that."

Anyway, the public performance that eventually followed was a personal success story. My name wasn't on the program, and the regent of Grisee, a high-ranking Javanese official who was seated in the front row, asked Mother Van der Steen to introduce the serimpi dancer to him. And here's my greatest triumph now: when I stood before him, I greeted him in Dutch. He stared sharply at me and said, "Oh, you're not even Javanese! May I congratulate you on dancing such an excellent serimpi, even though you're a European?" (In the Indies, Indos were officially classified as European.) I felt as proud as a peacock with seven tails! For I adore anything Indonesian, but especially its dances. But all its artistic expressions are in my eyes always more beautiful and better than those of any other culture. Of course, this is because they move me deeply, I feel the essence of Javanese mysticism in all its ramifications.

Naturally, I was still a virgin when I performed that dance, which may only be done by virgins. Had I not been, I am certain a Higher Power would have put a curse on me. Can you imagine me, such a demon for speed, performing the serimpi dance in exquisitely slow tempo and with all my heart and soul? I could do that because I felt that's the way it had to be done, and I didn't even find it difficult to be that disciplined.

As I remember it, it took hours to dress me. First, my arms and face had to be painted yellow; they call that *boreh*. Then the kain had to be draped just so between my legs, trailing to the back and held up around my hips with an udet, a long, woven belt. Then the gold-decorated, black velvet kemben (in Javanese court language, *kasemekan*) was wound to a tight fit around my upper body, leaving free my neck and shoulders, which also had been *boreh*ed. Then the beautiful, gold-painted headdress with its elegantly up-swept lines was fixed on my head, earrings were fastened to my ears, winged bracelets were put around my upper arms, diamond bracelets on wrists, and rings on my fingers. All these ornaments were made out of leather. Then my lips were painted red, my eyebrows penciled black, and a couple of beauty marks were placed on my cheekbones. A black line was painted right next to the lower edge of the headdress. A long string of kantil flowers hung down one side of my headdress, and another string, this one of arabian jasmine, was attached to the golden *keris* (a serpentine dagger) that was inserted diagonally in the kemben on my back. A green scarf was knotted around my waist and ended in two long slips, which I manipulated during the dance. My parents had bought me this costume. You may remember that I had worn it to great effect during my stay in Munich.

Mother Van der Steen died not long after putting on the play in which I danced. It was her last effort. She was famous for her Indies theatre performances, in which she always either acted or directed. Always impeccably dressed in sarong and kebaya, closely fitting around her wiry and skinny frame, she was a real character with strong principles. She was very witty and sharp, sometimes too sharp in her criticisms. Closely identified with Surabaya, where everybody knew her, Mother Van der Steen's fame extended beyond its borders, for she travelled far and wide with her troupe, giving excellent performances. At any rate, she provided me my moment in the sun.

134

Then, one night, my father suffered a light stroke. The doctor who lived next door to us, and later became our house-doctor, told him to move to a cool climate and to take it easy. We were all so concerned for our dear father. Fortunately, that stroke didn't have long-lasting effects. The doctor said that it was caused by severe diabetes.

My father having to move to a cool climate meant we had to leave another, by now familiar and cozy, house—we had to pull up stakes again. I went through a another difficult adjustment. Our old Koki had died some time before; now babu Sanem retired and went home to Pagah, where her married granddaughter lived.

My parents moved in a hurry to Punten, a small resort near Batu, in the mountains northeast of Surabaya. To visit them, I would take the bus and be there in under two hours. In Batu, the bus turned right, drove past Selecta, a popular vacation hotel and spa, and deposited me practically at my parent's door. In Punten, they lived temporarily in the pavilion of a huge, only half-finished house owned by my uncle, Frans Geul, my mother's brother. It had a garden to match, in which grew roses, various other flowers, and also orange and apple trees. It was named Sonnevanck, and indeed, it basked in sunlight.

During my parents' temporary stay in Punten, they had three houses built in Batu: one for my sister, for which she paid herself; one for my parents' grandchildren; and one for themselves. My parents' house was named Branggah, after the plantation where my father worked as an administrator at the time of their wedding. The house for my parents' first grandchildren was named Emcari, for their shortened names: Emmy, Carla and Rita. They were the children of my brother Paul and his wife, Annie van Lawick.

I already worked at the BPM, and stayed behind in Surabaya, where I found a boardinghouse in a hurry, a free-standing pavilion with a small vine-covered front porch and a very large sitting-dining room. I happened to know the family who lived in the main house. The lady of the house took care of my food—it was inexpensive, it saved me work, and above all, it was tasty.

I hired a maid to keep my house clean, and also to bring my noon meal to me in a *rantang*, taking the tram to where I worked on Societeit Street. She was joined from all quarters of the compass by a swarm of servants, all of whom were bringing hot meals to be consumed in the large employee lunchroom of the BPM. Lunchtime

135

not only provided a pleasant break, it was also fun to guess what each of us was having for lunch that day. We often shared food, and the room was filled with a cozy buzz of voices and the rattling of china and silver.

Our food was kept hot in that authentically Indies item, the rantang, which consisted of several metal containers, one on top of the other, and carried by a handle at the top. The rice was always at the bottom and the rest of the containers were filled with various side dishes. Napkins, spoons and forks, everything was included, up to the ubiquitous glass of iced water.

For me, my years at the BPM were truly the Roaring Twenties. That was the most fun and light-hearted period of my whole life. I went to parties, went dancing—I had become proficient in ballroom dancing in the meantime and had come to love it—went to restaurants, did sports, swam, took long walks, went to stay with my uncles in the mountains, went to Batu where my parents lived, or to Punten to stay with my retired uncle Frans.

Meanwhile, my dear little Oma Maria died and all her furniture was sold at auction. Her home too was lost to me forever.

I read a great deal in those days, especially when I started to slow my life down a little. I had had it with being away from home all the time. Strange, the way in which you can suddenly be caught up sharp like that. I became deeply interested in various religions and studied them by reading various books dealing with religious subjects. I had serious talks about various facets of religion with anybody who was willing, no matter what his or her religious background happened to be.

All this time, I was simply one of many employees at the BPM. I worked in the "confidential" department, where I had to keep statistics up to date on the sale of oil. This brought me in daily contact with one Henk Schenkhuizen. We would also meet outside office hours, either on the tennis court or on the basketball court. We quickly became friends, but I never for a moment thought Henk would one day be my husband. Although I liked him as a friend, I had found him physically unattractive from the start. Yes, I even thought he was ugly. Nevertheless, he was fun to talk to or to do sports with. Later on, we went out dancing together, and on those occasions he would always present me with an orchid, which I had to wear in my hair. Other girls started wearing flowers in their hair soon after, following my example. I don't know if *they* also got those from their friends or steadies, but it was true in my case.

In spite of all that, my heart hadn't quickened at all; I had experienced no extra thrill of any kind whatsoever. And then he asked me to marry him. I was dumbfounded. Yes, that's the truth; I was naive enough to think that all his special attention was done out of simple friendship.

Stumbling over my words, I explained that I didn't feel anything for him but friendship. As I said earlier, I really thought him quite unattractive. Here you see clearly that love, or so-called love, is based on outside appearances. If a certain man isn't handsome, that is the end of it; there is no sex-appeal and he isn't worth a second look.

Henk smiled very sweetly at me and didn't seem to feel hurt or anything like that. He was very composed and proceeded to tell me that he was convinced I *did* love him, that I simply hadn't become aware of that yet; furthermore, that he wasn't going to ask me to marry him a second time, but that I would have to go to him and ask him, once I had come to realize that I did love him. Well, that did it! I decided to turn my back on him right then and there. I went away for a month and stayed on vacation with my parents in Batu. But, as strange as it sounds, I did begin to think of him more and more, and I began to have a feeling of loss and emptiness inside of me. Anyway, to make this short, when I came home from vacation, there he was, waiting for me on my front porch. I had sent the lady of the main house word that I would be home at such and such an hour, and she, aware of what was going on between us, had alerted him. I felt so happy at seeing him, I put my arms around him and right then and there asked him without more ado if he would marry me. Fate had closed full circle.

The strangest part of all is that by that time I thought him the handsomest man, inside and outside, in the whole wide world. We were in love until the day he died, and he was the only man who made my heart beat faster throughout the long years we spent together. How was it possible that I ever thought him ugly or unattractive? You can't ask for better proof, right here, that true love changes everything and allows you to see things with unusual clarity: it combines inner and outer reality into a harmonious whole that leads to happiness.

We were officially engaged for a year while both of us kept our jobs at the BPM, putting money away for our future. Suddenly, I began to feel unwell. I became jittery, made lots of mistakes in my work, and, on top of that, suffered an outbreak of large, festering sores on my buttocks and around my vagina. These sores itched terribly and the pus soaked through all the layers of my clothing. The odd part was, that I never once considered seeing a doctor.

I had a good friend, an older woman whom I called "Aunt" Ivy, who was married to one of my fellow employees. Aunt Ivy noticed how jittery I was. She said to me, "Rita, I see that a part of your brain has turned black. I think you've been put under an evil spell. Why don't you visit Dr. Boekebinder? He has special powers and can tell you if I'm right." This Dr. Boekebinder was locally famous; for instance, you could hand him certain items, and he could tell you whom they belonged to and what lay in the future for him or her.

Strangely, we Indos who grew up with black magic, called *guna-guna* in Indonesia, were kind of sceptical about it and had the idea or the feeling, "Well, that won't happen to me. That can only happen when you're afraid of it, or believe in it." That was the general reaction.

Her comment shocked me, of course, and really shook me up. I went that same afternoon to see Dr. Boekebinder, who started right out with, "You probably feel you've been put under an evil spell. That's usually why people consult me," followed by a disdainful little chuckle. "But anyway, take a seat and let's see if it's true."

I sat down across from him. He took a small, gleamingly polished metal mirror with a handle and held this over my wrist. Immediately, the mirror started to tremble and its whole surface became heavily misted over. Dr. Boekebinder looked at me, his face serious, and said, "Well, no doubt about it. You've indeed been put under an evil spell. They've tried to drive you insane, but they would never have succeeded, for you've something that protects you. Do you pray a lot?" When I told him "Yes," he said that that was the best weapon against such dark powers. Remember, the biblical Paul taught us: "We aren't fighting against flesh and blood, but against dark powers. . . . I'll come to your home this evening. No servants, please," said Dr. Boekebinder.

138

Well, he arrived that evening around ten o'clock at my pavilion and, still standing on the front veranda, he said, "I can smell it already. It's inside, somewhere in your bedroom. It has a horrible odor!" Neither I nor Henk, my fiancé, smelled anything. I couldn't because I was still under that spell, of course, and Henk couldn't smell it yet. But when Dr. Boekebinder told him to pick up my pillow, we could see that it had been tampered with, part of the seam had been sewn closed with black thread. *Dukun* (Javanese experts in magic and healing) always use black thread to insure that a spell will take hold. By then Henk also smelled the bad odor.

Dr. Boekebinder told him to cut the black thread, stick his hand in the pillow, feel around in the kapok filling and to take out anything hard and solid. And yes, holding it as far away from himself as he could, my fiancé handed Dr. Boekebinder the thing. I just looked on, dumbfounded, and still couldn't smell anything at all.

Dr. Boekebinder explained, "This is typically what people use to put an evil spell on others. Look!. It's a *ketapang* nut, that has been hollowed out and filled with all kinds of stuff, designed to concentrate the power of the dukun. In addition, a magic cross has been cut out on top, to provide even more satanic power. Jesus' cross looks like this †, while the magic cross looks like this + ; it's a simple plus sign."

Very carefully, he folded this awful thing in a paper bag and assured me that he would destroy it that very night in a ritual manner and with it destroy the magic spell. He must have done what he promised, because the sores started to dry up immediately after, and they stopped itching, even though it took another month before they had completely disappeared and forever stayed away. At the same time, Aunt Ivy assured me that my brain had cleared up completely, not a spot of black to be seen any longer. This particular experience, however, gave me the God-given power myself to find things when other people were put under a spell, thus snatching them from the hands of the devil. Such a fight against evil is horrible, but the Bible recounts many cases of such fights. Satan is very powerful, but with the help of Jesus' powerful love, we can protect ourselves against him and overcome his demonic powers.

You shouldn't assume that guna-guna only exists in Indonesia. Satan has his finger in the pie in every country. You can read for yourself that such dark powers, sometimes called voodoo and sometimes by another name, are found all over the world, no country excepted. In one country it may be more out in the open than in another, but magic has been used as long as the road to Rome has been in existence.

In my time, people also believed in astrology and mediumship, read fortunes from cards, used needles to point out letters, and I don't remember what else. Be that as it may, one day when I was playing along with that nonsense once again, the following was ticked off by the Ouija board, "Why doesn't Rita pray?" (We would pray before we started the session.)

True, I didn't pray, because I knew it was Satan's work and that the Christ is more powerful than anything else. And the others kept praying while I kept talking to Jesus. Well, that ended it; the needle stopped moving.

The lady in charge said, "One of us is resisting this."

"Yes," I said, "It's me. To show you that this is false. If there were truly a spirit here, who had something worthwhile to say and wanted to tell the truth, then he, that spirit, would have persisted. But instead, he slunk away with his tail between his legs, because Jesus is here." She stared at me with angry eyes and never asked me to sit in again. And the others also learned a lesson and found out they were playing a dangerous game.

My sister was a medium. For a long time, she had played around with the idea that she saw spirits and had other powers. She studied all that occult folderol and one day she asked me to sit in on a so-called table dance. She wanted to convince me once and for all that she was indeed a medium and that these kinds of things *did* exist. Okay. We put our hands on a little table in our bedroom (my parents weren't home), and in a minimum of time the table started to rise. I looked up and glanced at my sister's face. I got the shock of my life!

I have already described what my little sister looked like, but I'll describe her once again, for good measure. She had a refined, gentle face, gentle eyes, and curly hair. But then, at that table dance, I saw an old, ugly witch sitting across from me, her lips pulled up into a snarl, uttering guttural sounds, sweat dripping down her face, her eyes glowing with hatred.

Instinctively, I said, "In the name of Jesus, be gone with you!" and at once the table fell down again and my sister sank back in her chair, half-fainted. She was her old self again, but was totally

140

exhausted. When she had regained strength, I begged her not to do this again and to ask God to take away her bad and evil fascination. She promised me this and she has kept her word. She overcame that fascination forever.

I'm sharing these experiences, to prove that Jesus is Almighty Power, and whoever believes in Him is empowered to lead others back to the right way. I'll never forget that witch, that devil, who took over my little sister that time, because he had the power to change a beautiful girl into a nauseating monster, whose only wish was to bring destruction and death. My husband had his own extraordinary experiences, which came to him unbidden and out of nowhere, and to this day we have no idea why. I'll tell you about this later, however. For now I'll return to our engagement.

Yes, following old-fashioned custom, I was officially engaged, for a year. Our official engagement was celebrated with gifts of flowers and an intimate dinner, while my fiancé presented me with a golden chain bracelet, symbolizing my being in love with him or "chained" to him in spirit.

One month before our wedding, we picked out our rings and had them engraved. They were plain, gold rings, without any decorative elements, only engraved with our pet names for each other and the wedding date. I have never taken my wedding ring off my finger since the day of our wedding on 2 January 1935—now more than fifty years ago. It is engraved with the word *Liefste* or "Dearest." He was dearest to me then and he is dearest to me now, and it says liefste on his tombstone.

After a year's engagement, and after I had worked for the BPM five years, we were married at the residential courthouse in Malang on 2 January 1935. Before that, my father had "married" us in a private ritual at my parents' home, by giving us his blessing and having us exchange rings, witnessed by my mother, brothers and sister. That was a beautiful and blessed moment. Henk and I became husband and wife on the same day that my parents had their wedding thirty-two years earlier.

I was twenty-eight years old, and the night before, I slept for the last time between my parents, the way I used to do when I was little. I felt tense and couldn't sleep at all. We talked together until late and I listened to my parents' advice.

That morning, my mother helped me dress in my full-length, white satin bridal gown with sleeves and a short train, a long veil gathered around my head, tailor-made for me. When I stepped out of the room, my husband-to-be was waiting for me already, dressed in a black, so-called swallow-tail costume, a huge and elegant bouquet of white phaleanopsis orchids in his hands.

In the meantime, lots of friends, acquaintances, and relatives had arrived, all of them planters, administrators of coffee, tea, and rubber plantations, who were either real uncles or whom I called "uncle." They all knew me from the time I was born. I had set my heart on marrying a planter myself originally, because life in the mountains looked so appealing to me. But, after two broken engagements with planters, it appeared this life was not meant for me, and, as it turned out later, this was all to the good. My mother wasn't too pleased with my choice in marriage partner. My father, on the other hand, was completely happy with it. He was able to look beyond the small paycheck and the job my future husband had. He was able to see the strong love Henk felt for me; he knew that here was a man who could keep a rein on his impetuous daughter; and he saw how happy I was.

I kept stumbling over my long veil while I walked arm in arm with my husband-to-be. He shook his head at me in pity and whispered, "You should have put on your sailor's suit instead of this gown. Try to walk slowly and with dignity and don't walk as if you're trying to win the one-hundred kilometer race." But I never like to walk slowly, like this, *sloyong-sloyong*, never; I always walk fast, even now. That's why it was very hard for me that day, to keep my legs under control. I'm sure, I didn't walk gracefully. Nevertheless, we had a wonderfully happy and fun farmer's wedding, what with all those planters surrounding me in that house called "Branggah" in Batu.

When we went on our honeymoon, driving first to Malang, in an uncle's Cadillac, three white doves flew over our car and they stayed all the way with us until we stepped out of the car in town, at which time they swooped around gracefully and flew away from view. We took this to be a favorable omen.

The day after, we started on our honeymoon in our own car, a little Ford, and promptly, on the very first day of our marriage, we had a big fight. All through that long drive, all the way from Malang to Yogya and from there to the Borobudur, we didn't say one word to each other.

Along the way, we stopped in Pagah, to visit my old, retired babu Sanem. We found her selling pecil, a Javanese vegetable dish, in the guard house so familiar to me, where the kentong still hung as of old. Unfortunately, she had grown blind. When I called out to her, she recognized my voice immediately, but her granddaughter had to lead her to me. Babu Sanem put her arms around me and felt me all over. My new husband underwent the same treatment, willy-nilly. She sent her grandchildren immediately on various errands, and took us to her new house in the kampong. There were some chairs, so we could sit down, and soon we were gossiping together in Javanese, enjoying a glass of *kopi tubruk*, ondeh-ondeh, kwee apem and nasi pecil. At that time, my city-bred husband only knew Malay; he didn't know the Javanese language, and I had to keep translating. All too soon, we had to leave again after a tearful farewell from babu Sanem, whom I saw there and then for the last time.

The frosty atmosphere between my husband and me had mellowed a bit by then. We drove past the sugar plantation Garum towards Blitar, where I left my bridal bouquet on the family grave in the cemetery in Blitar. We went on to the Borobudur, a centuries old Buddhist temple, where I finally made up and everything was okay again between us.

After visiting the Borobudur, we arrived properly beaming with happiness at the sisal plantation where we were to stay. This was managed by yet another of my many "uncles" and "aunts." I don't remember the name of that plantation. We stayed there for a week and then returned to our own little house on Reiniersz Boulevard in Surabaya. We had already furnished it before we got married.

What a wonderful homecoming! All the baskets with flowers from our wedding had been brought in from Batu; the food stood ready; and my maid, smiling broadly—she had been such a loyal servant during my maiden years—walked up to me with a german shepherd puppy in her arms, a gift from my new husband to me.

In our family room, other gifts from him lay waiting—no less than three cookbooks! Well, doesn't the love of a man go by way of his stomach? But it wasn't out of place in my case, for I didn't know the first thing about cooking, not a thing except for how to cook rice in a pot, which I had learned to do as a Scout. Anyway, at least *my* love didn't go by way of my stomach, it only went by way of my heart.

My marriage was at times difficult, turbulent, but it was also happy, through the twenty-eight years that it lasted, with terrible fights and wonderful making-up again, with various illnesses and other obstacles, but, time and again, the genuine love we felt for each other pulled us through.

1. Marguérite Lanzing, age 20, on a ski slope in Reit im Winkel, Austria, during her stay in Munich 1927-1928 (p. 124).

2. Marguérite Schenkhuizen on her wedding day, age 27, 2 January 1935 in Malang, West Java. From left to right: Paul Lanzing (father), Josje de Kruiff, Marguérite Schenkhuizen, Henk Schenkhuizen, Marga Hanfland (bridesmaid), Emmy Lanzing (mother). The children are Rita and Carla Lanzing, the daughters of Marguérite's brother, Pof.

3. Marguérite Schenkhuizen, age 28, with her first child, Doeshka, in front of the gate leading to the back yard of the house on Slamet Street in Surabaya. The child was born on 15 November 1935 (p. 148).

4. Marguérite Schenkhuizen, age 40, in the fall of 1947 at
the end of the Pacific War at the time she and her family
left Surabaya for the sugar plantation Kadipaten in
Central Java (p. 198).

5. Marguérite Schenkhuizen, age 49, with her family in Bandung 1955-1956. Front row: Henk, Marguérite, and their daughter, Pax. Back row: Doeshka, Guido, and Joy (pp. 206-12).

6.   Marguérite Schenkhuizen, age 85, in Pasadena, California.

NEWLY WED 1935

Henk, my husband, was slender, almost skinny. In my opinion, his head was big. He had the most beautiful large brown eyes, which could look at me in the sweetest way. He had broken his left wrist during a soccer match and it had been repaired with a steel pin; he still had a large scar there. He had sleek and stiff hair, which he combed flat to the back with pomade. Later, he had a haircut like the one that has been fashionable since the late 1980s—short and standing straight up, a crew cut—which looked very good on him. When I married Henk, his teeth were white and beautiful, but later, after he returned from POW camp, many of them fell out; luckily his smile stayed just as sweet as ever.

He was an excellent dancer and, before we had children, we would go out dancing a lot on Friday evenings, when only the so-called "chic people" went out on the town. That's nonsense, of course, but at that time in Surabaya, it was *the* evening to go out. In those days, we still had to work on Saturday, if only for half the day; the rest of the day was enthusiastically filled with sports.

Henk was very patient with me, and was very versatile. He read a lot, studied a lot, was a good bridge player, and played a fair game of chess. He taught me both games. He was, however, quite sloppy—not at work, but at home—really what you would call *srampangan* or careless. I would find his work tools everywhere, on the floor, in the garden, wherever. One day, I put the whole mickmack in a bag and sold it. He blew his top, but afterwards his stuff was kept where it belonged, even though he stayed as slack as ever otherwise. Henk wasn't nonchalant in dress or hair, mind you, but his books, clothes, and all that were left strewn around carelessly. A strange trait in a bookkeeper, which he was.

I have to tell you about my first cooking adventures. I used one of the most well-known cookbooks of the time, the one by Catenius van der Meijden. It contained Indonesian recipes, of course, but also Dutch ones. The book that I now have dates from

1942, fourth printing. I knew Mrs. Catenius personally. She and her husband were not originally from the Indies—they were totoks—but they had lived in the Indies for a long time. I'm not sure about this, but I believe "Uncle" Cat once worked in the mountain plantations. He was a terrible tease. Both Mr. and Mrs. Catenius were sweet, good hearted people, who also lived in Batu, where my parents had moved after my father had been diagnosed as a severe diabetic. Batu wasn't exactly a metropolis, so everybody knew everybody else, and that's how the Cateniusses became my parents' good friends. We, the children, called them Oom and Tante Cat.

It was curious the way in which both of them knew how to cook all kinds of cuisines excellently. Besides their interest in creating new recipes and in recording recipes from different cuisines, they also loved animals and gardening, especially the cultivation of orchids. As a matter of fact, my husband bought my bridal bouquet from them. You could arrange to have food delivered by them, and they also rented rooms to vacationers.

They were plain and simple, honest and hard-working people, who were busy from early morning until late at night. Here again, I feel proud to have known them. We always had a good time at the Catenius home.

I remember my painful attempts to produce our first meal as a ten-day-old new housewife only too well—my first rijsttafel, cooked in our own kitchen. First I had a talk with Minah, my tiny maid. She was forty years old and already a grandmother. She became my maid when I was still unmarried and stayed on after my marriage. I asked her what she ate in the kampong and told her I wanted to eat the same kind of food. Then I translated a recipe for a chicken dish from a cookbook for her and asked her to prepare that also. Indonesians in general, and Minah in particular, have an incredibly sharp memory; she had no trouble carrying out my verbal instructions.

Not only Minah learned to cook these new dishes; I did too. However, Minah was much the better cook because she was very ambitious. If you had left the choice to me, we would have eaten rice with fried salted fish every day; that tasted good and was easy. But Minah got acquainted in the kampong with various Indonesian cooks, who worked for trendy hotels or wealthy people.

She got them to share all kinds of delicious recipes and they showed her how to set the table with napkins folded in the shape of

146

flowers, among other things. Every time we sat down at our dining table, my husband and I found something different waiting for us. It wasn't just the tasty rijsttafel Minah cooked for us, but the table was set differently each time, with flowers and napkins.

Minah was truly our major-domo; she was much more than just a maid, for she did everything. In the morning, she went to market, then she washed our clothes, including my husband's heavy, white, cotton-drill office pants, and everything was back in our closets by day's end, neatly washed and ironed, spotlessly white, and proper. In between, she also cooked our meals.

To go back to my early years at home for a moment, I had noticed then how hard Koki and Sanem had to work for—what seemed to me—very little money. It's true, they also got free room and board. I swore to myself, however, that, if I ever had servants myself, I wouldn't pay them so poorly, and I always kept my word. That's just part of my ethical way of thinking. We paid Minah seven-and-a-half guilders a month in salary plus full meals. Moh, my loyal house servant/gardener during the Japanese occupation, received the same pay.

From the beginning of our marriage, Henk handed me his salary in the envelope it came in at the end of the month and he kept doing this until he died. This was entirely his idea. In those days, Europeans, regardless of rank or occupation, usually got a monthly paycheck, paid out in cash in envelopes. I handled the household finances and paid the bills. When Henk needed some money, he simply asked me for it. We always discussed large purchases together before making the decision, yes or no. We never squabbled over money.

From the start, before we sat down at the table, the servants would be given their food, and they ate exactly the same food we did. They would eat half their portion and take the rest home. The rest of the food would be brought to the table; there the children would be served first, then my husband, and last of all I. That stayed so throughout my whole life, and my children do it the same way in their own households. I never followed the generally accepted custom—it may have been specifically Indies, for all I know—to give the man of the house the biggest slice of meat, because he was the wage earner and had earned that right. What an absurd idea! The children, who still had a lot of growing to do before they were adults, got served first and got served most. We

147

adults were already strong enough to do with less. And the idea that only after we had eaten, the servants would get their share, I didn't like at all. After all, they worked the whole day long, and sometimes even into the night if we needed them to baby-sit.

Henk and I rarely went out after dark, however, because to us our children came first, and we liked to spend our free time with them, especially while they were still very young and needed us badly. When we first got married, Henk and I resolved not to have children until we had been married two years. In the first two years of our marriage, I became pregnant twice! So much for good intentions.

Our first child, a girl named Doeshka, was born the same year we got married, on 15 November 1935, in Surabaya. Everybody started counting fingers at once, to see if I hadn't been naughty and had been "forced" to marry. They were all disappointed—everything was nice and dandy. Our second daughter, Joy, was born on 4 May 1937. That year, 1937, would be very eventful personally, but more of that later. Guido, our son, had us waiting another three years—he was born on 11 April 1940. My youngest daughter, Pax, which means peace, was launched after my husband returned home from Japanese POW camp. But all of this still lay in the future for us.

So, my husband worked for the BPM while I assumed my duties as a housewife, and our life rolled on at a merry pace. Blitz, my husband's wedding present to me, grew into a large, strong, dog—a genuine shepherd. He was both protective and bright. I had soon taught him to pick up the papers and letters at the front gate. Nobody dared to enter our yard unannounced, because Blitz would have torn that person apart. He loved to play hide-and-seek and, no matter where we hid, he would always find us. We would put a hand over his eyes and tell him, "Find the little woman," or "Find the boss." He even found objects that had been thrown into the water.

Shortly after our marriage, we moved into my parents' house on Slamet Street in Surabaya, where we had all lived together as a family for so many years. After my parents left for a cooler climate, it had been rented for a while, but now stood vacant. Because it was a great deal larger than what we had, Henk and I decided to rent the house from my parents. This was a good decision, for Doeshka gave notice she wanted to join us.

THE EARLY YEARS OF OUR MARRIAGE
1935-1940

We quickly moved into the house I knew so well from my youth. The room in the middle, which originally had been my parents' bedroom, now became the nursery. Henk built a baby table himself. Together, we draped a cradle with blue-flowered voile. Luckily, my husband was very handy and versatile. I have two left hands myself. My husband used to say, I only knew how to play tennis, how to run fast, swim, or do any other sport that appealed to me. Well, he wasn't far off the mark. Housework didn't appeal to me, never has. But in the course of the years—especially now that my hair has turned white and I'm a bit wiser—things gradually went smoother, the more so when I remembered to sing the praises of our Savior, who made everything turn out so well for us.

I felt wonderful during my pregnancy and never suffered from morning sickness, or anything like that, which seems to accompany a first pregnancy. I refused to listen to any of the good advice given me by my well-meaning friends and even that by my doctor—you shouldn't do this, or, you shouldn't eat that—and allowed my God and Help to lead the way. Throughout all my pregnancies, I kept eating hot and spicy food. That was taboo, or else your child would be born with red and inflamed eyes. I kept doing what I usually did around the house before I was pregnant. I would often forget that I had a fat belly and would try to get in somewhere only to get stuck between a cabinet and the wall, for instance. I can still laugh about that.

My oldest child, a girl named Doeshka—which means "favorite of the gods"—was a plump but tiny baby, and she stayed small. This was my first experience with giving birth. While I was pregnant, my husband and I would put our hands on my belly, then pray together and talk to the unborn child, which was already kicking my belly from the inside with great force and vivacity. We did this with all

149

our four children, and I feel and know for sure that each knew and felt this, even as a fetus. This "ritual" undeniably left its stamp on my children's lives and for that I'm deeply grateful.

Then, Doeshka's birth. Everything was ready. Piles of colored diapers and homemade and hand-embroidered shirts had already been neatly put away in the baby dresser. I had white, pink, and blue diapers. Everybody, including the nurses later, thought that was quite original. I forgot to tell you, I was so ignorant, that Henk had to cut out the first baby shirts. He did this with a ruler and a compass, it's true, but he managed to cut out a shirt. Well, that was a little too embarrassing, so I asked my mother for help. She sent me some patterns, which I figured out how to use. Well, by then I had so much fun with it, I started to embroider all those baby clothes. I had learned embroidery in the girl's HBS. Doeshka got a truly adorable layette, which I used later for Joy too.

Suddenly, I was so caught up in sewing that I decided to surprise my dear husband with a homemade pair of pajamas. I only worked on it during the day when he was away at the office. I took apart an old pair of Henk's pajamas, cut out all the different components and sewed them together. When the new pair was finished, I wrapped the pajamas up and threw the package in his lap with the proud words, "Look what I made for you with my very own hands." Not knowing what to expect, he quickly opened the package and was happily surprised at seeing the red and blue pinstriped pair of pajamas. He put it on right away and we burst out laughing, for my husband stood there with the pants on backwards. It looked awfully silly. I had put the left leg where the right leg should have been and vice versa, so the fly was on the back! The top fit nicely, however. When we had stopped laughing, Henk hugged me and said, "It doesn't matter. I think you're very smart anyway." I set my mistake right and he wore those pajamas, my very first piece of sewing, until they fell apart at the seams. That's how he showed me how much he appreciated my efforts.

Another day, I set a homemade cake before him. It looked nice and promised good eating. My husband tried to cut it, but it was so tough the knife flew out of his hand and the cake fell on the floor. It was as hard as a rock. A totally bungled job. Fortunately, we could laugh about that too.

Early in the morning of 14 November 1935, I bathed Blitz, my dog. That evening, Tje's fiancé, Hans Nepveu, picked me up for

150

dinner at a Chinese restaurant. I don't remember why Henk didn't go with us; he might have stayed home to finish something or other. After a delicious Chinese meal, we drove into our yard, where Hans nudged the lamppost in passing while making the turn, causing the streetlamp to crash onto the street, where it shattered into a thousand pieces. The broken gas main kept swooshing the whole night through.

Early the next morning, at three o'clock: the first signs of impending birth. I hastily grabbed my packed suitcase, stepped wrapped in my housecoat, into the car, and was driven to the hospital, where our Doeshka was born at eight in the morning. For a first birth, it happened quickly and smoothly. Doeshka's birth took three hours, from the first cramps to when she triumphantly slipped out of my vagina, at which time I felt a certain relief, but also a feeling of emptiness. Most of all, I felt very happy.

She didn't cry. She just lay there between my legs, her eyes wide open, still connected to me with the umbilical cord. At birth, her eyes were blue, but they changed to greyish green when she grew up. She was pulled up by her legs, held upside down, and given a slap across the buttocks, but she didn't give a sound. Finally, after several slaps, she said, "Oh," as if to satisfy us, and that was all. It was apparently enough to get her respiratory system working.

I got to feed her for the first time the day after her birth. The milk gushed forth from my breasts. She got hold of the nipple soon enough and drank the life-giving fluid with gusto. This was happiness, the highest kind of happiness.

She would lie for hours without uttering a sound in her little bed next to mine, her eyes open. I would only hear soft smacking and sighing. The doctor thought it quite unusual. My husband and I couldn't get enough of watching this miracle of God. Henk could watch our child for hours, playing with her little fingers that held on to his workman's fingers. The strength of such a little baby!

In those days, it was the custom in the Indies for a woman to stay ten days in the hospital after giving birth. Well, I thoroughly approved of that custom. Even in the best of circumstances, giving birth is no picnic. Even though I had had a relatively easy delivery, I was happy to get some rest and, above all, professional attention. We, mother and child, received good care in the hospital, and at home the servants looked after my husband. By that time, I had two servants: Minah and her daughter.

People who knew dogs well had warned us that german shepherds are very jealous. They told us about cases in which such a dog had bitten a baby to death. Henk took the soiled baby clothes home every day and had Blitz sniff them. He would growl first, take another good sniff, and then his tail would start to wag while my husband told him, "This belongs to the little boss." Blitz seemed to understand it perfectly.

On the day of my homecoming, Blitz was waiting for me. Holding my precious little bundle in my arms, I called him, "Blitz, come to the little woman!" He ran up to me. When I bent down to show him Doeshka, he stood still, wagged his tail and licked her all over her face with his long, warm tongue. The ice was broken and I could trust Blitz with my child. From that day on, he never left the cradle in which Doeshka slept. He guarded her day and night, like the notorious Cerberus. No stranger was allowed to come near her. It made us feel very safe.

I still can't quite grasp the fact, that the Almighty brought two individuals together in love, at which time a child was created in the woman; a creature, so perfect and so sweet, a little person, a replica of the parents, who, joining forces with the All-knowing, brought another human being onto the earth. It will always be a miracle. Just for that one moment of birth, I would want to be able to conceive forever and ever. Giving birth is a release, a genuine deliverance, but at the same time a giving and receiving of great love.

That's why spiritually, to be born is to be be born again, as Jesus told Nicodemus in the Bible. To be born again in the spirit is an act of liberation; a being saved and a giving and receiving of the highest form of love, which changes the individual in such a way, that he or she starts to live differently, according to the laws given us by Jesus and which He Himself followed.

Giving birth to a child, is the loving giving of a new individual to the Omnipresent, so that His grace and works will continue to exist in never-ending happiness. I experienced His grace in so many ways, but especially in my four children, given me by God. When they grew up and started to understand things better, my husband and I always encouraged them not to set us apart as parents but to treat us as friends, with whom they could talk out everything openly and honestly. We did this so they would not refrain from telling us—out of a misplaced sense of respect—where we had gone wrong with them. "Surely, we're not infallible," we always told them. And that remains so to this day, resulting in beautiful and healthy relationships among my children, my husband, and myself.

But back to my early years as a married woman. Then the time came, that my sister had her wedding, also from our parents' house in Batu. So, we went there. Hers was a so-called high society wedding. It was all gold that glittered on the white uniforms of the officers of the Navy Air Force, my brother-in-law's friends and colleagues. My brother-in-law, Hans Nepveu, was dressed in a black, gold-trimmed uniform and tri-cornered hat himself. He looked very handsome and distinguished. My sister was pretty as a picture. Her slender body was dressed in a white silk gown with a very long train and a very long veil. Carrying a bouquet of Easter lilies, Tje walked with a solemn face at the side of her sweetheart and husband-to-be. She was a truly beautiful bride, totally conscious of the seriousness of the step she had taken.

Tje and Hans also went on a honeymoon, of course, but I've forgotten where they went. I have even forgotten the exact date of their wedding. It took place in 1936. Their first child, a boy, was born in 1937. Sadly, the birth was premature and their son had an insufficiently developed heart. He died when he was five months old. It was a grievous loss for my sister, and for all of us too. By that time, Tje and Hans lived across the street from where we lived in our fifth house. Here I'm running in front of myself again, so I'll get back on track.

Doeshka wasn't even a year old in 1936 when my husband was transferred to Mojokerto, also in East Java, where he was put in charge of the small local office of the BPM. We were assigned a huge, old-fashioned house with a large garden—one of those genuinely old Indies houses—so the transfer was fine by me. We soon made friends with other Indies families there. In such a small town everybody always knows everyone else.

One day, I received word that my father had died from a heart attack. Even though my father was a diabetic, he had always cheerfully and whole-heartedly discharged his duties as director of the agricultural institute from his home in Batu. He had never uttered a word of complaint. He had looked well. He gave himself daily shots of insulin, and followed the prescribed diet quite faithfully. So, his death shocked the whole family greatly, me in particular.

Thinking back, I remember vividly the day, several years before my father died when I was still single, we had seen an unusual solar phenomenon. In the middle of the day, we saw the sun encircled by two large, shimmering aureoles. It was extraordinarily beautiful, but eerie.

My father said at the time, "A ring around the moon, that brings luck soon; but a ring round the sun, brings sorrow to children and women." And, as an afterthought, he added quietly, "Child, I won't be here anymore by then, but you and the others will be. Our Dutch East Indies will fall into the hands of the Japanese, and it won't be a pleasant time at all." When I asked him how he knew this, he answered, "Because of the wretched politics of the Dutch government in the Indies."

Ten years after we witnessed that weird solar display—or was it indeed a warning in the sky?—Father's prediction came true and, as he had foreseen, he didn't have to experience it himself, luckily. My father followed politics closely, combined, deduced, and came to his final conclusion. I will never forget that episode.

Now, in 1936, I drove with little Doeshka from Mojokerto to Batu as fast as I could. I found my father already in his casket in the family room. He looked at peace and calm and sweet as always. He was seventy-two years old. My father was a well-known and popular man—flowers were piled high around the casket.

As an example of his notoriety, it happened once that a letter from Europe, addressed only to "P.G.A. Lanzing, the Indies," was nevertheless properly delivered to him. My father was not only good-humored, he was honest and helpful. Photographs of him clearly capture the goodness in his face.

Shortly after this sad event, my husband was suddenly transferred from Mojokerto to Bojonegoro, in the northern part of East Java. Here we moved into yet another large Indies house, with an even larger garden than the one we had left behind.

Bojonegoro was no more than a village in the middle of a poor region. That region was economically quite depressed. To give an example: if I bought nasi pecil from a street vendor for five cents, I would be handed ten packages, each containing half a cent worth of food. They didn't know how to prepare just one package of food, because they had no idea what five cents worth of rice looked like, what with pecil and everything else that went with that kind of dish. For years, Bojonegoro was known to be the poorest region on Java. To this day, I don't understand why the Dutch government never did anything to help. The poverty there was truly heartbreaking to see, surrounded as that region was by prosperous residencies. Truly, the strangest things were possible under the various governors-general. The Dutch government has not always behaved ethically, and the loss of its richest colony is surely an act of justice.

We didn't stay long in Bojonegoro, for my husband was suddenly let go. We had to move once again. He sent me and Doeshka to stay with my lonely, widowed mother in Batu while he boarded with relatives in Surabaya and looked for another job. Rather soon, he was hired again as bookkeeper in the office of Anemaet and Company, which owned and managed plantations, most of them sugar. He rented a small house on Carpentier Street, right across from the large house of my sister. That much was nice.

It turned out the reason he could rent that house so quickly was that it was rumored to harbor ghosts. Everyone who had ever lived in it, had moved out, helter-skelter, after a few months. However, even though I was an Indo, by that time I didn't believe in ghosts any longer. As a young child I did, but by that time, being a married woman and a student of the Christian religion, I denied ghosts existed.

This house had two bedrooms, a dining room, a sitting room, and a veranda, a complete utilities and servants wing, and a garage. There was even a small garden in front and back. Well, what more could I wish for? It was true, the quality of our houses was going downhill, but I was happy with our oldest child and a second baby on the way. My husband liked his new job. And so, life went on.

Not long after moving back to Surabaya and settling down in the two-bedroom house on Carpentier Street, our second daughter, Joy, was born on 4 May 1937. She was a long, fat baby. Once she could walk, it looked as if I had twins, for she was as tall as my firstborn. So, I made the same clothes for them. Yes, I did it myself with the help of the popular "Beier" patterns. There was nothing to it! Doeshka and Joy always looked fresh and cute, even if I say so myself. Because they both had blond hair and blue eyes in those days—inherited from their Opa Schenkhuizen and Opa Lanzing—people would assume all the time that I was their nanny or something like that.

By that time, Mentik, Tje's little Javanese playmate from Pagah, had found my sister again. They hadn't seen each other for more than twenty years and their reunion was something to behold. Tje immediately hired Mentik to become her maid and cook, and Mentik's husband, a neat and well-mannered Javanese, was hired as their chauffeur. The old, familiar pattern was soon re-established: Tje and Mentik would talk nothing but Javanese with each other when they were alone in the house. Mentik would massage Tje's legs while they gossipped. Tje's old playmate was a hard worker who not only kept the house neat and tidy, but also knew how to prepare simple but tasty food, just the way my brother-in-law preferred.

Tje and Hans would often join Henk and me when we hailed a street vendor, a man selling *tahu-tek-tek* or *tahu-campur* (tofu dishes), or a man who sold *soto*, a kind of soup. Hans Nepveu, my brother-in-law, was an officer in the navy and had to keep up appearances, as they put it. He was not supposed to eat from street vendors, which is why he and Tje came over to our house; even then we were careful to eat in the backyard, away from prying eyes.

Hans was actually a nice, unassuming fellow who adored my sister and couldn't do enough for her, showering her with loving attention and gifts of jewelry. He was a green-eyed Indo, the only child of a widow who lived in a rather downtrodden neighborhood of Surabaya. Mrs. Nepveu had earned barely enough to take care of herself and Hans, and though there was precious little left for extras, her little house was neat and clean and even had an aura of distinction. When we got to know her better, she told us that her husband, who died young, came from a well-connected Dutch family. His relatives refused to have anything to do with him after he married her, because they considered her to be beneath their social class. Hans felt unjustly rejected. When he was in Holland for his studies at the navy air force academy, Hans made it a point to look up his father's relatives. Once they got to know him, they changed their tune, acknowledging that he was an educated and well-mannered young man. When they finally met my sister, by then Hans' widow, they were charmed by her too, so much so that several of them bequeathed Tje substantial amounts of money in their wills. This unexpected largesse did not change my sister, who stayed just as sweet and unaffected as she always had been.

But we certainly had no inkling of this when we four enjoyed our forbidden food together in those days before the war.

Before I forget, I have to tell you about the ghosts in my house. If you can't share a ghost story, you're not a real Indo, so this is about our ghosts. One night, I was awakened by knocks on our dining room door, soft and repeated regularly. I thought, "There is our ghost finally." I tiptoed towards the sound, opened the door with a bang and . . . there stood the street guard. He had wanted to warn me that our door wasn't locked and was standing ajar. I ask you! That was that, the "ghost" went on its way, and I went back to bed.

Another ghost announced its presence not long after. Again, I heard knocking in the night, this time coming from the chest of drawers in the nursery. I crept up there, again on tiptoe. Whatever it was kept knocking stubbornly. Very carefully, I moved the chest of drawers filled with baby clothes away from the wall, and shone the flashlight I always keep near me, on the back of the cabinet. And what did I see? A small house lizard struggling with a moth it wanted to eat, trying to kill it by banging it against the back of the dresser, hence the knocks. This "ghost" was laid to rest too. If you just lie there, waiting in fear for a ghost to show itself or do something, that's what leads to ghost stories. Actually though, as you see, most of them are explained easily enough

On the other hand, my husband was indeed clairvoyant. He could always see either the *jaga rumah*—a benign house spirit—or an evil spirit in all the houses we ever lived in. He hadn't seen anything in particular in this house, so it was okay to move in. I would have moved in no matter what anyway, for, as I explained, I don't believe in ghosts. Moreover, I came to live across from my sister, which was great.

In this house, Doeshka one day became ill with a high fever, which didn't subside in spite of the medicine the doctor had given her. He was at a loss to explain this. Besides, he didn't quite know what ailed her. One night the fever had risen so high, she began to have hallucinations. She insisted on getting out of bed and being carried around, while she kept yelling, "There she is! There she is! And her belly is open! She's sitting on the wall!"

I thought, I'd better play along with her. So, intuitively speaking Javanese, I said to the woman with the open belly sitting on the wall, "Go on, scat!" And then I added in Dutch, "In the name of Jesus, be cursed for all time!" Doeshka immediately calmed down, and said sleepily that the woman had disappeared. The fever quickly abated. She slept that night like a rose, and was totally recovered the week after.

I don't know if it was fate or simply coincidence, but the very next day a *haji*, an Indonesian Muslim holy man, came to the door and asked my permission to set out some offerings at the foot of the wall. After he had prayed, he said to me in Malay, "With your prayers, you've banned the *kuntil anak* from this area forever. Thank you in the name of Allah." In the Javanese belief system, the kuntil anak is an evil spirit that steals little children. Can you imagine that? No matter how you look at it, there is so much that's mystical and mysterious in our land of birth.

I used to wish fervently that I too would develop the gift of seeing spirits or ghosts, as had my husband. One evening, I called him, feeling very excited because I was finally able to see a ghost in our garden. Would he please come and verify it. And indeed, we could clearly see the shape and movements of a dark, dancing woman. After watching it closely for a moment, Henk burst out laughing, "You and your overheated imagination! Look closely at your ghost. Go on, go over there. That's not a spirit at all!" I walked over there and then saw what it was: a rag that had been hung out to dry and was moving in the wind. From a distance, its shadow really did look like a woman dancing. Of course, we had a good laugh again.

The last episode with ghosts was the following: Every Thursday evening, offerings had to be laid near the branch of our neighbor's waringin tree that grew over our wall. And every week I was asked to contribute a quarter for the required flowers, yellow rice, incense, and other things. Finally, I'd had enough of it and I called out loud, "I curse that tree! Every Thursday it's the same nonsense!"

A week later, Surabaya was visited by a kind of typhoon, that swept off entire roofs and whirled them around in the air. I heard a terrific creaking noise and that waringin in the neighbor's yard lay there, roots and all. The servants ran up, knelt in front of me and folded their hands together respectfully, calling out, "Allah did as Mrs. Rita asked!" No more offerings on Thursday evening. That was the end of that nonsense.

Then 1940 came and with it the birth of our only son, Guido, causing great rejoicing in our household. By now, it had become impossible to ignore the ominous rumble of war in Europe. We were glued to the radio, listening for news, when we heard the chilling code, "Telegram Berlin! Telegram Berlin!" and we knew— Holland had been overrun by German troops. Within an hour all Germans in the Indies were picked up to the last man and jailed. This was done by the PID, the Dutch political information service. Later, those Germans and NSB sympathizers, who were loyal to Holland, were set free again.

Our anxiety rose. What next?

SURABAYA IN WORLD WAR II 1941-1942

For months the air had been filled with rumors of war. Then our turn came: the Dutch East Indies was called to arms. My husband was called up for military service, and with him all able-bodied men. I immediately volunteered my services for the civilian air watch. Its office was conveniently close to our house on Carpentier Street. Evenings, I sewed piles and piles of shirts of unbleached muslin for the war wounded, the Red Cross, and whatnot.

We were told to build air raid shelters, either out in the yard or by converting a garage by means of sandbags. There weren't enough helmets for the general population, so we had to make do with iron woks, with which we were told to cover our heads when bombs started to fall. Each of us was told to hold a big rubber eraser between our teeth to protect our eardrums. We had a training session once, using all these items, and we burst out laughing and couldn't quit, it was such a silly sight. Our family used our air raid shelter only once; we became claustrophobic and had difficulty breathing.

In the meantime, we heard all kinds of rumors. My mother wanted me and the children to come over to Batu and move in with her. I even went so far as to pack all my books on religion to send to Batu. Can you imagine! Not clothes or paintings or food, but my books. But I changed my mind, thinking of the wise lessons in the Bible, which teach you to have faith in God. As soon as I had decided to stay, I became calm. We stayed put in our own little house throughout the following years.

My sister, meanwhile, had moved to another house, that she had built herself, farther down Carpentier Street. There, the children of my brother, Pof, stayed in her pavilion; they attended the HBS. A married couple, friends I knew from my years at the BPM, by the name of Wasterval, moved into my sister's old house catty-cornered across the street from us. Eugénie Wasterval was

Armenian. During the occupation, the Wastervals sold delicious, home-baked cakes.

On 7 December 1941 Pearl Harbor was bombed. For us, it was December 8. The Netherlands, America's ally, promptly retaliated by sending out the few submarines it had. We heard they had been sent to Tokyo harbor where they reportedly sank three Japanese warships. I don't know if this is true or not, there were so many unsubstantiated rumors in those years. The Netherlands had declared war to Japan and the Indies had no choice but to follow suit.

My brother-in-law, Nepveu, flying his Dornier, met the attacking Japanese planes in mid-air. His last message was, "SOS, SOS, being attacked by eleven Navy Zeroes!" From then on, nothing but silence. Neither he nor his crew nor his plane have ever been found. This happened on Christmas Day 1941. Tje's and Hans' daughter was one year old.

All males, boys eighteen years and up, were now drafted. The older men were assigned to the Civil Patrol, the younger ones to the Indies equivalent of the Air National Guard. Others, such as my husband, were put under full alert in the Anti-Aircraft Guard. The Japanese came closer and closer. They seemed to be unstoppable. Singapore fell. They landed everywhere: in Sumatra, New Guinea, Java. We continued to hold fast.

At the very first air alert signal, I was by myself, alone on my post. The other ladies assigned to cover the same post with me, one way or the other had all found a ship and had escaped to Australia. At my post, I could hear the bombs fall, very close by—a terrifying sound. The sirens kept on howling and the telephone, which I held glued to my ear, kept relaying messages, "Hallo Heulang, hallo Heulang, send this message through via Pete. Send through via Pete." Suddenly the telephone fell dead—our boys, who had taken cover from air attacks in jungle and rice fields, had been routed by Japanese foot soldiers and taken prisoner. I waited. The telephones stayed silent.

Finally, the supervisor of my civil air watch unit came riding up on his bike, while the noise of planes strafing and bombs falling turned the earth into Dante's hell. Then, suddenly, complete silence. The supervisor told me to go home. Contact had been broken off. No orders anymore. This was 8 March 1942. The

161

Indies had surrendered. My soul turned to stone. My eyes stayed dry, but my heart pounded in my throat. It was all too much for me.

When I got home, I found my children huddling with the servants. They came running up to me, their eyes wild with fear. Our neighbor woman had shooed them all into the air raid shelter to quietly await the unfolding events.

The radio kept us abreast of the situation and one day a well-known radio announcer—whose name I have forgotten—told us that everything was lost and we had to obey our conquerers. He ended with the famous words, "Farewell till better times. Long live our queen!" after which the radio fell dead and he was taken prisoner. Later, all our radios were sealed to prevent us from listening to foreign stations. We could only listen to news broadcast in the Malay language, censored by the Japanese.

Anyway, I returned home from my last duty at that civilian air watch post and told my children that the war was over and Papa would be coming home soon now. I really, truly believed that, which was unbelievably naive. My servants, also reassured, went about their daily chores again.

I changed into a housedress and listened to the unnerving quiet that had settled over Surabaya like an almost tangible threat. I could see plumes of smoke rising up here and there, but otherwise, nothing but silence. The silence in my own heart was unbearable. I went over to a neighbor and we tried to give each other peptalks, advising each other that we had better keep low and follow the orders of the new authorities.

Then I picked up a book and sat down in our front yard. The children resumed their interrupted play. I settled down to wait for whatever would come. I was still convinced that Henk would suddenly appear before me.

Unexpectedly, we heard the roar of many cars, and yes, the first of the Japanese shock troops were driven past in open trucks: short men, dressed in tan, most of them heavily armed and wearing glasses. I looked on quietly but with pounding heart, wondering what would happen next. An officer was seated in each truck, accompanying his soldiers, and to my utter astonishment, each of them saluted me in passing. Automatically, I got up and looked along the street, and only then discovered that I was the only one sitting outside.

Why did they salute me, I wondered. Maybe because I was courageous enough to sit outside by myself, or what? Anyway, sudah, better to be saluted than to be shot through the head. But they wouldn't do that anyway, for now peace had returned between Japan and the Indies, right? Note my naiveté; you may well say, stupidity.

So, for the moment they drove past, but later returned to be quartered in the house next to mine, a huge mansion owned by the manager of Socony, an oil company. This was accompanied by a lot of unintelligible screaming and yelling and the sound of stuff being unloaded. Even now my irrepressible curiosity got the upper hand; I just had to find out what Japanese shock troops looked like up close and watched them avidly.

With the invasion of the Japanese came their own unique odor: a sensual, sweet smell that hung over the Indies for three-and-a-half years. Was this caused by eating raw fish? It hung around their clothes, it permeated their skin, it floated through the air. Their mud-covered shoes brought the eggs of the huge so-called agate garden snails along, and these snails would later cover our yards and our garden walls and devour everything in their path. They became such a plague, that every day everybody would fill up a bucket a person with these snails to get rid of them. Later I heard that people were known to eat them. Not me!

In those days, a friend was staying with us. We could hear trucks arriving and the rattling of bottles being unloaded in the dark. It made her feel scared to death of being raped at night.

"There, you see," my housemate would say, "Now they're going to drink beer and when they're drunk, they'll come and break into this house."

Pretending to be icy calm, I said, "Can't you tell from the sound that those are soda pop bottles, not beer bottles?"

"You're always so optimistic. How do you know for sure?"

"Well, if it's a beer bottle, you hear 'klonang-klonang,' and if it's a soda pop bottle, you hear 'kleening-kleening.'"

"Aduh, Riet, how do you invent such things in heaven's name!"

We stayed awake, of course, if only because the racket of their guttural language and the rattling of the bottles kept us on edge. It was true though, those bottles did make a definite kleening-kleening sound. But no matter how much I argued, I couldn't convince my

163

friend that it was soda pop. Actually, I didn't believe it myself; I just said so to reassure my friend.

I just had to take a peek through our hedge the next morning and, true enough, empty soda pop bottles were strewn all over the yard. I called my friend over so she could see for herself, and we burst out in hysterical laughter. Everything was okay again.

Then the racket in the house next to ours started up again. One of those slit-eyes shoved himself through our hedge, holding a couple of pots and pans in his hands. All his gold teeth glittering in a wide smile, he tried to explain something to me in his gibberish, which I—only thanks to my own sharpness of mind, of course!—finally understood: he wanted to use my kitchen to cook his meal.

Well, I hovered over him, listening to his babbling, both of us smiling amiably at each other, trying to communicate with gestures. Whatever he was brewing started to smell appetizing and I sniffed loudly, which prompted him to share his homemade hotchpotch with me. It tasted delicious, even though I have no idea what was in it. I thanked him and he thanked me and off he went again, as fast as his bent legs could carry him. Well, however you looked at it, that was hospitable and friendly and not hostile at all.

My housemate kept lamenting, "What have you done now! Really, you're much too kind to them. They'll rape you yet. Also, aren't you fraternizing with the enemy?"

I said, "I would rather befriend them and turn bad into good. That doesn't turn me into a traitor or provide them with any service that could hurt our country."

So, that went on for a couple of weeks. Sometimes the same person would show up, sometimes he would bring a friend along, but they always returned borrowed pots and pans nicely scrubbed, accompanied by lengthy shaking of hands, bows, and *arigatos*, as if I had presented them the 100,000. (We used this number to refer to the Indies lottery, the grand prize of which was one hundred thousand guilders.) And then, just as suddenly as they had appeared, they moved on. What a relief!

When they had left, a Japanese crew was sent to inspect the house, because it had to be readied to house a high hat. That's when we discovered that these soldiers used to relieve themselves wherever they were at the time. The house was so badly fouled, the fire brigade had to spray the whole house free of human excrement and the smell of urine. Lysol was brought in. They swept, sprayed, and scrubbed. All the windows and doors had to be opened wide; the furniture was piled up; and we walked around with a handkerchief pressed to our nose. Finally, everything had been made habitable again and a colonel moved in with two field aides.

This man was fat, mustachioed, and had a yellowish pale skin. After work, in the afternoon, he used to take a walk in our street dressed only in a loincloth. At that hour of the day, I used to sit on our porch with a cup of coffee and a book, the children playing around me in the garden. Every time he passed me, he would look at me and make the deep Japanese bow, and I, without getting up, would make a small bow in return.

Everyone asked me, "What are you doing there, anyway. Why don't you sit inside or in the backyard? You'll see, one of these days, he'll make advances."

I retorted, "I wouldn't think of sitting in that tiny, stifling backyard. Anyway, I'm not doing any harm, and this way, he can keep an eye on me and see that I'm not a spy or anything like that."

"Well, you know what you're doing."

I must have sat on that low veranda wall for a month, keeping an eye out for my husband, whom I felt sure was going to come home any time now. All my neighborhood friends would shake their heads and tell each other, "She refuses to accept the fact that our men are now POWs and will never be set free. She'll go crazy if this goes on!"

Finally, I got a note from Henk, smuggled to me at the bottom of a package of boiled rice—a mere scribble written on the inside of a crumpled-up cigarette wrapper. He wrote that he was all right but that the world had gone mad, and that he was shut up in a former hospital for the insane in Madura (an island off Surabaya) where his battalion had held out for another eight days after the official surrender, because they hadn't heard the Indies had been overrun. Radio contact had been broken off, everything had been smashed to bits. Because his battalion had fought on after the cease-fire, the Japanese military had condemned all of them to death by firing squad, and they had been ordered to line up accordingly. His note went on in Malay, "but if it isn't your time, it isn't your time."

We never found out what prompted the sudden reversal of orders. It was such a relief to know that he was still alive!

From then on, I had to go on without my "Dearest." The first few months, I still received my husband's paycheck, until that stopped too, because the managers of his company, Anemaet and Company, were put into concentration camps themselves. By that time, the Japs could handle everything themselves, helped by the hordes of civil servants who arrived from the Land of the Rising Sun to work in industry and other places. What now?

LIFE DURING THE JAPANESE OCCUPATION
1942-1945

I still remember several of my neighbors during the occupation. There was Galestin, an Armenian, who lived in the house directly across from us. Doeshka used to swipe a fat papaya from his backyard from time to time during the war years. Francine Crompvoets, maiden name Swaving, also lived near us with her five children. Francine was an excellent cook. Then there were Ab and Eugénie Wasterval, whom I mentioned earlier. Eugénie's maiden name was Vardon. The Vardons owned a locally well-known carriage rental business. Eugénie had the rather doubtful luck of having her husband with her. Ab, an Indo, had fought at the front with the other draftees. At the cease-fire, he had coolly walked into a nearby house, changed into civilian clothes, and walked home. He was a nice man, a great help to us. Later, he was the only Indiesman in our street who still walked around free out of camp. Otherwise, most of the free men were foreigners. Later yet, Ab did duty as our street guard.

Broer Carels and Zus Voogd were also neighbors. They started a corn bread bakery soon after the cease-fire. Broer asked me to do the bookkeeping for them. I made some money and also received a small loaf of hot corn bread in pay daily. It really tasted wonderful and the bakery got off to a good start. But what I made was hardly enough to feed me, my three children, and two servants.

Luckily, I received a call from an acquaintance, who worked for the Jap civil authorities. They needed furniture for their houses and had asked her if she could find the necessary refrigerators, ceiling fans, rugs, curtains, dinner sets, and other items. This lady needed go-fers, who, on foot or on the bike, were asked to visit wealthy people and ask them if they wanted to sell something, anything; although wealthy, they had no cash—all banks were closed. I grabbed this job.

167

What did I do? Well, for example, that lady told me to find a ceiling fan for her. The owner would perhaps ask five hundred Indies guilders—printed by the Jap—and I would tell the middle-woman that I needed seven hundred Indies guilders to get one. She would give that sum to me without hesitation, for she would sell it to the Jap for nine hundred or something like that. We didn't begrudge each other's profit, and each of us could make a good living. We called that *catutten*, from the Indonesian term *catut*. That money was easily earned and it kept its value. I've never before or after had so much money as then, in the time of the Jap. Sometimes, I would make such a profit, that I could take a month off and we could even splurge on a ciroflé-cirofla cake baked by Ab and Eugénie Wasterval.

We women went wherever the wind of fate blew us. In spite of our radios being "sealed" about three months after the cease-fire on orders of the Jap authorities, we managed to listen on a regular basis anyway. This sealing of radio receivers consisted of two wires being fastened to the front of the unit so that the choice of stations was limited to a few local ones. An official lead seal was attached to these wires as well as to the back panel, hence the term. This happened more than once, every time resulting in fewer stations being available, until finally all radios were called in. We learned to listen between the lines and thus find out what was really happening in the war, in contrast to what the Japanese wanted us to believe.

I knew a young Indo who repaired radios for the Japanese. He was a whiz in radio. Pretending to check if a radio had been repaired well, he would listen to foreign news stations. That way, he got news about the war firsthand from England, America, Germany, and Japan. He would tell me the latest news, and I relayed that the same evening to my neighbor across the street, and my other friends heard it the day after when they visited me specifically with this in mind. What we did was dangerous, but it was also exciting and kept our hopes up. Not one of our circle ever betrayed us. But we were very, very careful.

Newspapers were printed in Malay only. But not to worry. I had hired an Indonesian house servant/gardener in the meantime, a former Javanese grade school teacher, who had fled from the Jap and was looking for a safe haven. I told him I could only pay him seven-and-a-half guilders a month plus free room and board. He

168

would have to sleep in our garage. Moh accepted and moved right in. The name "Moh" may have been short for Mohammed, in which case he would have been a Muslim. Every day, Moh and I would read the paper together and he would translate it into easier, run-of-the-mill Malay for me. One day, while the Germans were fighting against the Russians in the midst of snow and ice, he said in Malay, "Remember what I'm saying. This Hitler is making the same stupid mistake Napoleon once made and so he'll suffer the same fate and lose the war." I stared at him in surprise and respect. My gardener with his nice but vapid face was actually a well-educated man. Moh turned out to be right. But I'm running in front of myself again. Strange, the images from my childhood not only seem to be sharper but they also seem to be in better order than those from later years.

Soon after the occupation started, the Dutch schools had been closed on orders of the occupying forces and we had started to teach our children at home one way or the other. Then the order came down that we were no longer allowed to teach our children— they had to attend an Indonesian school. But most of us ignored that order and got lesson material from teachers, who also had been thrown out of work but still knew how to get hold of textbooks.

Right under the nose of the Jap, in the person of my colonel-neighbor, I taught my children every day from eight in the morning till noon. This was done with a lot of yelling and screaming and hysteria on my part whenever I lost patience. Then we would eat, and afterwards I would entrust my children to my loyal Minah and Moh, or they would be picked up by the colonel's aides, allowed to ride the horses in his garden, and treated to sweets.

The love of the Japanese for children is legendary. Our children became our guardian angels, because you were left alone if you had children. There were exceptions, of course, but on the average it was true.

Everywhere you saw women on bikes, going in all directions to catut. They formed an informal street-telephone or telegraph. And that's how we learned that our men had arrived from Madura and were put to work among the ruins of offices in Tanjong Perak, Surabaya's port. We weren't allowed to go near there, however. But what happened? All of a sudden, my neighbor from across the street hurried over and told me that my husband was on her telephone. We didn't have a telephone ourselves.

"How's that possible?!" I yelled, excited and unbelieving.

"Hurry, hurry, go 'n talk!" she said.

I ran over to her house, picked up the phone and, yes, I heard Henk's dear voice. He was happy to hear that we were managing fine, and when I asked him if he had gotten permission to call his family, he said, "Well, up to a point." My husband was rather phlegmatic. "I'm working here among the ruins and noticed a telephone on the floor next to a smashed desk. Well, I tried it and darned if it didn't work. That's how I managed to reach you. But now I've to leave, somebody is getting suspicious." He managed to call me several times afterward. I was truly luck's favorite child.

Not long after, we read in the paper that Tenno Heika, the Japanese emperor, was going to have a birthday. And, as a favor to us, we would be allowed to visit the POWs and bring them food. The whole country burst out in jubilation. On the appointed day, we lugged a big suitcase full of food and goodies and another smaller one with clothes onto the trolley: destination Tanjung Perak. Minah insisted on going too. There we went, with my three children. Guido, my son, was only two.

In the trolley, we were seated next to Japs, who asked us by means of gestures and a smattering of Malay where we were going. We folded our arms over our breast to signify POWs. Oh, they knew exactly where those were housed and they would take us there. Well, I ask you! One of them carried the heavy suitcase, Minah carried my son in her slendang, and, as if we were the best of friends, the Japs did indeed take us to the gate of the POW camp, where many men were already waiting for their relatives to show up.

My husband's eagle eye had already seen us and he signalled us to walk to such and such a place. Soon after, we were all being hugged by him, and the first few minutes were spent asking each other how things were going and how the war was proceeding. Minah couldn't stop crying and kept stroking my husband's lower legs. Then he fell upon the food. Each of the men had made himself a small food chest, from wood salvaged from the bombed-out offices, to store his belongings.

At nightfall we went home again, with empty suitcases and heavy hearts. Nevertheless, I was deeply grateful for Tenno Heika's gesture. For even though saying goodbye was sad, on the other hand, you were happy to know that your husband was still alive.

170

And you had been able to hold him again, feel him and kiss him, oh yes, especially kiss him. Tired and a bit down-hearted, we went home, to pick up our own life of waiting, hoping, and working to keep the children and ourselves fed.

But work was good medicine for us women; it kept us busy, and it was good for our bodies, because we rode lots of kilometers on our bikes. We helped each other as much as we could. We also took food to the totok women, who by then had been put "behind the gedek" (our slang for concentration camp, because these camps were invariably surrounded by high gedek walls to isolate the prisoners from the outside world).

All the Dutch people still outside the camps were ordered to get an identification card. To stay outside the camps, we had to prove that we had some Indonesian ancestors. We helped those Indies women who had light eyes and blond hair by rubbing their skins with cocoa and putting scarfs on their heads. Even though we laughed a lot when we did this, all of those we disguised like that did indeed remain free.

When it was my turn, the Jap said in Malay, "OK, passed. Indo, without any doubt." And I went on my way, relieved that I didn't have to say a thing. You can see now what a godsend my brown skin and eyes were.

We wanted to stay out of camp at all costs, and this drove the totok women—whom we had provided with food at considerable danger to ourselves—to call us "Nippon whores." The occupying forces generally forbade charity work of any kind and punished them severely. We didn't say anything back and just went on doing what needed to be done.

One day, we received news through the grapevine that our men had been moved to the *Jaarbeurskamp* (Fair Site) and would be working on the outside on such and such a date. If we wanted to see them (from afar), we had to be at a specific spot at a certain hour. We rode our bikes to the designated location. However, it was strictly forbidden to talk or wave or whatever when you saw your man, you knew you could only look, period. But we were grateful for every little bit.

And yes, there they came, standing up and crowded together in open trucks. I saw Henk immediately and naturally, impulsive as I was, I waved at him and called out in Dutch, "I love you." Hardly had those words left my mouth when I heard a strident voice, promising hell and damnation. I saw Henk's face stiffen, and I knew I had done something stupid for the umpteenth time.

I jumped on my bike as fast as I could and dashed away as if the devil himself was after me. This was only too true in this case, for a little Japanese, his short legs pedaling furiously, was after me. To be chased scared me to death. But, of course, I knew every nook and cranny of Surabaya and was able to shake him off soon enough and got home safely. I was completely out of breath, but had a feeling of triumph—my husband had heard me loud and clear.

That very same evening, another note was promptly smuggled to me, again written on the inside of a cigarette wrapper. It told me to show myself without fail at the same spot and at a certain time. Henk wanted to see if the Jap had mistreated me. When I saw him, and had escaped unharmed, I should only shake my head, "No." Well, I did as asked, and Henk smiled and shook his head over my genius for stirring up trouble. But his mind was set at ease as I stood there in the crowd, unharmed and steady as a rock except for my shaking head.

That way, we were able to observe our husbands at work, until we heard the rumor that they were going to be transported away from Java. Indeed, the men were moved, and we didn't know where. We could "correspond" with them via the Red Cross by means of postcards written in Malay, however. We had a lot of fun with that, for it meant literal translations of Dutch into Malay.

I finally got a postcard from Henk, from Pakan Baru in Sumatra, where the POWs had to repair an existing airfield that had been destroyed. He was doing okay, but the food was bad and scanty. Henk wrote, "It's not what you eat but how you eat that gives strength and health." He had smuggled in hot peppers, sown the seeds around his barrack, and they had grown up in abundance and bore masses of fruits. He shared those peppers with his buddies; not only did it make the food more palatable, but it was very good for their weakened bodies. Hot peppers contain a lot of vitamins.

You might say that I kept in rather regular contact with my husband during the Japanese occupation by means of postcards. Several of his I have kept to this day. The translations into Malay, the official Indonesian lingua franca, were really quite funny because, being Dutch, we rarely used that language and most of us spoke it poorly. For instance, I invariably ended my messages with, "*tjioem, tjioem pedis dari tertjintah mu,*" (hot kisses from your lover). That went from mouth to mouth in Henk's barrack. He said, "Something like that can only come from my wife."

One day, I was called over by a totok lady. I believe her name was Mrs. De Neef or De Neve, I'm not sure which. She, and a couple of other ladies, had been given permission to stay free in order to help wives of imprisoned military men, who had lost their only source of income. Mrs. De Neve, as I'll spell her name, asked me if I would be willing to take some money to the Amboinese wife of a POW. This particular woman lived far away from the city in a communist kampong. They had decided to ask me because I was dark-skinned and spoke the local language. I promptly said yes, keeping in mind that God has assured us in the Bible that each of us is surrounded by guardian angels.

So, I grabbed my bike and went on my way—it was quite a distance—and I found the little house, smack-dab in the midst of rice fields. I had to wrestle my bike through the mud, but I arrived safely at her door. I asked her if she was so-and-so and if she could prove this. She showed me some kind of identification of her husband. I quickly handed her the money, at least three hundred guilders, as far as I remember—living expenses for the next month or so—and urged her to hide it in a safe place. In the meantime, as always happens in Indonesia, the locals had gathered around. I greeted them with a wave of my arm and a wide grin. They returned my greeting coldly, and I jumped on my bike again. I still carried quite a lot of money with me, for I hadn't finished all my errands.

I have no idea what kind of story that Amboinese woman told the crowd to explain my visit (this Amboinese woman was herself an outsider in this Javanese region and was the wife of a colonial soldier into the bargain). I never heard from her again, but this may be due to the fact that the funds shrank rapidly. Moreover, the ladies of the auxiliary were put away in camp, but not before the *Kenpeitai* had tortured them terribly. The Kenpetai suspected us of being involved in some subversive action.

Their suspicion turned out later to be based on fact, even though *I* knew nothing; I had simply delivered the money. Nevertheless, I too had to appear before the Kenpeitai. And again, my being Indo saved me. They asked me a lot of questions and then let me go home, after barking at me never to get involved again with the bad Dutch enemies. I rode my bike home as fast as I could. There, my children, my housemate, and the servants were waiting for me in tense anguish: was she coming home or not? In case I wasn't released again, I had already taken steps to ensure the safety of my children and my cats and dogs.

Mrs. De Neve, apparently the leader of an underground network, had been betrayed, of course. First, she was beaten half to death, then stretched out on the floor and her belly filled with water, after which a Japanese jumped up and down on top of her. She screamed in pain, but she never told them any of the names of the members of that underground. To top it off, the Nippon pushed a bamboo into her vagina and twirled it around and around. She fainted, but was brought to again and again, doused with buckets of water. Still, she did not give them any names. Yes, she screamed and yelled in pain and terror, but she never betrayed anyone. At last, Mrs. De Neve was thrown into a cell and here she was discovered later by the English, fortunately still clinging to life. They got her on her feet again eventually. I don't know how long she was able to enjoy her newfound freedom and the medal she received for her courage. I salute this lady!

And so our life under the heel of the Jap went on. We learned a few words of Japanese. We learned to bow low for the guards in front of buildings or whenever we passed Japanese in the street. And they would bow condescendingly in return. "What bends doesn't break," said Father Cats, a well-known Dutch folk philosopher, and I kept that in mind. On the inside, none of us bowed low for the oppressor. Instead, we would laugh in ourselves. I, for one, knew for sure we would be liberated one day.

We were very optimistic. Together with my house servant/ gardener, Moh, and my friend, the radio repairman, we could clearly read between the lines—it wasn't going so well for the mighty army of Dai Nippon. The Americans had jumped into the war after the attack on Pearl Harbor. Every time the Americans conquered an island, the Jap would announce in the paper or on the radio that the Japanese forces had retreated from that particular island in order to be in a better position to defend another one—in other words, for strategic reasons. When I relayed that to the people round about, they wouldn't quite dare to believe it, but a flicker of hope would appear. When we exchanged news, I was usually the only one who insisted that the Americans would land in Japan and would bomb that country, for that would be the only way to stop those ants once and for all.

Life wasn't totally grim. We did fun things among ourselves. For instance, we started a classical dance club, decided on a program, and then invited the whole neighborhood. It was just for fun and to have something different to do. It didn't cost a cent. In that way, we kept our spirits up. The Jap used to tell us that, if we women had made up the army when the Jap attacked us, they would have lost for sure.

In our daily conflicts with Indonesian pedicab drivers, the Japs always took our side. The driver would be sent on his way with a vicious kick and wallop, cruelty I loathed. The Japs were just as cruel and strict with their own people; that may be the only way to keep control over such a huge army. They must have been tired of the war too.

A couple of civilian Japanese tried to befriend us, by knocking on doors at night and asking if they could visit, even though this was strictly forbidden by the Kenpeitai. One of them came to visit me. As soon as he sat down, it was funny the way in which Moh would suddenly appear and start to dust or mop the floor, keeping one eye on the man from the Land of the Rising Sun. I had never asked Moh to do that, but he knew these customers. And so the Jap couldn't do a thing. I was and still am so grateful to Moh for his loyalty and caring, and the way in which he voluntarily protected the lady of the house and the children. After boring me a couple of times with his visits, the Jap stopped coming, because Moh would be hovering in the background dusting the chairs. Those moments are unforgettable.

Another time, we were again surprised by somebody from the Kenpeitai, a member of the Indonesian Intelligence at his side. He asked me all kinds of questions. Among others, whether I was pro-Nippon or pro-America. I answered promptly that I was neither pro-Nippon nor pro-America, but only pro-God, who holds the whole world in his hands. Those two were dumbfounded. They didn't know what to fill in on their questionnaire. So, they packed up their stuff and left, shaking their head, to bother other people with their stupid questions.

The Kenpeitai showed up again one day, out of the blue. We could hear them coming from afar on their motorbikes. Even that was easily recognizable, because only the Japanese and their cohorts

175

had access to motorized vehicles. I had no guilty conscience and waited calmly when the Kenpeitai man strode up to me.

Straight away, he barked out in Malay that I was accused of being a spy. I asked him why. Pointing at a tall rain tree in the garden of the colonel next door, he said, "Well, you ordered many branches of that tree removed, didn't you? So that you could better signal American planes!"

I almost started to laugh. Instead, I asked him to follow me indoors, where I would show him the damp spots on the walls, caused by the shade of the tree that didn't let any sun through, in turn causing my children to be sick a lot. I added the last comment as a brilliant afterthought. You know, they are known to be very soft on children. He went in and inspected the spots and saw that I had told him the truth.

He berated the Indonesian who had removed the branches, because he had neglected to ask the Jap for permission, and, with a deep bow, allowed me to keep the wood to use in cooking for my children. As soon as they had disappeared from sight, I gave the wood to the woodcutter, for that was his pay.

That's the kind of crazy stuff we had to endure. The Japanese were very suspicious and could act very silly. On the other hand, you can't entirely blame them, for they must have been aware of the silent but determined resistance on the part of us women.

Then, all of a sudden, we had to plant sweet potato, en masse, reportedly because of the shortage of food. Each of us was assigned a certain plot of land and, with lots of joking around, we happily planted the shoots upside down in the soil. A poor harvest, what else.

Next, we each were handed ten castor beans to be planted too, reportedly because the Japanese lacked airplane oil. Graciously obeying, we promptly dropped all the beans save one in hot water before planting them out in our front yard. The uncooked pit sprouted magnificently, flowered abundantly, and beautified our garden. The castor bean, with its large, hand-shaped leaves, is a handsome shrub. Here too, we joined the Japanese in being sadly surprised at having only one seed sprout. I think they must have suspected us of engaging in silent resistance. The only thing they did was berate us in their unintelligible language. Well, we couldn't care less. We couldn't understand what they said anyway.

176

Another time, we were called up to learn to extinguish a fire bomb. We had to bring buckets. Then the show could begin. Everyone had brought their own pail. Some were large, some were small, but the one carried by one of our neighbors, Ludie van Zele, outshone them all—he had brought a small toy bucket decorated with an orange bow. Orange is the color of the Dutch royal house, the House of Orange.

The first bucket was filled at a fire hydrant, and we had to hand this on, quickly followed by another one; the last one in line had to empty the pails over the pseudo-fire bomb. Every time that little bucket with the orange bow came past, we would laugh our head off and say in Dutch under our breath, "Long live the House of Orange." The Japs, who had no idea why we laughed so hard, followed our merry example and also got in a good mood.

Ludie van Zele is the brother of Lilian Ducelle, the former publisher of the Indies magazine, *Tong-Tong* (now renamed *Moesson*), and was married to Dany Bearts. An excellent pianist, Ludie played in a well-known orchestra that performed in fashionable hotels and restaurants. He also gave solo piano recitals. He had beautiful hands with long, slender fingers. Ludie bore an uncanny resemblance to a certain Alexander Brailowsky, who happened to be my favorite foreign pianist.

So, we certainly had our moments of fun. Then, one day, the colonel next door sent me an order to come over for dinner that evening. I was dumbfounded and my friends told me, "Now you're in for it! That comes from bowing every morning, now he wants more and quite something else!" Well, I didn't like it, even though I felt a great deal better when the aide said that the children were also expected.

However, the hand of our Savior upset the applecart once again. Near dinnertime, the same aide came running up all in a dither. The dinner was called off. The colonel and all his troops had been called up unexpectedly and had to leave immediately, destination unknown. I was told to take the contents of the refrigerator and all the prepared food.

Thanking God for his timely interference, I went over with my servants and plundered that refrigerator. It even held a delicious cake, and, of course, raw fish, which we enjoyed fried. I shared as much as possible with our nearest neighbors. All of us got an unusually good meal and everything was wonderful, enhanced by the suspicion that somewhere something was happening.

For the past several days, we had already been able to read between the lines that America was coming closer and closer to liberating us from Japan. The air alert system was put into use and soon after the first Boeing 25 planes started to fly over the Indies, launched from aircraft carriers. At the sound of the alarm, all lights had to be turned off and everyone had either to go inside or duck into an air raid shelter.

Nobody liked the rickety air raid shelters, so we would all gather on the back porch and await the coming events. Everywhere, Japs giving orders; cars driving up and down; and then the sirens wailing in one constant tone—air alert! You heard the rumble of airplane motors in the distance, and the shower of bombs here and there on spots that were important to the Japs. We were completely convinced America would never bomb civilians, so we stayed where we were, full of tense anticipation and trying to see where the bombs were falling. Those were terrible moments no matter what. Many bombs fell nearby, because the Americans were trying to destroy the oil refinery, Wonokromo.

I'll go back now to the first American attack, to show you how God's hand protected us. That time, they came not only with bombers but also with attack planes that sprayed bullets over everything that was Jap. The air alert service had told us, "When you don't have an air raid shelter, lie down in the grass as flat as possible." So, we lay down in the dark on the lawn in our small backyard. Not a cloud to be seen in the beautiful starlit sky. Suddenly and to our great surprise, it started to rain hard. We ran inside and took cover under our concrete kitchen table. Not long after, airplanes flew over, shooting off their machine guns with a thunderous ack-ack-ack. It was short but powerful, for we could hear thundering and rattling on the green in our backyard.

The next day, we looked around there and found several pieces of shrapnel about four inches long. If it hadn't rained, we would have stayed there on the lawn, and that shrapnel would undoubtedly have killed us or at least wounded us severely. It was only a very short rain shower and it was quite local to boot—it was a real miracle of God.

AFTER THE OCCUPATION, THE REVOLUTION
1945-1946

You could set your clock by it: every night at ten o'clock the American bombers came from what we assumed to be their carriers to bomb Java. If we were chatting together, having a nice visit, we used to say, "It's ten o'clock, guys! The Americans are coming. The sirens will go any moment now." And, yes, those words would hardly have left our mouths when the sirens would begin to howl and we would run back home. All lights out; dark-blue draperies drawn tight over our boarded-up windows; then we would sit back and wait.

Soon enough, the oil refinery, Wonokromo, as well as other Japanese-occupied areas were bombed and partially levelled. I would always sit outside on the veranda with Moh. All tensed up inside, we would avidly watch the sky where the Japanese were trying to catch the American bombers in their searchlights. Sometimes they succeeded, but usually they didn't. Invariably, the American planes deftly evaded the anti-aircraft guns. Moh and I would whisper together and clap our hands soundlessly. Don't forget, even though the colonel had departed, we still had Japanese neighbors, who would run nervously back and forth, driving off in their cars, jabbering in their guttural language.

Moh and I would see the bombs fall, looking like large, glittering cucumbers, in a chain-like procession from the plane—a truly chilling sight. But we felt the day of our liberation approaching, and—with only American planes in the air above us—we felt safe.

One day, I slept through the air alert signal, the windows open and all the lights on. Loud knocking on the door and a rough voice, "Kenpeitai!" Political police searching for spies!

I flew out of bed, jerked the door open. Yes indeed, there stood a Jap. He pushed a gun in my belly. I thought my last hour

179

had come. But I had forgotten about my rescue team, my three sleepy-eyed, scared toddlers, anxiously clinging to my pajamas.

His face softening, the Jap asked me in Malay if I had been asleep.

When I answered "Yes," he asked me, "Didn't you hear the air alert?"

"No," I said, "I was sound asleep."

He turned me around, pushed his gun in my back, and marched me to every light switch in the house to turn it off. Walking around like that, the only thing I could think of was my husband: if Henk were here, he would shake his head and wonder how I got myself in trouble, again. I felt like an actress in some B-grade cowboy movie, and couldn't help laughing within myself, even though my heart was pounding madly. At last all the lights in the house had been turned off. The gun was taken off my back, and I heard the front door slam.

I didn't know if that Kenpeitai man had left, or whether he had closed the door and had stayed in the house, only to finish his act of bravado in the dark in some unspeakable manner. Not to wait too long! I quickly turned on one dim light. No Jap! Light out again. Locked everything and jumped into bed with my chickens in tow. I wondered, what next with this yellow race?!

In our husbandless state, we women had organized to meet every evening. I then would read the Bible aloud and try as well as I could to explain the golden rule or to answer any questions. Those sessions were truly soul satisfying. Besides being educational, they also helped us focus our mind on higher and better planes, away from the war and the Japanese. Of those who came together this way at Anneke de Roock's house, the faces and names of Hetty Willems, Mrs. Muller and her two married sisters, and Zus von Fehm, whose husband was Finnish, somehow stand out in my mind. There were several other women present, whose names (but not their faces) have slipped my memory. Well, those were very tense times and all this took place quite a long time ago.

Actually, we weren't allowed to have meetings of more than five people at a time, and there were thirteen of us—I and my twelve "disciples." Moreover, the Japanese were very serious about enforcing such rules. However, this too must have been God's will. After all, we were sharing God's word; we never doubted he would protect us. And not even once did the Japanese interrupt us.

At that time, Minah and Moh were still with me and they watched the sleeping children in my absence. That was a truly soul satisfying time, that period in which we read the Bible together, in the time of the Japanese while the Americans were coming closer and closer.

During the day, we would often be visited by Chinese, who bought up gold, jewelry, and so on. I sold everything, the little that I had, so that my children, and Minah and Moh never had to go hungry.

Actually, the real saviors were Madurese women. They bought up just about everything: old clothes, shoes, ball gowns, bottles, empty tins . . . I had a special customer, who paid good money. She was a tall, dark-skinned Madurese woman, ramrod straight, sharp faced, with thick, silver Bengals encircling her slender ankles. We would haggle about prices until both of us were satisfied—both of us would profit, enough to live on. These women were called *tukang botol*, because they originally bought up only bottles. But by the end of the occupation they could use anything and everything.

We still had our sealed radios and one day—first to our great consternation, but later with great happiness—we heard the atom bomb attacks announced. And then we heard that Japan had conceded to an unconditional surrender, making my earlier conviction come true that the Americans eventually would land in Japan. All Japs were quickly disarmed, I believe by their own officers. Dutch planes flew low over Surabaya and threw out pamphlets, "The war is over and we'll come soon to set you free and to bring food," among other messages.

Without further ado, I opened all my windows wide and nailed the Red-White-and-Blue against a wall. Everyone was taken by surprise, confused, and at the same time happy and relieved. We didn't see any Japanese any more, not a one. But neither did we see any Dutchmen nor any Americans. That night, hundreds of powerless, disarmed Japs were slain by Indonesian troops who had been called together somewhere by Sukarno, the future, first president of Indonesia. They had been waiting for just such an opportunity. Even though we heard Sukarno's proclamations over the radio, nobody understood what was happening. It was eerily quiet all around. The air was thick with dark foreboding and suspicion.

At the same time, the totok civilian male and female concentration camps had been opened. These POWs, set free by the Red Cross, streamed back into town, where they were welcomed by those who had remained free and had made room for them. I myself had totok relatives, who stayed with me one after the other, only to move on to their final destination elsewhere or into empty houses down the street.

Then America was stupid enough to leave the liberation of the Indies to the English, who loosened their British Indian soldiers against the *pemudas*, the newly formed rebel army. This ended with the East Indians being driven together in a school in our neighborhood—no ammunition, no water, no food—caught in a trap. The British troops were forced to lay down their arms. They tried to transport as many Dutch women and children as possible to the harbor, Tanjong Perak, by trucks with white flags on top. There, one English warship lay ready to take them to Singapore, where refuge and medical help awaited them.

Shortly before this evacuation, I had received a letter from Henk via the Red Cross. He begged me not to go to Singapore, for he stood ready to leave for Indonesia leading a group of Amboinese soldiers who would free us from the *pelopors*, the Indonesian revolutionaries. These Amboinese troops, although also Indonesians, had stayed loyal to the Dutch. So we stayed behind, waving good bye to the women who were leaving. Of the six trucks filled with women and children, only two arrived at their destination. The others were caught in an ambush and shot to pieces by the pelopors. It was horrible! We were grateful not to have gone along.

Thus began the infamous *bersiap* time, the freedom fight right after the Pacific War. Nobody knew on which side the other was. We tried to adjust ourselves as best as possible to this queer situation, waiting for the actual liberation, which kept us waiting and never really arrived for us. Moh was recruited too, and had to stand guard in our street.

As if this turmoil was not enough, I had to take Minah to the hospital, where she died a week after, from cancer. All this grieved us deeply and put a damper on our expectations.

Then the order came down that we, the Dutch, would no longer be allowed to shop for food in the open-air market, the pasar, on peril of death. Ab and Eugénie Wasterval who lived across the street from us, had fled, leaving the contents of their cupboards and bakery behind. The officer in charge of the TRI* (the official Indonesian army), had moved into my sister's house farther down Carpentier Street. I asked him, "May I pick up the food left in my friends' house?" Permission was given, and I got my hands on a lot of rice, dried meat, butter, cheese, et cetera, which I shared with people in our street.

The totok women, only recently set free, were put in camp again, and many Indies people voluntarily moved into those camps too. Our street showed one empty house after the other, still guarded by dogs which had also been left behind. And while the English and Indonesians were still fighting each other furiously around us, Doeshka, my oldest daughter, and I tried to feed and water those strays. There must have been at least twenty of those dogs in our street alone. I myself ended up with six dogs and eight cats.

From the alley, Moh would smuggle us food, throwing it over the wall. In addition, two little Amboinese girls brought us food daily for a small fee. Here, too, the hand of God, praise be to him.

I had an amusing experience very early in this bersiap period. One day, a gleaming black limousine stopped in front of our house, the red and white of the Indonesian flag flying triumphantly in front. A TRI soldier opened the door and an Indonesian jauntily jumped out. He was dressed as if he were d'Artagnan come to life again—tight-fitting black pants, white shirt, red cape, head covered with a large, white-plumed hat. I stood at my front door.

Noticing me, he swept off his hat with a deep bow. He walked up to me with mincing steps, greeted me politely and coolly walked into my house, opening all the cabinets. Then he commandeered my wallet. That day it held only a couple of *rupiah* and he told his aide with a gesture of grandeur, "*Oh, nyonya ini miskin. Tulis surat permissi beli dipasar*" (Oh, this lady is poor. Write her a permit to shop in the local market). Robin Hood himself, it seemed.

I was duly handed the permit. Then they left to visit the neighbors, where they *did* take all the money and valuables. I never used that permit—the pasars were much too hostile to my taste, and who was this fool giving orders left and right anyway?

*[Actually TKR. See glossary. Ed.]

183

Not long after the uproar following this visit had subsided, a motorcycle of the feared Kenpeitai stopped at my house. The man wanted to know if I had seen so-and-so individual, exactly describing *Pak* d'Artagnan. I told him what I knew, and he in turn told me that the man was a robber, who had stolen the black car from a high hat. The whole act was a con game. He was locked up the day after, having enjoyed his sport for one day.

During this time, low-flying Dutch planes scattered pamphlets, stating in English and Dutch that the Dutch would land soon to set us free. I grabbed one of those pamphlets and stuffed it in my blouse, standing neighborly next to a TRI soldier, who tried to read his upside down. I took it from him and translated it into Indonesian. Then they suddenly got very active and noisy and chased us all inside. In a wink all the streets and yards were swept clean of pamphlets. None of the people in our street had had the time to read the message well. So, that evening we had a big neigborhood meeting. I took the pamphlet from my blouse, smoothed it out and read it aloud. Hope rose again. But it would turn out to be premature.

Finally, all the English troops had gone. Only the TRI was left, as well as the extremist branch of the Indonesian troops. They couldn't stand each other and each constantly issued orders contradicting the other.

It was the evening of 18 November 1945. The full moon shone bright. We sat talking in the family room, enjoying a coffee tubruk. Loud knocking on the door. A uniformed Indonesian ordered us to evacuate—the extremists were getting the upper hand and were planning to kill us all. We were to gather at the corner of our street.

We had already figured out this might happen, so everybody got hold of his or her suitcase; my daughters got their pillows, my son grabbed his guling, and I my large suitcase. At the designated street corner, army trucks stood waiting and we got on.

I'll never forget that peculiar feeling of unreality, as if caught in a bad dream, surrounded as we were by a world bathed in greenish moonlight, as if in blessing.

Five trucks or so took us to the Simpang Club, where we had to find ourselves a spot. My children and I staked out a place to sleep under the piano in the ballroom. Like stray dogs, each of us prepared a makeshift bed from blankets and other stuff we had brought with us. We could hear planes fighting overhead and a bomb exploding nearby. We huddled close, trembling. My son was five years old, my daughters were nine and ten.

Then, as if there weren't enough pandemonium and terror already, Bung Tomo himself, the infamous leader of the local extremists, honored us with a visit. The TRI soldiers, taken off-guard, looked on in disbelief and fear. His voice cracking with hatred, Bung Tomo ordered the TRI to behead all women and children that same evening.

Can you imagine how we felt, knowing as we did that in the past few days other Dutch women and children had been slaughtered by the same bullies? Strange to say though, deep in my heart I was convinced God didn't want this for us. Our heart pounding with fear, we waited in resignation.

Bung Tomo had left. Daylight was beginning to break through. A number of jittery TRI officers ordered us to pack our stuff and gather quickly and without any talk, and off we marched, to Gubeng Station and a heavily shuttered train. We were pushed in like cattle. Women screamed hysterically for their children, who had gotten lost in the crowd. But I had ordered my children to hold on to my pants and at no time to let go. The way in which my children kept totally quiet was remarkable. Only once did they ask me what was going on, that was all. They followed my orders faithfully and we stayed together.

The TRI, which was friendly to us and didn't wish us any harm, transported us by train to Mojokerto—TRI country—about sixty kilometers from Surabaya. Everything around had been divided into sections of TRI country and extremist country. The TRI also wanted Sukarno's *merdeka* or freedom, but without needless slaughter of the totok and Indo Dutch who had been left behind; hence the flight to TRI country.

We entered the train in Gubeng at six in the morning, and rode in total darkness and at a snail's pace, constantly fired at by extremist machine guns. We arrived in Mojokerto at noon. It had taken us six hours to travel a distance which normally took an hour.

On arrival in Mojokerto, we were unloaded lightning-fast and taken to empty houses, which had no water or anything else for that matter. We were left without any food or water for thirty-six hours, but none of my children complained. They said only once that they were hungry and thirsty. After I had assured them that we would get food and water soon, they kept quiet.

Around four the next afternoon, we were herded together again, now to walk under the broiling sun to our final destination. After we had walked for an hour, I quoted, "How hot it was and how far!" from the *Camera Obscura* (a well-known Dutch literary work), not only eliciting all kinds of angry comments but even curses.

People bitterly asked me where my optimism and unending trust in God had led all of us now. I forgot to mention that I had also talked others out of fleeing to Singapore with the English. Convinced either the Americans or the Dutch would come to free us soon, I had persuaded them to stay where we were in Surabaya. Instead, we were now walking under the supervision of the TRI to an unknown destination.

When people asked me where I thought we were heading, I answered, "Oh, it won't be long now until we see green meadows and waterfalls and tall shade trees," a remark met by caustic comments and disbelief. I didn't have the slightest idea where we were going either. I was just trying to pick up our spirits.

Not long after, we stood before a high, iron gate. It was pushed open. And what miraculous sight met our eyes? Two huge waringin trees shading a vast, green lawn, and two Indonesians pumping water, sending it gushing from a pipe! Every last one of us threw down our stuff and, screaming with unrestrained joy, we ran for the water. The two Indonesians didn't know what was what. All they saw was a horde of disheveled women running towards them. So, holding their sarongs high, they ran as if the devil was after them.

And then the questions came. "How could you have known this, Rita?"

"Are you clairvoyant, or did you talk with the TRI officers?" And more of the same.

We refreshed ourselves and then lay down in the cool shade of the waringins, where a soft breeze brought us even more relief.

After a while, the TRI officers came to tell us that we had arrived at the Brangkal sugar mill, and that we were free to pick where we wanted to live in the available houses. We would stay there for a while.

Well, it was "Let's go!" The women stormed into the houses and each laid claim to a spot in one of the rooms. There we spread our beds on the cool, stone floor. Without more ado, I lay down and fell in such a deep sleep nobody could wake me up. Only very late at night did I finally open my eyes. I stared straight at a package wrapped in banana leaf. Women from the surrounding kampongs had brought us some food. My children having finished their portion already, I fell upon mine. The food woke me up completely and returned my strength. It was white rice with meat and vegetables, pecil, wondrously good.

I surveyed our environment in the dim light of an electric bulb that hung from the ceiling. Earlier, we had been given gunnysacks, originally meant to hold sugar, for bedding. Most of us had brought some blankets or sheets, but of course, not I. Fortunately, a couple of my friends had extra blankets and shared those with us. It could get quite chilly in that region.

In that camp, we had pasar day or market once a week, at which time we could shop for food with what little money we had on us. We also could barter stuff: a pair of underwear for a couple of packages of cooked rice, something like that. Some of the women had brought kitchen stuff with them, and prepared snacks they would invent themselves with the little they had available. We would buy those, and with their profit they would continue their little enterprise.

We loyally shared everything. But since I hadn't brought any food, I was always on the receiving end, for instance, when we had coffee tubruk in the evening, outside or on the back veranda, when we would tell stories. Usually, everyone was sound sleep by ten at night.

From the many people I was in camp with, I remember only a handful. Strange, isn't it? I do remember that Zus Voogd, a former neighbor, was there with me. She had her two sons and one daughter with her. Then I remember Miss Wilson, a teacher, who told fairy tales to our children every evening before bed. She was an excellent storyteller. As soon as we mothers discovered how good she was, we would come to listen to her just as eagerly as our children. Poes Meyer, whom I knew from the Scouts, and her mother, Otje Meyer, were also in camp with me, as were Anneke de Roock and her two sons, as well as Anneke's aunt, Mrs. De Roock. Then there were Zus Schalks, Mrs. Muller and her two sisters, and my cousin, Hanny Lanzing. Hanny was taking care of two children, strangers. In a previous camp, they had been separated from their parents, while they were with their nanny. Seeing that they were lost and alone, Hanny had taken them under her wing.

One day, I decided to check my suitcase with a couple of ladies looking on, and we all burst out laughing. What we saw in my suitcase drove my friends to say, "That's just like you, Rita! Everyone else brings food or clothes and you cram your suitcase with sanitary napkins!" Really.

I laughed hardest of all. And, as it turned out later, I didn't even need them. Doctors say it seems to be something psychological which causes women behind bars to stop menstruating, with some exceptions. After a while, all of us walked around with distended bellies and we would ask each other, "How far along are you?" We all looked quite pregnant.

Besides sanitary napkins, I also had packed a couple of exquisite, full-length ball gowns. These proved to be very valuable when I started to gedek. To gedek, we would stand next to the (gedek) fence and barter our dresses for food. It was forbidden. But we did it anyway, on the sly. On the other side of the bamboo wall, the Indonesians found it quite profitable and would come eagerly to exchange their food for our clothes, clothing being quite scarce in their kampongs. I also had many bars of soap in my suitcase, as well as toothbrushes and toothpaste, all of which came in handy.

We had far too few vegetables and so we ended up "grazing." Every scrap of edible green was harvested and put in the sayor, the vegetable soup. The well-known *daun kentut*, also called *daun sembuan* grew there. It was very nutritious and tasted good, but it did stink of fart, for which it was named. Soon enough, the whole camp smelled of daun kentut. Everyone needed vegetables, so, why not daun kentut? When that herb was completely picked clean, we turned to lamtoro, of which we used the young leaves as well as both young and ripe seeds. Not long afterwards, we discovered a small cassava field, and the day after, that field looked as if a herd of wild pigs had rooted around in it. We not only took the fat roots of the cassava, but also the young tops, until there was nothing left to harvest—it looked as if a swarm of locusts had come down in that field. A tree with yellowish leaves, called *kol banda*, was also stripped bare.

188

I wonder what our guards thought of this. Once we started devouring anything that was green and edible, the whole area turned into an empty desert. Only the grass was left to grow green and lush as before.

One day, my oldest daughter, Doeshka, discovered how easy it was to steal sugar. A railroad car, filled with bags of sugar, had been left behind in the mill yard. As soon as it got dark, she, her sister, Joy, and other eager takers went out, armed with a knife and an empty can. A firm push of the knife would rip open the bloated belly of a bag of sugar and the contents would pour into the can. The hole was neatly stopped up again with a handful of grass, for the next time. We were starved for something sweet. So, every evening after our meal, I would dole out one teaspoon of sugar per person. It tasted as good as cake and it gave us the necessary energy.

Another day, we got hold of freshly made trasi (fermented fish paste). We ate that, roasted over a fire first, with rice—it tasted divine. Not long after that, trucks filled with cassava were driven into the yard and we were told to get as much as we wanted. Now, that turned into a real looting party. Nevertheless, everybody got a fair share.

Now and then TRI officers would come and eat in a large barrack in camp, which had been converted into a kitchen for the TRI. Often I would stand there, waiting until they had finished eating, and then I would snatch the scraps of leftovers from the serving bowls like a starving mongrel and collect them in a can I had brought with me. I shared these scraps—first serving my children, of course, and then others too—and they tasted delicious. That had been going on for a while until one day one of the cooks walked up to me in a bad mood, spat me in the face, and tried to wrestle the food from my hands. But I stood my ground and, after wiping the spit off my face, I stoutly defended my food. She finally went off, still screaming and cursing.

Sometimes, leftover rice would be dried in the sun on woven bamboo trays to be fried later for a snack for the guards. That wasn't safe from us either. Time and again, a couple of those trays would be emptied and then we would eat fried rice crust that evening, delightfully gurih!

One day, we discovered that everyone had head lice and that our beds were crawling with bedbugs, which sucked out our precious blood at night and caused us to get up in the morning covered with itchy bumps. We got rid of the bedbugs by scrubbing our bedsites with kerosene and airing our blankets and what have you in the sun. The TRI gave us the kerosene as a gesture of goodwill. We were told to rub it on our heads and on our hair too. But it burned our scalps terribly, so we stopped that quickly.

I was first in cutting my children's hair off close to the skin. Their hair was already full of nits. Their "bald" heads looked so clean and cute. Recognizing the humor in the situation, they started "slapping" each other on the head, not real hard, of course, it just sounded like a slap. They were rid of head lice forever. Soon after, other mothers followed suit and cut off their children's hair. It looked funny, but at the same time clean and fresh. We ladies also cut our hair, short but not quite bald, and regularly used the *serit*, (the Indonesian, half-moon shaped, fine-tooth comb). We never got completely rid of head lice that way, but at least we could keep it under control. Now that I write this down, I feel my scalp itch again. It was a real scourge.

A creek wound its way down the far end of our camp—that was my very own latrine. The real toilets were always occupied, or there would be people around and then I couldn't "go." I have to move my bowels in peace and privacy and that's what I achieved: squatted down Indonesian-style on a board placed over the creek, while I observed butterflies flying from flower to branch.

Suddenly, my group was forced to vacate our "home." We had to crowd in with others in the administrator's house, where all of us had to share the one bathroom. There was room enough to sleep, but only one huge bathroom, in which everybody seemed to take a bath simultaneously. The children made a game out of it and urinated or defecated all over. You can imagine the stench!

After our evening meal, we would walk around the camp and visit or would sit down under a tree with a clove cigarette and kopi tubruk, both of which we had received by illegally bartering. The TRI guards pretended not to see us and thus Camp Brangkal wasn't too bad.

Laborers freely went in and out of the camp, and we talked a couple of them into smuggling in some corn on the cob in return for a handful of money. You would never guess where they hid that corn: wrapped in a banana leaf between their legs right under their "bell," where it stayed nice and warm. And who looks down his nose at this is a prune, for it tasted extra good!

We even observed Christmas in that camp. A long time beforehand, we had collected tinfoil from ladies who smoked. One of the ladies was very attractive and spoke the native language well. She arranged to have plenty of cigarettes brought in regularly and also extra food. On Christmas Day, we stuck a branch of a casuarina tree in a can filled with sand, and decorated it with stars and balls of cigarette foil and a sprinkling of wildflowers. That evening the village chief sat down among us and listened quietly while we sang Christmas carols. When I picked up my Bible and began to read Luke 2:1 aloud, he left, and we were free to observe the true spirit of Christmas, which is Jesus' power, love, and good news, giving us strength and hope.

However, the extremists threw sand in our soup again. They were gaining ground and had pushed through into our region. We packed our stuff lightning-quick and were loaded like cattle onto trucks to be transported to a weaving factory in Dinojo, already crowded with seven hundred men, women, and children. It's a miracle the extremists didn't machine gun us there. They placed barrels filled with kerosene along the walls of this camp and threatened to light these as soon as any *belanda* (European) be he Dutch or American, showed up to free us. It didn't look good, but I said we would be saved by one or the other belanda sooner or later, netting me some more angry stares.

Here our daily food consisted of rice and *kankung*, a leafy vegetable, cooked with a dash of salt in large barrels—a kind of Dinojo rice porridge. Here, too, we had pasar day once a week, offering a welcome diversion as well as respite from our dull diet.

Then we were given some medicines, making us wonder why the extremists got so soft-hearted. Were they perhaps losing ground against advancing troops that would liberate us? Hope rose again. By then, we had used all the weaving looms for firewood.

191

BITTER HERBS 1946

One day, one of the women sat down next to me on my mat. She was known to be an active prostitute. She saw me reading the Bible and she said to me, "You know who I am. You're religious, you're reading the Bible. Can you tell me if I'll end up in hell?"

I said, "No, you won't end up in hell, for you've kept from harm all the girls between thirteen and eighteen years, whom the Indonesians might have wanted to rape. You offered yourself in their place to satisfy the Indonesian camp guards. In that way, you saved these girls from possible harm. I'll tell you the story of Rahab, the whore, who was named in the genealogy of Jesus. Even though she was not of their race, she protected the Jewish spies, and therefore God forgave her her sins. God will forgive you too because of the good deeds you've done, but ask God for forgiveness and stop being a prostitute. Come, let's pray."

We prayed together and she felt relieved, knowing that God had taken her under his wing because she had promised not to sin in that way any more. Then we parted and went our separate ways. I don't know if she kept her word.

And thus the weeks rolled by. Several babies died. The Indonesians permitted a group of women to put the babies to rest in mother earth, outside the camp. Our most heart-breaking experience in camp was to watch these babies die, to see the sorrow and helplessness of the parents!

Suddenly, I got malaria. A former nurse kept plying me with quinine from Red Cross parcels. I was still shaking with fever and feeling miserable, when we were told that the Swiss Red Cross had arranged for us to be set free the next day. We and all our stuff were loaded onto old, creaking trucks which had holes in the floor, destination Sumobito, yet another idled sugar mill.

Somewhere, at a small local station, we were transferred to trains. Because I was still feverish and very thirsty, friends had filled a bottle with water for me for the trip. Joy, my second daughter, carried it. Stepping down from the truck, it slipped from her hands and shattered. Gone was the water. This enraged Doeshka and she scolded Joy. My friends and children were very concerned about me. We got on the train and I had my children sit down on the bench while I lay down on the floor at their feet.

At the next stop, I asked a passing train guard to bring me some water. I was burning up with fever and thirst. He brought me a bottle of water and this time Doeshka held it. Other friends welcomed us at Sumobito, installed us on large, grass-filled mattresses, and brought us some food.

The day after, we were transported to Semarang, Java, in warplanes from which the doors had been removed, flown by English pilots. Soon, we were asking each other what kind of food we would ask for on landing. Most of us called out, "Me, a cheese sandwich! Aduh, cheese, mmmm, so delicious!" It was strange that we craved cheese above all other foods. Not nasi goreng, fried rice, *sambal* trasi or anything like that, but cheese.

On landing, we could already see our beloved tricolor waving in the distance. Our throats tightened. Many wiped away tears. A loud and grateful hurrah spontaneously burst forth from our happy hearts, accompanied by lusty applause. When we were led to the canteen that had been set up there, I was among those that went for the cheese. Heavyset, round-breasted, blond Dutch women hugged us and asked us promptly what we wanted to eat. We could pick out what we wanted.

"A cheese sandwich!" people yelled.

Famished after the poor food we had been fed the past several months, we wolfed down the tasty bun with its thick slice of cheese. We were also served water and tall mugs of hot Ovaltine. Everything went down like cake. After a short rest, each of us, one after the other, was given a shower of some stuff, designed to get rid of the lice and to disinfect us. Then we were housed in large, empty school buildings.

The day after we were taken to the harbor and there we climbed up a rope ladder, bringing us on deck of open LSTs, a kind of landing ship. There were cabins available below decks. Our boat, still roped to the shore, wobbled so much, I promptly got seasick. We put up a makeshift tent on deck with the blankets and pieces of material we had with us. There we stayed throughout the day, while the boat made its way to Surabaya, broiled and parched by the copper terror, which unrelentingly sent its heat down on us throughout the day. Once in a while, we were offered something to eat or drink. I only wanted water.

At long last, the next morning, Tanjong Perak, Surabaya. Everybody hung over the railing. Many friends and relatives were waiting for us. Like miserable, very undernourished cattle we stumbled down the gangway. As we arrived on familiar soil, the air was filled with sounds of noisy kisses and crying.

We were loaded onto trucks once again. This time our destination was the HBS school building on Ketabang, near Slamet Street, where I had lived as a child with my parents, and where Doeshka was born. Some time later, we found out that my mother was in Camp Tegalsari, together with my brother, Pof, his wife, and their three young daughters. Elsa, my sister, had already been transported to Holland.

My mother had been taken by Indonesians from her house in Batu to an internment camp in Malang, Java. From there, she had been moved to Camp Tegalsari in Surabaya. When my mother heard from the Red Cross that we were in the HBS camp she asked us to join her. That was some reunion. We were particularly moved at seeing Pof again, a Japanese camp survivor. He was skeleton-thin and seemed depressed. He had been sick a lot. During the last few months, Pof and my husband had been in the same camp.

Pof told me that Henk was fine, but that he had stayed behind in Singapore, where he had been promoted to paymaster. Henk had to provide women, taken there from the various camps on their way to Holland, with money and food.

I thought it strange, that he hadn't written me a welcome home letter, not even a telegram. Pof explained, "The Red Cross had told Henk you and the children had all been beheaded. So, it jolted him to hear you are all very much alive."

However, when I tried to get my brother to tell me more about Henk, I realized after a while that he evaded all my questions. I wondered why. Also, one of my brother's friends, a man who had spent his life in radio stations, tried everything to contact my husband, but couldn't get hold of him. I felt my heart getting anxious and heavy and I got more and more nervous.

What I'm about to tell you is more heart-wrenchingly painful than you can ever imagine. What I experienced, was so terrible, strange and incredible, that I find it hard to put into words. But—if this is to be a truthful life story—I have to put down everything: the fun and wonderful times, but also the sorrowful times.

Finally, the long-awaited letter from Henk arrived. It was a long one. But its contents hurt me as if someone had shot an arrow straight through my heart. It started without any of the sweet terms he had always used. It started chilly and business-like, as if we were strangers. Instantly, my husband thrust the knife deep into my soul, already bruised by dark forebodings. His letter proved these to be all too true. He wrote that he had heard that his whole family had been wiped out, and a mutual friend—years younger than I and much prettier too—had taken pity on him. This relationship had changed into love, and so "I've decided to divorce you. I want to marry her." I read that letter in a room at the refugee center. My mother and nieces happened to be present. They told me later, I had screamed out my sorrow like a wounded deer.

I completely lost my bearings. I only felt a deep emptiness within me and around me. I who had stayed so loyal to him throughout this whole ordeal. No Japanese nor Indonesian had ever put a hand on me. All around me in that same camp were women with babies from Japanese and babies from Indonesians, and still, when their husbands came home, they hugged each other close and everything was forgiven and forgotten, and the illegitimate child was lovingly accepted by the ex-POW. I looked on in dazed disbelief.

I had stayed loyal, had kept my virtue, and now I was being discarded. "Why, God? Why, Jesus?" kept hammering in my head. Nobody who knew me and had seen me cope could comprehend what was going on. Ours had been such a happy marriage, with an unshakeable belief in our future together; we had worked so hard together to protect the children and to raise them correctly. And I had lived with only one goal before me: to hold Henk, my husband, safely in my arms again and start our life anew after the war. "Go with God, for it was not to be, it was too much to hope for," even though it would have been wonderful.

I walked around like an animal in pain. When I had calmed down, I heard God say to me, "My grace should be enough for you." I resigned myself to the situation.

When my husband arrived a week later with the boat from Singapore, I was waiting for him on the quay in Tanjong Perak. He had come over to arrange the details of the divorce and to see his children. From where he stood at the railing, I must have been quite a sight when he first saw me again: a woman, who looked prematurely old, her hair turned grey with sorrow, ravaged by camp life and a recent bout with malaria. Such a contrast to the pretty young thing, ten years younger than we were. No doubt, I looked unattractive and pitiful to him.

Anyway, our reunion was not exactly the way I had imagined it all those years. Fortunately, Henk's reunion with our children was unaffected and loving on both sides.

I walked around camp like a zombie. And then I made a God-inspired decision: I threw down the gauntlet and told Henk that I was giving him his freedom—he was free to return to his sweetheart immediately and marry her. Speechless, he followed me with his eyes when I left him, my head held high, to go to my job in the kitchen of the refugee center. I even managed to smile, sing and joke around. But inside me everything had turned dull, lifeless, burned out.

Henk lived somewhere else, not in camp, and had resumed work at his old company, Anemaet and Company. About a month later, he looked me up to tell me that it had all been a momentary delusion. He—a man who had been in camp for three-and-a-half years, during which time he never saw a woman or had any relations with a woman—had been told that I was dead, and so on, and so forth. And, if he could come back to me, for he really loved only me. . .

I felt as if struck by lightning. I didn't feel happy or glad. First down in the valley of sorrows, and then up on top of the mountain—this was simply too fast for me. That cruel wound wasn't able to heal so quickly.

READJUSTMENTS 1946 ONWARDS

Then we went through a difficult period together: my husband trying his best to win me back, and I doing my darndest to find myself again. Finally the day came that we felt good about trying for another child—love had come back at last.

We moved from Camp Tegalsari into a large, vacant house across the street. We furnished it with rattan furniture from AMACAB, the Allied Military Administration Civil Affairs Branch. Our old house on Carpentier Street had been picked clean, except for a couple of Bibles, which I was happy to retrieve.

My aunt, Dien Geul, came to live with us with her youngest daughter, Noesje. And a young, married couple moved into the pavilion next to our house. All in all, we lived there quite contentedly and cozily. But not before we had rid the house of rats as large as cats. We hunted for them with guns until the very last one had been killed. The city of Surabaya had become terribly run-down during the war. Peace and quiet had not completely returned to Java yet, however. Extremists were everywhere and they continued their fight against the Dutch.

Our third daughter was born without a hitch on 25 July 1947. I was forty years old. We named her Pax, because she sealed the peace between my husband and me from that time onward, and because she was born in peacetime.

Not long after her birth, my husband was transferred to the sugar plantation, Kadipaten, in Central Java. There he was bookkeeper for his old company, Anemaet and Company. A couple of months afterwards, we followed by boat; first to Cirebon, a port city on the north coast of Central Java, and from there by car to the sugar plantation.

At first, we had to share a large house with a totok employee whose wife and children were still in Holland. When his wife and family returned to Kadipaten, we moved into our own home. This was a really huge Indies house, with an open front veranda, a long breezeway leading to the servants' quarters and utility wing, high ceilings, a large sitting-dining room, and three large bedrooms. It was wide, light and sunny. The front yard was smallish, but the side and back yards were spacious.

In the side yard grew a so-called honey mango tree, which was continuously in fruit. These mangos were delicious. We ate the young fruits in *rujak*, a spicy fruit salad. The ripe fruits were sweet and had a unique flavor.

There we had four mongrels, a monkey named Krelis, a cat, and several fish in a pond. All these animals got along well with each other. It was something to see them playing together. During the rainy season, the pond would overflow and the fish would flop around on the street. The children had a lot of fun catching them and putting them temporarily in another, safer place.

We observed the sugar-making process with interest. The sugarcane was brought in by oxcart, transferred to large carriers and crushed farther down the line, including everything on and around it. One day, for instance, we saw first a snake and then a mouse being crushed together with the sugarcane. Who knows what else was crushed. Admittedly, the resulting cane juice underwent a lengthy and thorough purification process. It was truly miraculous the way in which dirty sugarcane was turned into pure, white sugar crystals.

Once a week, I would take food and old clothes to the poorest families in the kampong, each time choosing a different one. The result was, that at *Lebaran* (the end of the Muslim fasting period, which we Dutch called the Indonesian New Year), we were showered by them with gifts of food, either presented as beautifully decorated food parcels, or on a tray covered with a white, crocheted doily. Our friends in the kampong thus showed their appreciation.

Of course, we were not the only employees living on the plantation. Besides ourselves, there was the administrator, Mr. Holsbergen and his wife; chief machinist, Von Hombracht and his wife; first employee, Schuurman and wife; second machinist, Van der Horst and wife; field employee, Horstman'shoff and wife; employee in charge of the young cane, the so-called *bibit-planter*, Westhoff and his Indonesian wife; and finally, the chemist, an Indonesian named Sawal.

This was our first experience with life on a sugar plantation. It was fun, but also filled with anxiety because the political situation was still quite unsettled. It was so unsafe, a detachment of the *"Huzaren van Boreel"* of the Dutch army, was encamped on the plantation. These soldiers were engaged in daily skirmishes with the local extremist pelopors, and would often suffer casualties when they walked into a trap.

The plantation had no school, so I resumed teaching my children at home, as I had done during the war. One day, Frans Buts, a private who liked teaching, took over. When it was no longer practical to teach our oldest three at home, they were boarded with the Harry van der Steur family in Bandung. Harry is a close relative of the well-known Pa van der Steur who had a famous orphanage in Magelang.

Bandung was a two-hour drive from Cirebon and Kadipaten. When school started, Doeshka, Guido, and Joy were driven to their boardinghouse in Bandung in armored carriers guarded by soldiers. At vacation time, they were transported home the same way, each child in a separate carrier to lessen the chance of all three children being wounded or killed together. Invariably, they had to take cover several times due to machine gun fire from pelopors. Even for that period, such trips were quite stressful to all of us.

Two of the enlisted men, Frans Buts and Wim van Hees, his buddy, visited us almost daily. They were Catholics, and they and I would often talk religion after supper. These discussions could get quite heated, but we always parted as friends. Wim, especially, was like a son to me and we corresponded for a long time after he returned home to the Netherlands.

These Dutch soldiers were all young—I would guess between eighteen and twenty-five—and taken from their mother's apron, as it were, to serve in the Indies. I treated them all as if they were my own sons. I made sure that they didn't overpay for fruit, and taught them the local manners and customs. In return, they shared their rations with us, such as canned ham, cheese, chocolate and so on, which at that time were still scarce and expensive. Soon, I was "Mom" to them all and was able to keep many boys away from the kampong, and the women there engaged in the oldest profession in the world.

Often up to a half dozen of these soldiers came to share our meals—rijsttafel—which they loved. Most of them ended up with either kidney problems or constipation as they drank no water at all, even though they ate a lot of salty snacks with their beer, coke, or whatever else they drank. When I got wind of their complaints, I told our cook to buy six gendihs, unglazed-earthenware carafes, from the pasar, and filled these with potable water. From that time on, I would always keep three of those gendihs available in the encampment, which was located next to our house. They loved that water, drank it regularly, and slowly their physical condition improved.

One case stands out in my mind, that of Heinz Jansen, also an enlisted man, who suddenly fell seriously ill. Kidney stones. He tossed back and forth on his bed, writhing with pain, showing no improvement even though he was under a doctor's care. One day, I saw a young man crawling on his belly in the street, groaning and weeping big tears of anguish. He crawled through our gate and up on our veranda. Recognizing Heinz, I ran up to him as quickly as I could to help him into our guest room, where he fell exhausted on the bed. I picked a handful of *kumis kucing* leaves and brewed a tea from it. I had Heinz drink two full glasses of this tea daily—once in the morning and once in the evening.

Naturally, I told the doctor what had happened. Even though he wasn't enthusiastic about herbs, he nevertheless consented to their use. He also asked me if Heinz could stay with me, so that I could continue to treat him with Indonesian herbs, mostly because the poor boy himself begged to be allowed to stay in his "adopted mother's" care. After a week, the fever and pain were gone. Heinz could walk again. We fed him well to bring him back to health. After ten days Heinz was able to return to normal duty.

His colonel, or whatever he was, sent me a very correct thank you note. I'm not sure of the rank of the officer in command, for I'm always confused as far as military ranks are concerned, just as I don't know a thing about car models—it's all the same to me. Heinz himself never forgot his "debt" to me and we became good friends.

While we were also friendly with the officers, we were closer to the enlisted men. Even after the unit was transferred and then sent home after the Second Military Action, we kept in contact and corresponded with several of them for quite a long time until that petered out with the years.

These soldiers managed to sweep the whole of West Java clean of insurgents in one day. Many combatants were killed or taken prisoner. And for what! Not long after, Holland betrayed the soldiers and us by signing the Round Table Conference Agreement and surrendering the Indies to Sukarno and his compatriots.

After three-and-a-half centuries of mostly good leadership, the newly elected government in Holland suddenly came to all kinds of confusing decisions. It was a given that the islands would attain freedom and independence sooner or later, just like all other colonized countries. But the way in which this happened truly reached a new low and was very disappointing, especially in view of all the loss of life among the Dutch soldiers, for nothing.

Besides befriending lonely soldiers, I also developed a close relationship of another kind during our stay at Kadipaten. I already explained that at our arrival, we were first asked to share a house with another employee of the plantation. Only after his family returned from Holland were we assigned our own dwelling. Curious to inspect the premises, I went over and walked from room to room. I left the so-called service wing for the last.

In the old days, dwellings were traditionally divided into two parts: the main building, which held the bedrooms and the living quarters, and the service wing, which comprised the kitchen, store-room, servant's room(s) and also the bathroom and toilet facilities. The latter were always at the end of the long porch on which the various utility rooms opened, with the WC at the very end. In turn, the service wing was usually connected to the main house with a short breezeway. Obviously, that location of the toilet often resulted in people having to hurry when they were in pressing need of relief.

On my round I had finally reached the restroom. In the Indies, doors were rarely locked and often stood open to "air the room." When I stepped into the restroom, a huge warty toad jumped up against me. It was a *kodok bangkong*, who had chosen a strategic spot in the center of the floor. I'm fond of toads and frogs, so I simply picked him up and deposited him gently in the grass in the backyard, not expecting to see him again.

The first time I used the restroom, there was that toad again, right where I had first found him, directly in front of the toilet. I ignored him and sat down. Right away, he—I assume it's a he, what else could it be?—hopped up to me and stared me in the face. His bulging eyes had an intelligent look. Secretly, I'm intrigued by the mystery of the frog prince of fairy tale fame, so I stared back and began a conversation with him. After all, there was no one around to snicker, right?

201

I asked him if he was in fact the prince who had been turned into a frog, who could only resume his human shape if somebody smashed him down against the ground. My answer was a croak that appeared to be brought forth from deep down in his belly, followed by a hop that deposited the toad squarely on top of my bare feet.

I looked him over from up close. He kept turning his eyes this way and that, all the while flicking his tongue out at me. His back and sides were somewhat warty and his skin was greenish gray. His head was full of character. For a toad, he seemed quite sharp. I decided to call him "Opa," and shared that information with him. I was rewarded with another resonant "ggrroack" and a slight move of his body, his icy-cold toes firmly fastened around my own.

Suddenly, he jumped up against my right leg, his tongue touched my skin, and then he fell back again on my feet. This was repeated several times, leaving me dumbfounded at his weird behavior. What was the matter with him? Finally it dawned on me. The houses in Kadipaten crawled with insects. I was being attacked on all sides by mosquitos lusting for my precious blood. Of course! Opa was only trying to quiet his grumbling stomach and here was his chance to fill his belly. From his position on my feet, he would lurch forward every time he saw a mosquito land on my leg, catching it with his tongue. While I sat there, going about my business, the toad kept up his rescue mission.

I thought, well, I found my prince after all. Here he was, ugly and cold to the touch, but nevertheless a knight, for didn't he defend me with ardor against the chemical warheads of the enemy? I thanked him for services rendered with a gentle tap on his back, which he acknowledged with a soft "ribbit."

Thus Opa was offically installed as the guard and rightful inhabitant of our restroom. Not without fretful protests on the part of my children, however. They loathed frogs and toads. Every time one of them had to use the restroom, came the yell, "Mammie, Opa is here!" Then I hurried up and deposited Opa outside, where he waited patiently until the restroom was vacated and he could hop in again. It didn't matter where in the large garden I put him down, he always found his way back. It was an uphill battle for me against the united front of my children, but . . . Opa stayed.

He seemed to feel I was on his side, for he kept defending me against all insect attacks. One day, I noticed a huge centipede crawling out of a corner. My toes curled with loathing and horror.

I instinctively pulled up my legs, jeopardizing my balance in the process. I was stuck. My knight errant, however, audaciously hopped up to the invader and promptly engaged him in—what seemed to me—an unequal fight. I was greatly concerned for Opa, but unnecessarily so. With the patience of David in his confrontation with Goliath, Opa waited for the right moment. Then, with a strategic insight worthy of General Norman Schwarzkopf, he attacked from the front and, with one mighty bite, grasped the centipede by the head.

I thought, now the centipede will use his tail to sting Opa in the back and that will be the end of poor Opa. Not so. The centipede suddenly went limp, and slowly but surely its heavily armored body disappeared into Opa's wide mouth. His belly round and full, Opa croaked in triumph, flicked his tongue and hopped back on my feet. He stared at me with his moist eyes as if to say, "Ain't I something!" I gently picked up one of his front paws and thanked him. His mouth moved slightly. Was Opa smiling back at me? Whatever, I was able to finish my business in peace and quiet. I have to confess, however, that nothing in the world would make me choose to be in Egypt when Moses cursed it with a plague of frogs. Frogs or toads in my bed? Brrrr, never, not on your life, prince or no prince!

Of this period, I also remember another, totally different, episode. One day, Henk had to pick up money in Cirebon for the plantation. He was accompanied by the chauffeur and one armed guard. I was permitted to go along to do some shopping. I left my youngest daughter, then one year old, in the care of my loyal servants and the Dutch soldiers. On receiving the money from the bank, my husband hid it under the car seat and we drove home. And yes, as expected, a pelopor stopped us along the way and asked where we were from and where we were going. My husband quickly handed him a unopened pack of cigarettes, talking to the man in fluent Sundanese or Javanese, I forget which. We were allowed to resume our trip unmolested. The pelopor had no idea my rear end protected a million rupiah, safely to be delivered in Kadipaten.

What a period that was. Full of anxiety, but also very interesting. The hand of God was clearly visible. He guided us according to his will by means of unexpected events, some of them admittedly unsettling.

Among the employees of the plantation was a lot of jealousy which led to a surfeit of nasty gossip. When the bosses of Anemaet and Company in Surabaya investigated these rumors, it resulted in the immediate firing of both my husband and the administrator. Neither one had been willing to let things slide, and they had worked well together. The men at the top didn't like that, and thus the easy way out, "Fire them!," to the consternation and disappointment of the Indonesian workers and locals.

What had happened was this: my husband had somehow or other managed to prevail upon the locals to keep Kadipaten free of sugarcane fires and pelopor attacks. His intervention was said to be "going to bed with the enemy." At first glance, it may indeed have looked that way, but it really wasn't that at all. But how can you expect totoks to understand the way in which Indonesians, pelopors or not, like to be approached, that is, in a sensitive and courteous manner. My husband, who spoke several native languages well, put his own life on the line and took the initiative to talk with the local leader of the extremists. At that time, the pelopors were known to cut off the male organ and stick this in the mouth of the dead enemy, as a sign of their deepest contempt. My husband risked that. The only other person to know about these talks was the administrator. The result: no more fires in the cane fields, no more attacks, everything was peaceful. Unfortunately this was leaked somehow or other and the information quickly sent through to the administration in Surabaya. This initiative apparently required the firing of the employees involved, even though it was done to benefit the plantation, the administration, and the local population. The very next week, several hectares of sugarcane were set on fire again.

By coincidence, the Van der Steur family in Bandung with whom our children boarded happened to move out, and we moved into their house.

Later, again, rumors were spread that my husband had been fired because of fraud. That was the easy way out—no honest explanation, nothing. My brother, Pof, investigated this matter personally, and he found no sign of fraud. By that time, however, we were already settled with all our stuff and our four dogs in Bandung after setting our pet monkey free in the forest.

BANDUNG 1952-1957

So, we settled down in Bandung. With the bonus which employees of the sugar plantation received once a year, Henk bought a motorcycle with sidecar. It was a Harley Davidson, which could hold all of us: I and Pax, our youngest, in the sidecar, and the rest behind the driver. The children were all quite small and skinny, so it was a perfect fit. It wasn't easy to find another job but, after many frustrating setbacks in his search for a job, my husband finally found a permanent position as bookkeeper at the GEBEO, the public electricity company.

I can't resist sharing with you my husband's adventure with a so-called Achehnese "prince." At the time, we assumed the man to be who he said he was. He spoke Dutch well, was well-mannered and dressed with exquisite taste. He persuaded my husband to accept "a magnificent position" in Batavia (Jakarta). Fortunately, my husband's married brother lived there, and Henk could board with him. The *teungku* (prince) made high-faluting promises, had his fingers in several pies, and even treated us to a fancy dinner at the locally renowned Hotel Homann. But the salary he had promised Henk never materialized. He turned out to be a slick con man and was ultimately jailed. Henk was a witness for the prosecution when the case was taken to court.

In the meantime, all the children went to school. Doeshka and Guido went to the Christian Lyceum, Joy attended the MULO, a vocational high school, and the youngest went to elementary school.

When my husband was hired at the GEBEO, he sold the motorcycle, and we moved to a larger house. It was put up for rent even though it was still occupied. Any other woman would have refused to move into that house. Newsprint covered the front windows; the air was heavy with the stench of dirty dishes; spiderwebs hung from lamps and ceilings; the floor hadn't been swept in years; the cans in the kitchen had grown legs—they literally moved with the hordes of bugs and cockroaches that lived in them; overgrown shrubbery hid the open veranda round about from view. In short, the house could have been a set in "The Munsters" television series. You can't imagine how filthy that house was.

Nevertheless, we immediately saw possibilities, in spite of the mess. Fortunately, my children had lots of friends, who volunteered to help us clean. With great enthusiasm, the paper was torn from the windows; the live cans were thrown in the trash can; the shrubbery was cut down and the clippings put up in piles; buckets of water and Lysol were dumped on the floor; the windows scrubbed with alcohol; and the spiderwebs removed with long-handled brooms. Our gardener and two maids joined wholeheartedly in the clean up. We worked like people possessed. At day's end, we went to bed in an empty but clean and fresh-smelling house.

The most recent inhabitants of that house had been an old woman and her son. Rumor had it that this son had been in hiding from the Indonesian army. He had desperately wanted the house to disappear from view. That's the reason, it was said, why they had plastered the windows with paper and let the shrubs grow wild. Mother and son finally escaped to Holland under the protection of the Dutch commissioner, who had been hastily installed himself.

We had finally settled down. I had three servants: a maid, a cook, and a gardener to take care of our rather large garden. I helped with the cooking and made the beds. The rest of the day, I spent reading the Bible.

My second daughter, Joy, had graduated from the MULO and was already working as a stenotypist in the office of the Dutch commissioner, a kind of local Dutch consular office headed by the lawyer L. van Straten, who came from a similar position in Makassar (Ujung Pandang) on the island of Celebes (Sulawesi). Joy's immediate supervisor happened to be one of my second cousins, Loekie Geul.

One day, I too came to work in the same building with Joy and Loekie, because the office of social services in Bandung, a division of the office of the Dutch high commissioner in Jakarta, hired me as a social worker. The Dutch high commissioner in Jakarta officially represented the Dutch government after Indonesia was granted its independence on 27 December 1949. It oversaw seven local consular offices dispersed over the various islands which comprise the Indonesian archipelago. One of the offices was the one in Bandung which hired me and my relatives.

After the end of the Pacific war, there were several waves of repatriations of Dutch citizens to the Netherlands, comprised of both totok and Indo Dutch. The high commissioner looked after the interests of those Dutch citizens who remained in Indonesia. I was hired to visit indigent Dutch living in kampongs round about Bandung, all of them Indos, to ascertain whether they were entitled to repatriation and financial support. I ask you! I found this easy to decide, naturally. My reports were such that the people I visited were granted financial support and were put on the list for repatriation. Mind you, I never lied. The condition in which these people lived was truly desperate, each case worse than the other. I fought hard for them and opened my mouth when necessary to convince the commissioner's high hats of the soundness of my recommendation. I would invite them to step into a becak with me and visit those people, so they could see for themselves. Anyway, I got them to see it my way.

On quite a different level, my husband had an extraordinary experience during our stay in Bandung. It came unbidden and out of nowhere, and we still don't know why it happened. Through his job, Henk got acquainted with a young Indonesian. One day, that young man came to visit us unannounced and handed my husband a *keris* (a native, serpentine-bladed weapon that is often thought to have magic powers) with the compliments of his father, who had died recently. Surprised and moved, my husband accepted the keris. It would later lie on my desk in its beautiful, carved, wooden scabbard.

Every evening at a certain hour—I've forgotten what time—we would hear a loud bang on that desk. My husband and I would investigate and my husband would say, "I see *haji macan* standing next to the desk."

I have forgotten to tell you, that, when we still lived in Kadipaten, my husband often had to visit the administrator's house in the evening. On the way, he would pass a large waringin tree. One evening, he could clearly see a haji, who held a tiger (macan) on a leash. He smiled kindly at my husband and then faded away into the dark depths of the waringin. My husband told one of his fellow workers, the Indonesian chemist, Sawal, of this encounter. Sawal said that a haji was indeed known to have been buried with his tiger next to that tree many, many years before. From time to time that holy man, called haji macan, would appear on certain occasions. His appearance signified good luck and prosperity to the one who saw him.

So, that same haji macan, whom Henk first saw at Kadipaten, would stand next to the keris lying on my desk in Bandung. I asked Henk, "What is haji macan doing?"

"He just smiles."

"And the tiger?"

"Nothing. Just stands there swishing his tail back and forth."

"Well," I again, "I'm going up to him. I want to know what he's doing here and what he wants."

So, directed by my husband, I went up to the haji and, according to Henk, stepped over the tiger and was then in the haji, who, Henk said, kept smiling serenely.

"Well, I don't feel a thing and I don't see a thing either. This is meant only for you, it seems. Sudah, al!"

At the time the young Indonesian brought us the keris, he had also said that my husband would receive three gifts in all. The keris was the first gift.

Not long after, my husband had to go on an inspection tour. He had to inspect the work of an Indo, who did the bookkeeping of a subdivision of the GEBEO in a small town. This Indo lived with his Indonesian mother in a nice house in the kampong. He invited my husband over for supper at home, also to meet his mother. The front door had hardly been opened to admit Henk, when the mother ran back inside and returned holding a small box. She said, she had to give this to him, an order from Above. Just so! "This" was an old-fashioned, exquisitely worked ring, which he had gotten as a gift, just like that! That's how he received the second present.

The third gift came to my husband much later, when he worked as a bookkeeper for the Wilhelmina Gasthuis, a city hospital in Amsterdam. There he ran into a nurse whom he knew from Indonesia. During that first warm reunion, and without any preliminaries whatsoever, she pulled a ring from her finger and gave it to him. "I'm not sure why," she said, "but I feel I have to give this to you, this very minute."

I tell you, the strangest things can happen in that realm which we call the occult, and who knows the reason for all of this. Even now, we still don't know what this means. My husband accepted all these gifts and put all of them together in a safe place. Much later, when he slept the sleep of death in his casket, I laid everything at his side to accompany him. To me, this was, and remains, totally incomprehensible.

But my husband would see things all the time, which would later turn out to have really happened. He would not have heard or read about them in advance in any way, so that you could say he had been influenced somehow. One day, for instance, he was on the top level of an apartment building somewhere in Amsterdam, where he was visiting a friend. It started to rain hard and the door—which opened to the outside—had to be closed. When my husband tried to close the door, he felt something holding it back. He looked to see what was wrong and saw an old woman standing at the door. She obviously wanted to come in. My husband stepped aside to let her in. Without saying a word, the woman walked quickly to a certain spot in the room and suddenly was gone. He found out later that she was the former owner of that apartment. She had committed suicide in the same spot where she disappeared from view.

These episodes, and those I told you about earlier, are the only things from another world I experienced myself in Indonesia. Otherwise, our life in Bandung was nice and uneventful. Suddenly, and out of the blue, we got word that Henk was eligible for a merit vacation in Holland, the family included. My husband had worked that well and that hard.

When we approached the ship which would take us to Holland, I heard loud screams and hurrahs coming from the deck. People I'd recommended for repatriation stood there at the railing and they were yelling, "Mrs. Schenkhuizen, Mrs. Schenkhuizen, here we are! Thank you! How nice that you're going to Holland too. You saved us!" There they were, fourth-class passengers, some in their best clothes, some in sandals, some in tattered coats, but all of them peppy and happy to be going. I myself also felt happy, because these almost-forgotten Indos had been granted their heart's desire.

In contrast, we were travelling second-class ourselves. But, no matter, I looked up all my former clients anyway, to listen to their stories of deliverance and their gratitude—we shed many a tear.

Didn't I tell you that my husband was a witness for the prosecution against the teungku? On the day of our departure, a subpoena arrived ordering him to appear before the court the next day. I tore that order up. I thought, too late, we won't be here then, we'll be on our way to the cold country. When he came home, I told my husband that I had torn up the subpoena. It upset him terribly, and he ranted, "What a stupid thing to do!"

Fortunately, my husband had a friend who was a high hat at the Department of Justice, an Indonesian. He drove as quickly as he could to see that friend, who happened to be in, and explained the matter. This man arranged for Henk to provide a written statement, swearing on the Bible that he was telling the truth. Nevertheless, our consciences didn't rest easily. As long as we remained in Indonesian waters, the authorities could haul him off the ship for malfeasance. With a sigh of relief, we finally set foot in Singapore for some sightseeing—that adventure fortunately ended well, too. I admit that I know next to nothing about legal matters, especially nothing about legal matters in the chaotic Indonesia of that period.

I promptly got seasick and stayed seasick just about the whole voyage through. The only exception was at Captain's Dinner, when we all showed up wearing our best clothes—we had the most beautiful dresses made to order specifically for that evening. But my stomach turned again when I saw the abundance of food: pigs with lemons in their mouths; whole lobsters with their fearsome claws draped over green lettuce and red cabbage; thick slices of meat floating in greasy gravy, and much more. I forced myself, eating only food that wasn't greasy, and felt great relief when the "orgy" was behind us and I could go on deck, where I gulped the fresh air.

Did I mention we travelled on the *Oranje* (Orange)? Together with twenty-four other ships, we were the first to pass through the Suez Canal after the end of the conflict between England and Egypt. We went at a snail's pace, if I may use that term for the cautiousness with which we navigated the silted-up canal. At either side of us, at a distance of a couple of meters, we were surrounded by desert. We could see sand dribble down from the banks. During our passage through that canal, we were part of a flotilla of twenty-five ships, the *Oranje* in the lead—which is only fitting, after all it's "orange above all." From our ship, we had a grand view of the other ships when we went around a bend in the wider lake sections of the Suez Canal.

In Port Said, you had those well-known, funny, Arab magicians, who, pokerfaced and with lots of prattle, got my children—especially Joy, my second daughter—involved in various tricks. As if they knew, of all people it was Joy—she who hated to be touched by strange men—who was touched by one of those magicians when he "put a spell on her," after which she felt something scratching around on her chest. Screaming at the top of her voice, she plunged her hand into her blouse and plucked out six adorable yellow chicks. She pushed them back into the magician's hand and ran off. You wonder how the man pulled that off. You can't help laughing at those magicians' antics. Lots of Arab vendors came on board, too, selling all kinds of knickknacks. People all around talked, laughed, and dickered with great good humor among buyers and sellers alike.

I believe each of us received some clothes in Port Said. This distribution of clothes was mostly designed to help the repatriates. In fact, we ourselves weren't repatriating. We were a family proud of being on a merit vacation. For it meant that our husband and father had done such an excellent job, that he was awarded vacation abroad earlier than his contract stipulated. In addition, Henk had been given a year's sabbatical to give him time to get a certificate in electronics. Heretofore, he had studied electronics on his own. All in all, we had great expectations.

My husband, even though he had "only" graduated from the MULO, had a lot of irons in the fire. He read a lot, he studied a lot, and he could be a good and interesting partner in conversation. And he was a real whiz in electronics. While I was born with two left hands, he was a born handyman. He could repair anything and everything, and not only electrical items. Really, he was an all around whiz, this Indo urchin from a family of eight.

STRANDED IN HOLLAND:
SUMMER 1957 - JULY 1962

In the summer of 1957, we arrived safely in Amsterdam, where my mother and sister welcomed us. I hadn't seen them in ten years, so we had a terrific reunion.

Doeshka, our eldest, had left for Holland earlier. She was enrolled in a midwife course. She too was on the dock to welcome us. We had sent her a telegram, that I would be coming together with her brother and sisters, but that her father would follow later. That had been the original plan. But then came the surprise of the merit vacation after Henk had worked at the GEBEO for five years. Predictably, she was elated to see him and wanted so much to hug us all, she kept hopping up and down with impatience. What a happy reunion we had!

First we ate a delicious meal in a restaurant. Then we went to Lairesse Street in Amsterdam, where they'd found us a place to stay in a kind of boardinghouse. At first sight, we hated the narrow and steep stairs leading to the third level, where we were to stay. The rental consisted of a large, light and airy combined dining room, sitting room, and bedroom area. A separate, small bedroom opening onto the hall was assigned to Guido.

As could be expected, of the whole family, Joy was the first to slip on those high and steep stairs. Those stairs weren't the only problem. We also thought the rent too high. Eventually, we checked advertisements and found an address in the "Gold Coast" district, also in Amsterdam, at the house of a totok family who had lived a long time in the Indies. It was called the "Gold Coast" district for the number of wealthy people that lived there. Nevertheless, we were able to rent cheaper and nicer rooms there, on Michel Angelo Street, than the ones we had on Lairesse Street.

Doeshka, who was in the second year of the midwife course, left school. She preferred to be with us. She immediately got a job at the Giro, a bank.

Our vacation in Amsterdam was a lot of fun. We looked up several relatives. We also stayed for a month in Naarden, where we house- and dog-sat for cousins, a married couple. Amongst others, we listened to beautiful concerts in the Amsterdam Concertgebouw (the Amsterdam concert hall), and went to a one-man show by Wim Kan, and also one by Toon Hermans, both of them well-known Dutch stand-up comedians of that period.

At the Toon Hermans show, I made a fool of myself for the umpteenth time. We sat in the first row, for we wanted to miss none of the jokes and tricks of this comedian. At one point, he said, "French isn't hard to learn at all. Just listen to this: a pipe is *une pipe*, a sack is *un sac*, and if you put those two together . . . " Before I knew it, I'd yelled: *"Piepzak!"* (a play on words: the Dutch term piepzak refers to being scared).

The audience shook with laughter and Hermans said, "Exactly, M'am, you there on the first row. You listen well, you are very intelligent, you have no trouble learning French at all," and in that vein he went on, and on, and on. I laughed loudest of all, even though I felt hot with embarrassment. My family looked shyly around, my husband shaking his head as always, even though he, too, grinned wide.

That whole evening, Toontje hauled me in by the collar so to speak—whatever subject he poked fun at, eyes dancing with fiendish joy, I was at the receiving end. The audience loved it. Well, sudah, I thought in resignation, as long as you're having fun. I seem to be the butt of the jokes, but that isn't too bad. Back home, we had a good laugh again. "Of course, it had to be you again, Mom!"

I could be found in the Bible Museum almost every day. I was especially fascinated by the exact replica in miniature of the Jewish tabernacle in the Sinai desert, as described in Genesis 26. To see God as a cloud by day and as a light by night! And then the way the tabernacle had been set up: the wall of curtains, the sacrificial table, the ark in the Holy of Holies, and all the other details. I felt a certain resonance with God's purpose with this tabernacle, depicted exactly the way God had told Moses to construct it. Its message mystified me at the time, but it made me feel joyous anyway. I didn't know then why it affected me that way, but now

213

everything is clear to me. It's amazing, the way in which such a display, put together from scraps of wood and fabric, can be a source of enlightenment!

Naturally, we toured all the Amsterdam canals by boat, crossing underneath ancient bridges, seeing the most interesting old houses, leaning this way and that against each other, as if the riches of the East Indian Company were too heavy a load to carry for them. Tiny windows, large doors, wrought iron façades, it was a treat to look at them, all the while keeping in mind that the Lords XVII, the seventeen wealthy and powerful underwriters of the Dutch East India Company, put on the dog there with their profits from the riches of the East: coffee, tea, pepper, tobacco, cloves, and the spices from Banda—nutmeg and mace.

In short, we enjoyed our vacation as much as possible, even though Guido attended the Spinoza Lyceum, Doeshka had a job, Joy attended the Schoevers school of business to get her business certificate, and Pax went to grade school.

We had hardly settled down late that same year when a telegram arrived from Bandung and GEBEO; my husband had to return immediately because his replacement had had a nervous breakdown caused by the increasing tension between the Indonesians and the Dutch and they needed Henk badly. We looked at each other in dismay and disappointment. My husband was particularly upset because he had set his heart on continuing his studies in electronics and had already had several talks with various instructors.

We decided to take only Pax, our youngest, with us to Indonesia and to leave the oldest three behind in Holland. In a hurry, we looked for a boardinghouse for them which we could afford and found one with a totok family. We immediately felt these people and their home weren't quite right for us, but we were squeezed for time and decided to go ahead anyway. With the telegram from the GEBEO in hand, we were quickly booked on the *Ruys*, leaving from Rotterdam.

The morning of our departure, I left for Rotterdam with a heavy heart. I found it tremendously difficult to leave three children behind. My mother, sister, and the children came along to see us off. Worried about the unsettled situation in Indonesia, none of us looked happy. Suddenly a public-address system was turned on and a man announced in a loud voice that passengers with Dutch passports and Indonesian visas could not return to Indonesia, except at their own risk. He continued, "You can safely travel to Singapore, but from there you continue your journey to Indonesia at your own risk."

I immediately burst out in joy, "Wonderful! Wonderful! I can stay with my children!" Delighted at the news, we hugged each other. Both my mother, already at an advanced age by then, and my sister were as relieved as we were. My husband was perplexed, however. He looked concerned. The first thing he said was, "What about a job? Now I don't have a job!" I said promptly, "Dear, this is a miracle, God's miracle! No doubt, He'll take care of a job too. don't worry, be happy that you can stay here with us."

At my words, his face relaxed. He then hastened to the visa office to get additional information and also to get our trunks taken off the ship, so that they wouldn't be taken to Singapore and back. As always, there was a lot of bureaucratic red tape, but my husband bought a box of cigars for the stevedores and in a wink we had our trunks back. The luggage of most of the other passengers went all the way to Singapore and back again.

So, there we stood. Everybody was excited, laughing and talking, I most of all. We phoned our boardinghouse on Michel Angelo Street to find out if we could return there. After we explained the situation, they were happy to have us back. Back we went to Amsterdam and our old boardinghouse. We drank a cup of coffee together and then we reclaimed our old rooms.

Next, my husband went to the Ministry of Social Work to get things moving. Here, my husband was told that he was not entitled to financial support or housing, because, officially, he was not a repatriate. "Well," said Henk, "You'll hear more about this."

Without more ado, he went straight to the head of the Ministry, Ms. M. A. M. Klompé. At first, she, too, shook her head—we were not classified as repatriates, but as people that had run aground, flotsam. We weren't entitled to the benefits repatriates received. My husband said calmly, "You are mistaken. My family and I have indeed run aground and become flotsam, but that is due to the same political situation that resulted in repatriates coming here. What is the difference? I insist that I receive the same benefits as the repatriates."

After consulting various laws and all kinds of papers, my husband was judged to be right and he was immediately assigned to a halfway house (pension) run by half-Indies people, on Van Baerle

Street. By the way, this was on the same street as the concert hall, making it easy to attend performances. We got a huge sitting room-bedroom with cooking corner on the second floor, and another bedroom on the third floor. Once again, we had to climb steep and narrow stairs to get to our rooms. Stairs in old Dutch houses are such unlovely contraptions.

We had moved into a so-called *contract pension*. The home's owners had contracted with the government to provide temporary housing to people from the Indies; they were paid for this service. He was an Amboinese and she was a totok. They were nice, jovial people. We received a government stipend and were permitted to cook an extra dish or so when the mood struck us.

My husband immediately started looking for a job. He found one soon enough in the office of the Wilhelmina Gasthuis, a local hospital. I got a job too, cleaning toilets and bathrooms at the address on Michel Angelo Street, where we had stayed during our vacation. First I had stayed there as a paying guest, and now I came back as daily help. I walked from home to work and back, thus saving enough to buy extras. In the meantime, my husband kept sending out applications left and right.

After half a year, he got an excellent job at the *Oosterbeekse Tegelfabriek*, a tile factory. Overjoyed, we quickly moved to Oosterbeek, one of the most beautiful places in the Netherlands. Henk had rented the upper floor of a house on Schelmse Way. The owners were Hollanders. They lived on the lower floor of the house.

Schelmse Way was a beautiful, wide street lined with nice houses. The sitting-dining room, bedrooms, and kitchen on our floor were "Indies" large and we felt immediately at home. The only drawback was that we had to share the bathroom with the owners, but it wasn't that much of a problem, for—common to Hollanders—they only took a bath once a week. Fortunately, we had our own toilet facilities. We didn't have to set out cebok bottles there, for the toilet was equipped with a water sprayer, turned on and off by means of a handle on the side—the occupant could spray him- or herself clean. A nice and hygienic invention. I wonder why they don't have that kind of equipment here in America.

Our bedrooms opened onto a large balcony, where we could hang our wash to dry and where a tall apple tree generously offered us its juicy fruits. The owners gave us permission to eat the apples.

216

Within the shortest time, that tree had been picked as clean as if a swarm of fruit bats had visited it.

Doeshka got a job at the Giro bank in Arnhem, the same city in which Guido attended the Lyceum, a high school, and where Joy got a job as a bookkeeper in an import-export company. Everybody used a bicycle, including myself when I went shopping.

Our whole family was together again, and we all lived under one roof in a picture-pretty environment. I was so happy I could burst. Soon enough, the children's old friends, also repatriated from the Indies, came to visit us. And Pax brought home a friend, a very Dutch, white-skinned blonde girl from a working family. The two of them were nicknamed "Black on White," after a popular licorice you could buy by weight in paper twists. Pax's friend felt immediately at home with us and shared our rijsttafel without hesitation, even though she had never seen or tasted it before. She liked everything and ate enormous portions. She became a regular customer of our rijsttafel and was a loyal and sweet friend of our Pax.

Even though we were happy where we lived, we still yearned to have our own house. A Dutch family happened to have emigration papers for Canada, but needed a buyer for their furnished house. My husband again consulted the authorities in charge of repatriates, and they bought the property for us on the condition that we pay them back in monthly installments. The whole transaction was done "with closed wallets," as they say, and we could move into the completely furnished house, at 6 Parallel Way in Oosterbeek.

It wasn't that big, but it suited us nicely. My husband and I shared one large bedroom, and there were two smaller bedrooms. We rebuilt the huge attic into yet another bedroom.

The previous inhabitants didn't seem to have used the bathroom. We found a bathtub in the attic, however. We laboriously carried that bathtub down the steep and exceedingly narrow stairs and put it where it belonged: in the bathroom, next to the toilet and the washing machine. After connecting the water to the bathtub, we had a real bathroom. I was particularly happy with the washing machine, for my hands would get wrinkled from washing our clothes by hand on a washboard. We also had small gardens in front and back, completely separated from our neighbors by an iron fence all around.

Doeshka had been going steady with one Humphrey Schmidt in Bandung, but she had broken off the relationship shortly after moving to Holland. When she heard on the grapevine that he had arrived in Holland, she somehow finagled to get his address, contacted him again, and invited him to her birthday party. After that party, their relationship was as solid as ever. Soon after, Doeshka and Humphrey got engaged and he came to live with us, sharing the attic with our son Guido.

True to its name, Parallel Way lay parallel to the railroad tracks running deep below the level of our house. Whenever a train went by, our house would quiver as if caught in a gentle earthquake. You could reach the railroad tracks by clambering down the broom-covered slope. After crossing the tracks—quickly!—and climbing up the opposite slope, you would find yourself in the Oosterbeek woods. Our house was in an excellent location. It felt to us as if we lived out in the country: no neighbors behind us, and our view of the woodlands changing with the seasons. In fall, that forest flamed with fiery color, and in winter it was blanketed with sparkling-white snow.

Now that we lived in our own house, we promptly got ourselves a dog, a lassie or collie. We got him as a puppy, but he soon grow to normal size. His name was Blitz, too, and he was very smart. Soon enough, I had taught him to get the paper and to open the door with his paw and close it behind him with his hip. I took walks with him, rain or shine, at five o'clock in the morning. I found the cold hard to endure, even though I was swathed in thick coats and woolen cap, and wore sturdy shoes. But I did it anyway, just to please Blitz. He was such a magnificent dog. We all loved him.

I walked through the woods no matter what the season, deeply enjoying the changes in nature. I would often drop by the special cemetery for those who had died in the war, mostly Americans. They had died in the fierce fighting around Arnhem, a fifteen-minute tram ride from Oosterbeek. That cemetery was marvelously quiet and still. Whenever I gazed over the white crosses in the green grass, I felt sure that these men hadn't sacrificed their lives for nothing, for the Lord had let their souls pass before his throne and had breathed on them, saying, "Well done my children. Come, enter my house."

Oosterbeek lies in a particularly beautiful area of green woods and meadows, not far from the "Veluwe," which we often visited.

We couldn't get enough of that region, where we would see deer and wild pigs, and heather in purplish bloom stretching to the horizon, which was sprinkled with stately pines. There, we could sit outside in a sidewalk café and enjoy the environment.

A few houses down the street from us lived another Indies family. We got to know them, because their son went to the same Lyceum with Guido. We became friends. It was nice to have friends close by, especially for me. We visited back and forth. Because the wife tended to be rather depressed, I often visited her to open her eyes with the help of my Bible, so that she could learn to see things differently. We grew very close that way.

Humphrey Schmidt, my future son-in-law, rode, first on a bike, and then on a motorbike, to Nijmegen, another town. But when winter really set in, he wisely switched to the bus. He said, *"Ke-te-kout-en*, it's too cold; *kekittelen*, I get goose bumps all over."

Another group of friends from the Indies brought us in contact with the world of flying, providing us with another son-in-law. This time, it was an Amsterdammer, born and raised, one Jur van der Woude, a pilot. Jur would come along with another pilot we knew from the Indies, and he too loved our rijsttafel. You guessed it, Jur visited us more and more often, and finally asked my second daughter, Joy, to marry him.

In the meantime, Guido graduated from the Lyceum, was called up for the draft, and assigned to Ermelo. This was not far from Oosterbeek. Guido would often come over for the weekends, bringing *his* friends along, and they too shared our rijsttafel. These were all Dutchmen, who had never, or rarely, tasted genuine Indies food. Our meals, enlivened with anecdotes about a soldier's life, were crowded and noisy. We would hear various Dutch dialects spoken, some of them quite difficult to follow. Guido made many good friends among his fellow soldiers. He has stayed in contact with two of them, both of whom have come to stay with us here in America from time to time.

Guido was soon promoted to sergeant. It was cute to see his enlisted friends having to salute him. When you are a soldier, you have to salute, it doesn't matter whether you are friends, on penalty of spending Sundays and holidays in the barracks. They would address Guido as "sergeant," as required, until they were all safely in my house, when they called him by name again.

We had a good time in beautiful Oosterbeek. Naturally, we gave our house an Indonesian name, which Jur, my totok future son-in-law, neatly lettered on the front in airplane paint, "*Bumi Suci*," meaning happy or sacred house. The present owners have tried to remove the name, washing it and scrubbing it to no avail—"*J'y suis, j'y reste*," (I'm here to stay), as Marshall MacMahon said during the Crimean War—a truly indelible reminder of those strange "Moors," us!

The day of my oldest daughter's wedding arrived. All our friends and relatives had come over. Doeshka wore a lovely, short bridal dress and held a bouquet of stephanotis, handed her by the pale, nervous bridegroom waiting for her at the foot of the stairs. She was a beautiful bride. My husband blessed Doeshka and Humphrey there, and then, surrounded by relatives, they exchanged rings. Everything was done the old-fashioned way: lovely, with dignity, and with a warm outpouring of love from father to bride and bridegroom, and from the mother and all the assembled relatives on both sides of the family. Only then did we leave for city hall in open, horse-drawn carriages for the official ceremony, the signing of the marriage certificate. Afterwards, a beaming bride and bridegroom rode in the warm sunlight to the restaurant we had reserved in advance, to feast, eat, and drink. The festively decorated dining room was filled with relatives and friends and we had a fun and noisy party.

Then Doeshka and Humphrey went home and changed clothes to go on their honeymoon. They rented a car to drive through Germany—along the Rhine and so on—and had an unforgettable honeymoon.

So we lived pleasantly, until my man came home one day with the unexpected news that the tile factory had laid him off, his umpteenth lay off. The cause of his firing was a younger man, a totok, who had been hired to supervise Henk at the salary which originally had been promised my husband. Hot words were exchanged, resulting in Henk's firing.

Shortly after, a business office came on the market at a reasonable price in Heusden, an hour's drive from Oosterbeek. It handled the bookkeeping of the surrounding farms. Against my advice, my husband bought it. Joy gave up her job in the import-export company in Arnhem and became my husband's assistant in Heusden. Every day at seven o'clock in the morning, they would leave together for the village of Heusden. However, the hardheaded farmers didn't trust the "blue boy" from the start, because he introduced all kinds of newfangled ideas and methods, all to get the office to work faster and more efficiently. As could be foreseen, they resisted his innovations. So, this venture, too, ended in a fiasco. As a result, my husband became very despondent and sickly. He was no longer the dependable breadwinner he used to be.

Joy married Jur van der Woude not long after, one year to the day after the wedding of our eldest. By that time, Doeshka had already emigrated to America with her husband and their three-month-old baby boy, Brady.

Again, my husband first blessed this marriage at our home, and then looked on while Joy and Jur quietly and seriously exchanged rings. Joy looked beautiful, just like her older sister. She was dressed in a short wedding gown and a long veil, and carried a bouquet of red roses. The reception, held in the restaurant used for Doeshka and Humphrey's wedding party, was again well-attended and joyous. Joy and Jur went on a short honeymoon to Terschelling in the Netherlands, where his parents had a house in which they could stay for free.

A year had passed since Doeshka had left us and she, settled in California, pleaded for our immediate emigration. She was very concerned about my husband's chronic sickliness. His doctor had advised him to move to a warm climate, and what would be better than America, in particular, California?

Under the Pastore-Walter Act, a large number of refugees from the Indies were allowed to immigrate, being refugees of war. We could only move to the United States, however, if we had paid all our taxes and could prove that we needed to emigrate. A note from our doctor helped the authorities to decide quickly that my husband indeed needed to move to a warmer climate. This decision was made even easier, when they heard that our oldest daughter lived in the United States already.

Acquaintances wanted to buy our house with all its furnishings. They offered enough to pay our taxes and finance various other expenses. We could finally start to pack. Our papers were in order and all of us, including the newly married Joy and Jur, left for Amsterdam. From there, we would fly to the United States with a DC-10 on the eve of 4 July 1962.

It was icy cold, in spite of the time of year, and it rained buckets. We were dressed in our heaviest winter clothing, looking like emigrants. I was airsick throughout the whole plane trip and treated the other passengers to the loud noises accompanying the act of throwing up. My children and husband were terribly put out with me and thoroughly embarrassed. As if I could help being sick. To this day, my family has no idea how horrible it is to be seasick or airsick.

LIFE IN CALIFORNIA: 4 JULY 1962 -

New York. 4 July 1962. Here we were, my husband, myself, Guido, Joy, and her new husband Jur, and our youngest daughter, Pax. It was ninety degrees Fahrenheit. Our winter clothes suffocated us and the towering skyscrapers on Broadway made us feel even more overheated. The customs people were nice and bid us welcome with a few well-chosen words. A lady from the church which was sponsoring us handed us $150 to tide us over—we had no other money with us—and loaded us into taxis, which took us at top speed to a refugee center to await marching orders.

We removed as many layers of clothing as possible, then decided to explore the city a bit. Everybody had fled the heat—gone to cooler regions; New York was totally deserted. Joy kept me company. We would find out later that she was in her early weeks of pregnancy. What with the heat, my airsickness, and Joy's still unknown pregnancy, we were not exactly in top form there in New York. Nevertheless, everything interested us. We were eager to get our first impressions of our new country. We walked past grocery stores. There! Both of us saw it at the same time—a couple of boxes on the sidewalk filled with mangos. What a delightful surprise. We quickly bought a couple of them and later ate them in a café, where we ordered some food. Totally unexpectedly, we were served glasses of ice water—ice cubes tinkling refreshingly—free and not ordered by us. The mangos were delicious. They were a treat for us all, but especially for my totok son-in-law, Jur, who had never eaten one before.

We had to kill a lot of time in New York—six hours—before the train would leave for our final destination, Pasadena, in southern California. The building in which we waited was not air-conditioned. My husband, physically quite weak already, was terribly bothered by the heat. The doctor had said, "You've angina pectoris. But you may get to be a hundred if you take care of yourself and move to a warm climate." But this heat was too much of a good thing.

Finally, we could board the train in the afternoon, with many other refugees. Oddly enough, all the trains carry names here, and ours was called the Erie Lackawanna, an Indian name. And, true to its name, it had Indian traits, about which more later. It was pleasantly air-conditioned, and there was even a faucet near the toilets where you could fill a paper cup with ice-cold water and drink as much as you wanted. I felt immediately content and happy with everything.

Once the train began to move, however, I understood the meaning of its name, for it shook from left to right as if dancing an Indian snake dance in a perpetuum mobile. You went to the toilet in a drunken walk. Once there, you had to wait until the train righted itself a bit, quickly sit down, and do whatever you came to do. We had a lot of fun with that crazy train, destination Pasadena, California, where my daughter, Doeshka, lived with her husband, Humphrey, and son Brady.

In Chicago, we had to transfer to the Santa Fe, a much better train. It had a normal and pleasantly gentle ride—delightful. Here we had one car almost to ourselves. All in all, we spent three nights and two days on the train.

Along the way, more passengers got on. Our sixteen-year-old Pax soon made friends with two American girls. They had approached her in a friendly way, giving Pax an opportunity to try her school girl English. We later found out they were Pax's age. At first, Pax felt shy and afraid of making mistakes. But soon enough she could keep the conversation going, albeit with a lot of hemming and hawing, the American girls pleasantly correcting her where necessary.

The time went quickly for everybody except my husband, who was visibly exhausted and in pain. Thank God, he could stretch out full length because of the many empty seats.

In contrast, I enjoyed every moment of the trip. As I explained earlier, I adore trains and train rides. Moreover, I had to pinch myself once in a while to assure myself that I had indeed arrived in the country of my dreams. I sat glued to the large windows, drinking in the expansive grandeur of America's wide open spaces. In my mind's eye I saw wild mustangs galloping up to us, half-naked Apaches with colorful feathers sitting on them, bows and arrows at the ready to slay the white dogs and scalp one and all. I heard their war cries and I saw Winnetou, tall and dignified, his arm raised high and his dark eyes boring into mine . . .

"Hey, what are you staring at like that! Do you see something special in those prairies, that yellow grass, and those high hills and endless plains?"

Oh dear! Henk! Shaking me out of my fantasies. When I explained that I had met Winnetou and Old Shatterhand, he smiled, and he, too, got sucked into the world of Karl May's stories. Together, laughing a lot, we embellished on. It was great fun. But soon my husband got tired again and had to lie down, poor dear. It was so pitiful and sad.

And thus we thundered on, passing various towns and unfamiliar places, night turning into day and into night again, until we neared Pasadena. We stopped at the little station of Santa Anita, an old and historical building; at that time it was still in its place near the railroad tracks, but since then has moved to the Arboretum in Arcadia. I thought I recognized sweet potato there, its rank growth and large leaves covering the ground. I called my family over to see it. Everybody was wildly enthusiastic. "Just like at home in the Indies!" "And it grows wild here, just like that!"

I asked one of our fellow passengers what that plant was called in America, and she answered pleasantly, "Ivy." Our faces fell. You might say that I was dumbfounded.

When you are used to the beautiful stations in Europe, you expect to find even larger and more beautiful buildings in America. We had finally come to a full stop. Signs proclaimed Pasadena. Well, who of us hasn't heard about Pasadena! So, we all stuck our head out of the car and all we saw was a small porch with a subfloor of smooth cobbles!

Soon we saw Doeshka and her husband accompanied by several Indies people walking alongside the train. We called out to them. As fast as we could, we ran down the high train steps and fell in each other's arms. We hadn't seen each other for a year. What a reunion! We were surprised and happy to find old friends also waiting for us there: Henk Gaspers, Carla and Hans Keasberry, and Ben and Ida Swart.

All our baggage was quickly collected and loaded into the various cars, and then we drove along the streets of Pasadena to Doeshka's house.

I asked her immediately, "Is that really the Pasadena station?" She answered, "Yes." Keenly disappointed, I exclaimed, "How's that possible! And that in this rich and big America!"

Not long after, we stepped into Doeshka's white, wooden, little house on Mar Vista Street in Pasadena. It had two bedrooms, a nice family room, a dining room, a full bath with toilet, a kitchen, and a rather large garden. Henk, I, and Guido shared one of the bedrooms; Jur and Joy slept on a convertible sofa bed in the family room; and Pax stayed temporarily with a good friend of our children, Micky de Vogel, who lived nearby. In the dining room awaited us a complete nasi kuning, a special and festive kind of rijsttafel, upon which we fell with great appetite and joy. We talked each other's ears off!

Our first grandson, Brady, who was a year old, accompanied his oma the next day on a walk around the neighborhood. And then, after a couple of days rest, we started looking for our own house and jobs. Not long after, we—that's to say, Henk and I, Guido, Pax, and Micky de Vogel—moved to a large house on Flower Street, also in Pasadena. It came completely furnished. The refrigerator was filled to overflowing with good food, the beds neatly made, the carpet brushed. There was china, glassware, pots and pans; in short, nothing was missing to make it comfortable. Doeshka, and her husband, Humphrey, had taken care of all this, helped by the Presbyterian church in Pasadena, our official sponsors.

Our new house had a small, open porch covered with roses; a nice front yard with a large pine tree, one of those old giants; a spacious family-dining room; three bedrooms; and a large kitchen with breakfast nook. It had a huge backyard with wall-to-wall lawn, a couple of storage rooms, and a garage. All in all, it overwhelmed us. Within fourteen days of moving in, my husband landed a job as a bookkeeper with Fairchild Cameras in the City of Industry, which he enjoyed very much. Soon we bought a secondhand car for the daily hour's drive to my husband's office. Guido attended the Pacific Airline School, and Pax walked to Pasadena High School. Micky de Vogel, who was now boarding with us, had a job and drove her own car back and forth.

In those days, we didn't own a television yet and every Tuesday evening, we visited Doeshka and Humphrey to watch the famous roller skating show. We found it riveting, and we felt the same way about the wrestling show. It wasn't long, however, before we discovered it was all a sham. Nevertheless, the being together was enough in itself to make us feel happy and content.

Joy and Jur stayed with Doeshka and Humphrey for a while longer, but then both families found their own houses and they went their separate ways. From that time on, my husband and I had two homes to visit. (Joy, my second child, was expecting her first child, and Doeshka, my eldest child, was expecting her second.)

This wasn't the only time my oldest two moved. It's so easy to move here in America. You can easily find a reasonably priced rental house and friends can help you on moving day. They moved several times, either to a house with more rooms, or to a cheaper one, or to a house with a larger yard, and so on. And the actual moving always went smoothly enough; with a lot of nonsense and joking around, the new home would be ready for supper and sleep that very same day.

And so our new, American life got under way. We went on a lot of picnics with other Indies families we had gotten to know. We either went to the beach or to a park. Each family would bring its own playpen for the toddlers, food, and ice chest, but we would all share whatever we brought along—such great fun! Here we were, Indos, seeking out each other's company under these unfamiliar skies, all enjoying California's wonderful, sunny climate. It was such a delightful experience to be able to find foods here that you remembered so well from your old home in Indonesia, and such a good feeling to be able to hear and speak your own language again in a strange, new country. Our get-togethers in our new country, our country of choice, were always so joyful and harmonious!

It was 1962. Our first Christmas in America was approaching. On 19 December 1962, I got a call from Henk during office hours: he was in the hospital—he had fainted after experiencing severe chest pains—but I was not to worry. "Please come and visit."

Fortunately, Micky had taken the day off and she took us to the hospital right away. There we found my husband, quite relaxed and really not looking bad at all, sharing a room with another patient. As soon as the doctor appeared, I asked him a thousand and one questions. He wasn't sure what was wrong and wanted to observe my husband for a couple of days longer.

Henk came home on 24 December. He was apparently well enough to celebrate Christmas with us. We kept it quite simple and

227

low key. Christmas evening, he went to bed early, feeling exhausted. Out in the garden with us the morning after, he fainted again. Back he went to the hospital and there he had to stay again. On 29 December he was released again from the hospital. He got up the next morning, 30 December, in excellent spirits. I could hear him whistling and singing in the bathroom. It was Sunday, and everyone else was still asleep.

Stepping outside, he said: "I feel wonderful! I have no chest pains. I'm completely well again. Why don't you fix me some toast and fry me a couple of eggs?"

We were sitting outside on our front porch. I got up to get him the food when he fainted again. This time it took longer to bring him to. I yelled for help but nobody came. He regained consciousness and I asked: "What's wrong?!" He said: "Oh, nothing. It must be the heat." Nevertheless, I carefully led him back inside and had him stretch out on the sofa.

"I really want those eggs," he said.

I got up to do as he asked. His eyes followed my every move. I thought that very strange and finally asked him, "Why do you stare at me like that. Is something wrong?"

"No, nothing," he said, "I just love watching you. You're such a busy bee."

Those words had hardly left his mouth, when he called out, "Goodbye dear, I'm going," his eyes rolling back in his head and his body jerking in death.

I ran up to him and held him close, alternately begging God to save him and calling for my son. At last, Guido heard me and called an ambulance. The ambulance crew, accompanied by police, stormed into our home a couple of minutes later. But my husband had already left us. I myself had closed his eyes for his eternal rest. My grief turned me to stone. I couldn't even shed a tear.

After taking all the steps designed to revive a person and a final check, the doctor said: "Your husband is gone."

Even though you already know, you always cling to even the slimmest hope, that he might yet live. So, that dry, "Your husband is gone," was like a hammerblow on my numb brain and felt doubly painful. And so, this event ushered in yet a different stage in life, for all of us but particularly for me. It was 30 December 1962, five and a half months after coming to America.

The people in charge of my husband's funeral took his body away to be prepared for burial. But not before all of us had witnessed a miracle: before the undertakers placed a white sheet over him, we saw Henk change into the slim young man he was during the time of our courtship. It was both miraculous and weird. We stared, filled with awe and surprise. This change may have lasted no more than a couple of minutes, and then he changed back to the way his body looked when he took his last breath. What could it mean? Was this meant as a sign to us, assuring us that Henk was happy where he was, young and reborn in the glory of the Almighty? We hope so. Whatever it meant, it surely provided some comfort, and I myself will never forget it.

On 1 January 1963 we watched our first Rose Parade on television with the constant thought in the back of our mind that a dead, beloved member of our family was still above the ground, waiting to be buried the day after. The following day was somber and drizzly. There were few people in attendance. We hadn't been in the country long enough to make close friends, and we hadn't really shared the news of my husband's death with many of those we did know. The graveside ceremony was short and simple. Numb, we returned in the cold of the day to Doeshka's house, where we stayed that night. 2 January 1963. On that day, twenty-eight years before, Henk and I were married.

The down-to-earth task of taking care of finances and my husband's estate awaited us on 3 January. My two sons-in-law and my son took away all my husband's clothes and everything else that could remind me of him, except for the one pair of blue pajamas he had slept in the last night. I wore the pajamas until they fell apart.

I didn't want to stay in that large house any longer. It reminded me too much of Henk, in particular the cologne he used to wear, which I smelled everywhere I went. In addition, my financial situation forced me to live smaller and more cheaply. So we moved from the house on Flower Street in Pasadena to one on Alameda Street in Sierra Madre. The Flower Street house was large and comfortable. The new one, a Spanish-style house, was small, here and there rather cramped, but it was snug and cozy. It was just the right size to house us all and its upkeep was easy. It had an open patio in the back and a small front yard; everything was just big enough and it did not demand a lot of care.

Both Guido, who was still going to the airline school, and I had to find work, because Pax, my youngest, still had to finish high school and, later, college. We put my husband's life insurance payment in the bank. It was enough to provide some extra cash when needed, but not enough to cover the daily expenses.

Members of the Presbyterian church that had sponsored us soon found me a job—playing the role of maid in rich people's homes. That was really the only job I could do. After being married for twenty-eight years, during which time I had never held an office job, I had completely lost my former skills in stenography and typing. I went to evening school for a time, but gave that up, being much too tired to study in the evening.

I worked five days a week, eight hours a day, for families in Arcadia and San Marino, all of them wealthy, all of them nice and helpful. I didn't have a car and couldn't drive one anyway, so these good people picked me up and took me back home. Thus began a new period in my life in which I learned the American way of keeping house from A to Z. Soon I was treated like part of the family, trusted completely. I would always be all by myself in those mansions, for the family would be off to work. I was fifty-five years old, still young and strong enough to move mountains if needed, even though the loss of my husband left a permanent hole in my life. But that only made hard work even more healthy for me.

Guido accepted any and all jobs he could get, either offered to him in person or gleaned from newspaper help wanted columns. All of them were low-paying jobs and didn't suit his skills at all. Finally, he ended up in the real estate business. He started out very low and small, something like worker number 1001. But he steadily rose through the ranks, changed employers a couple of times, until he arrived at long last where he is at present, holding down a position as legal advisor at World Title Insurance Company. In California, a title company assures buyers of real estate that they own it free and clear, and are legally protected against any future claims made against that property. It requires exacting research.

Life went on its merry way—our household income augmented by what our girl boarder, Micky, paid for room and board—always with many youngsters around the house, most of them Pax's friends. She knew them from school or from dance parties. Pax's school was an easy walk's distance away, another plus. And so we went on with our lives, each of us working as hard as he or she could. My other daughters and sons-in-law all had their own jobs. In the course of the years, several more children were born to them.

We moved a third time, this time from Alameda Street to Michigan Street, and a larger house. That move also brought all of us geographically closer together, which was all to the good, for, while we have always been real monkeys-stick-together, after my husband's death we grew even closer.

OUR CLUB, "DE SOOS," (1963-1988)
AND OTHER MATTERS

Another interesting page in my American adventure book has been my involvement with the Indo club, the Soos, a name which is simply the traditional abbreviation of the Dutch societeit, meaning organization or club.

Tjalie Robinson, an Indo activist and writer well-known in Indies circles, started this club, calling us to our first meeting at the house of Paul and Ida van Ligten in either March or April 1963. Those present were, as far as I remember: our host, Paul van Ligten, Sr.; John Couwenberg; René Creutzburg; Tjalie Robinson; Eric and Mona Klinkert; Frans Elliott; myself, and perhaps some others.

Tjalie explained why he had assembled us, and we not only decided to go ahead with our own club, we also chose its first, temporary, board: Paul (Paatje) van Ligten, president; Frans Elliott, vice-president; René Creutzburg, treasurer; I, secretary; Eric and Mona Klinkert and Roy Steevensz, commissioners.

Although our new club was primarily Tjalie's idea, and although his wife, Lilian Ducelle, served a term as commissioner, he never accepted an official position on our board himself. Tjalie continued to function as our behind-the-scenes advisor, however, until he and his family returned to the Netherlands.

It was Tjalie, for instance, who insisted that only subscribers to the Indies journal *Tong-Tong* could serve on our board. Article fourteen stipulated that only Indos and their relatives by marriage could become members of our club. Tjalie explained that this restraint was essential if the new Indo club was to be spared a possible take-over by non-Indo elements, and a subsequent dilution of Indo culture in what was envisioned as a specifically Indo environment. He had witnessed such a cultural take-over happen in other places. Thus our "infamous" Article 14, described above; years later it was rescinded by popular demand.

Our focus was on preserving our own identity in Uncle Sam's country, not only for our own benefit, but also for that of our offspring, our children. We wanted to share with them our love for our country of birth, and to make clear to them why we are who we are—Indos, knights in shining armor.

We got off to a flying start, putting together a temporary list of rules and regulations and setting the amount of the monthly club fee. Our first general members meeting was held on a Sunday afternoon, 2 June 1963 at the Jefferson School in Pasadena. About three hundred Indos showed up. I'm not sure how we spread the word initially. I would guess that Tjalie had alerted the subscribers to his own magazine, *Tong-Tong*, and we had also placed flyers in various Dutch bakeries and stores. In addition, the infamous Indo grapevine may have played a useful role for once as people came to get to know one another in this new country of settlement. They were also curious to find what Tjalie had in mind in starting this group.

At arrival, we all deposited our special rijsttafel dish in the kitchen for our potluck preceding the official meeting. It was wonderful to see so many old acquaintances again, and friendships were renewed on the spot between old and young alike. Most of all, we simply gossiped our hearts out. It was truly a treat to meet other Indos in America! However, we could also choose to play soccer, chess, checkers, read a book, or borrow one. The gathering ended with a formal meeting in which we made plans for the next Soos day, deciding to have one once a month.

That first Soos day stands out for me especially because I was reunited with a couple of old friends, Ruud and Fredje van der Horst, whom I knew from the Kadipaten sugar plantation. Fredje later turned out to be a talented comedienne. Many of the people I met there for the first time became not only good friends, but also reliable supporters of our amateur theatre.

Aimlessly walking around at that first meeting in Pasadena, I was suddenly accosted by a lady, who put her hand on my arm, exclaiming, "Serimpi! Serimpi!" We smiled broadly at each other, embraced and introduced ourselves. She was a Weynschenk. She had recognized me as having danced the serimpi that one time in Surabaya, way back when. That pleased me no end.

Our next Soos gathering took place in Los Angeles at the International Center. It was the women's turn to show how good they were in theatrics. It was nothing but fun. Booths constructed of bamboo had been erected along the walls of the hall and decorated with ivy. We also took care of the food ourselves—Indos love to eat!—and it disappeared quickly, as usual.

I was the first secretary of the fledgling Soos, but in time more and more meetings and elections took place, and I voluntarily stepped down in January 1964 to make way for younger Indos. Their sense of identity as Indos newly awakened, they too wanted some input in the Indo Community "De Soos," the formal name decided upon during one of our meetings. At that meeting, we chose a new board, which basically stayed the same, except that René Creutzburg took over as secretary, Eric Klinkert became treasurer, and Ruth Creutzburg was elected to fill the commissioner's post vacated by Eric.

From the first, I got to work closely with Ruth, René's wife. She quickly and decisively took charge of our club meetings and events. She was an indefatigable and skillful worker, who excelled in creating all kinds of original decorations. Ruth brimmed over with enthusiasm. It was a grievous loss to all of us when she died, all too early, all too young. Our club meetings and parties were never the same afterwards.

Soon, the Young Indo Circle was started by the young adults in our group. This offshoot concentrated on furthering the artistic talents of Indos, specifically in order to keep the tradition of the so-called stambul alive. Originally, stambul (folk theatre) was invented by an Indo in the Indies of old. The young adults discovered my son Guido's artistic talents and he was put in charge of the theatrical productions. Helped along by many other Indos, the first play was put on. The first attempts at acting, during the rehearsals, either at our house or at somebody else's house, were hilarious. However, Guido stuck to his guns and showed the amateur players verbally and physically how to speak and move about. He was a very strict taskmaster, due to his tendency to want everything just so. People gradually adjusted to his authoritarian ways and they really did their best to put on a successful stambul. Every one of them discovered some latent talent, to their surprise and pride. They now felt the urge to regularly attend the day and evening rehearsals, not only because it was expected, but because they really had fun. They would laugh out loud when one of them made a mistake, or they would laugh in approval at the new variations in dialect, which were the backbone of the play dealing with the life of an Indo. The dress rehearsal was invariably a total mess, nothing went right, nobody knew his or her lines, and Guido would get more and more upset. This was true for every dress rehearsal bar none. Nevertheless, everything would be smooth as silk once the play was put before the public. You couldn't help wondering sometimes why it had to be that way.

My son produced many humorous takeoffs on old fairy tales or other stories, adjusting them to reflect the world view peculiar to the Indo. He freely borrowed the musical scores from operettas or operas, writing the lyrics himself; the singers among us would then give them lovely expression. We would always have sellout performances and the auditorium would shake with the loud laughter constantly ringing forth from the public. Often, the audience would applaud during the scenes.

We would always invite the Dutch consul and his wife to our performances and, of course, give them extra nice seats right in the front row. Later, he called the president of our club out to the front, telling him, "I have never seen a better group of amateur actors. They're even better than our own Dutch amateur actors. They have such wonderful twists of thought, where did they get the inspiration for them? My sincere compliments! I had a very good time and I wish you and the Indo Soos a happy future!"

Naturally, that reaction made us swell with pride. We were even asked to perform elsewhere, in San José, California, among other places. It was a great deal of trouble what with having to transport backdrops and what else, but we had an even more successful performance there than here in Los Angeles.

Of those that got involved in our amateur theatre, I remember quite a few, but unfortunately not all. If I overlook certain individuals, it is not because they are not worthy of mentioning, it is simply because my brain did not retain their names. There were so many! To name just a few, there were Roy and Marijke Stevens (she developed into a good actress); Rudy and Joyce Cohen (Joyce was also an excellent seamstress); then there were Curly and John Rijnders, and Curly's sister, Marjolein Ripassa. Marjolein and René Ripassa, husband and wife, sang beautifully. John Rijnders was a real joker. Ludicrously misapplying well-known Dutch sayings and proverbs, he got a laugh every time. Another jokester was Ineke de

Frétes, who never knew her lines but invariably ad-libbed herself out of any tight spots.

I must not overlook my own three girls: Doeshka Schmidt, and Joy and Pax Schenkhuizen. Neither should I forget to mention my grandchildren, Brady, Randy, and Scott Schmidt, and Mijanou, Michelle, Monique, and Mark van der Woude, all of them good dancers and all of them actively involved in our club.

Before I forget, I have to mention that besides our own theatre, we also had our own seamstresses, who, with great creativity and flair, designed and sewed our costumes. These were Rose Pasqua, Zus (Mathilde) Pieplenbos, Stans van Raalten, Nicky Rivère Verninas, and Joy Cohen. Minnie van Frankfoort once cleverly painted flowers on the skirts used in one of our Hawaiian dances. We also had our own backdrop designers, among them Victor Ripassa, who created imaginative sets time and again. He certainly was one of our treasures. Another time, Meiti and Guus Rivière designed the decorations for a luau with great flair.

It was truly odd the way in which so many diverse talents were discovered and put to good use. One of those who always jumped in with two feet at once was my former son-in-law, Jur van der Woude. A totok born and bred, Jur nevertheless felt great affection for Indos. He understood and embraced our culture. Naturally, he was often the obvious choice to play the "totok" in our performances, and he did this with gusto. He often came up with ingenuous ideas for our comedies or artwork. To top it all off, Jur could sing well. We had our own musicians, of course, ably and patiently directed by Gerrit Doppert, who was truly indispensable to the success of our stambul. All in all, things got done in the spirit of sublime cooperation and with taste and professionalism.

Besides our theatrical performances, we also had various so-called "nights," such as Oriental Night, Bali Night, Arabian Nights, Carnival in Rio, Halloween Night, Disco Night, Space Night, Roman Night, and so on. On those nights, you could feast your eyes on the self-made costumes and self-choreographed dances attributed to the various countries spotlighted. They were quite beautiful and done in such good taste.

And then we had our co-called "kinder cabaret," which was designed to showcase the talents of our youngest members. On one of those occasions, Debbie Seeman, for instance, displayed a natural talent for the dance. And Vanessa Westplat and her friends, Dawn,

Lisa, and Natalie must have trained for hours to do their drill routine so smoothly. And I remember fondly the performances of Nicole Soesman, Kimmie Florentinus, Ruby Creutzburg, and the twins Mijanou and Michelle van der Woude. These youngsters mostly performed dances they had invented themselves or Hawaiian dances. They always looked so sweet.

I should mention that Donnée Creutzburg, Ruth and René's daughter, often gave up her precious free time to teach us Hawaiian and Tahitian dances. At the 1979 luau we had the fun of seeing mothers Margo van Ligten, Riki van Lommel, Ruth Creutzburg, and Zus Pieplenbos bravely dancing the hula together with their nimble daughters. I applauded them all! On other occasions, Meiti and Nicky Rivière Verninas, my oldest daughter, Doeshka, Ingrid, Ruby and, of course, Donnée Creutzburg, and Hanne Westplat boldly showed off their curves and moves. They always drew an enthusiastic response from an appreciative public, and deservedly so.

And thus we managed to struggle onward and upward, intent on preserving our own identity in Uncle Sam's country, not only for our own benefit, but also for that of our *turunans*, our children, to share with them our love for our country of origin and to make it clear to them why we are who we are. Our club had many, many successful parties, and up to this day, people keep asking us to perform again. However, the anima slowly dissipated over the years. Guido lost interest because of a lack of inspiration, and all of us got to be a few years older too. We couldn't hand it over to our *bibit*, our children, either. Most, if not all of these, were born in the United States, thus spoke little or no Dutch, not to speak of the Indo jargon, the juicy pechoh, so peculiar to our group and so well-suited to express Indo humor—we are often unintentionally funny.

Be that as it may, our play *En Toen Al* (the end), for the twenty-fifth anniversary of our anemic Soos was the very last gasp of our aging actors and their director. The title was full of meaning for us, Indos: good-bye forever, the last farewell to and of our Soos on its twenty-fifth anniversary in 1988. We gave our club a worthy send-off, admittedly not without bloopers, but fun, as of old.

So now we Indos don't have a social club any more in America. The only thing that still ties us together is the old Soos magazine, *De Indo*, in which we can express ourselves by telling little stories and even writing an occasional serious piece. Then there is

237

our bowling club which keeps contact strong among a small group of us.

Another group of Indos started the ROSI club, a kind of offshoot of our defunct Indo Community "De Soos." They have many members. Their goals are different from those we had, however. Their main focus is on sports and trips, either to Las Vegas or cruises to Mexico and so on. Everything is always well coordinated and fun, lots of fun. Many former Soos members now belong to the ROSI club and enjoy it. ROSI Indos don't feel an urgent desire to transmit the Indo world view to their children, or even to put any extra effort towards doing so as part of a special calling. I say this, not to speak ill of ROSI, but simply to show the difference between the ROSI and the Soos. The latter was more skewed towards an idealistic bond with our former homeland and the consequences of that bond; this was our leitmotiv.

I myself belong to the ROSI bowling club and feel quite at home there, surrounded by old and new *kenalans*, friends, all of us finding a lot of relaxation and enjoyment in this great sport. However, I feel people use too much English in that club, with only now and then a slip of the tongue into our own pechoh.

I'll now describe my daily schedule and my present family circle. I get up at five in the morning, to study the Bible and to be alone with my Creator. Then I scatter seeds in the front yard and throw some old bread on the roof of the tool shed for the birds. My front yard is regularly visited by up to thirty *derkukus*, spotted doves, eating their fill from my handouts. I love to watch them, they are so beautiful with their mauve-tinted feather coats and soft-rose throats. The food on the tool shed is meant for the sparrows and starlings. Everything is gone in a jiffy. If I happen to be late with the birds' food, the sparrows will scold me loudly, while the derkukus sit in a row on a telephone line like soldiers on parade, the very image of patience. The fish in our aquarium also has to have its food. Spiritually nourished, I then start my daily chores: getting breakfast for my dear son and fixing his brown-bag lunch. I wave good-bye when he sets off for work in his car.

Next I make the beds and cook. I always do that in the morning; all I need to do in the evening then is heat the food. The rest of the day I can spend however I want: to go shopping, to go to church for some additional Bible study, or to visit a sick friend and give her a moral boost. At three in the afternoon, I usually take a nap after reading a good book or watching a good television show. When necessary, I *siram* or water the garden, and by that time it's close on five in the afternoon, time to feed my three large dogs. That is also the time to collect dog droppings in a brown bag; it can weigh as much as a pound!

By then the day is almost over and I wait for Guido to come home at around six thirty in the evening, and we can sit down to our rijsttafel. Afterwards, we settle down for a cozy evening of watching television, listening to some beautiful music, or doing some reading. I go to bed at nine, leaving Guido to finish his own schedule.

Sometimes I may be home by myself while Guido is out on the town with some friends or away on vacation with his buddies. There is more than enough variation in our daily life. I'm grateful to have a son who lovingly cares for his old mother, and that we live in America with all its happy consequences, especially the fact that my whole immediate family is concentrated in this area, which makes life so much more enjoyable and happy.

We now have the extended Schenkhuizen family, which has grown with three great-grandchildren already. When all of us are together—which is not always possible because one or the other of us may have to work or be called elsewhere—there are sixteen of us. New members are added gradually, spouses of my granddaughters and grandsons, and my great-grandchildren.

So far, we have always managed to have Christmas with all of us together. We try to share as many of the holidays as possible, in spite of the obstacles described earlier. We also go on joint camping trips. Our family, enlarged with friends, loads our cars with food and stuff. Then we drive into the mountains, to Lake Tahoe, Twin Lakes, Mammoth Lake, and various other vacation spots. We are in happy moods, looking forward to communing with the beautiful environment, relief from the heat, and being together once again.

We sleep in tents or in cabins which we reserve in advance. When evening comes, we tell tall tales around the campfire and plan the next day's activities. At night, the stars are so large and low, one can almost pluck them from the sky. We sleep like roses, and each morning we delight in awakening at sunrise to the bracing scent of pines.

I remember how on one of our outings, bears paid us a visit at night, luckily without harming us. It was quite an adventure.

Those bears looked so adorable to me, but goodness, they are very dangerous! You have to be careful with wild animals. Like those lovely deer I tried to feed, even though a sign on a pole nearby warned in giant letters not to do that. Numbskull me, I never even noticed those warnings, and with my love of animals, I forgot all caution. For all my trouble, a deer adorned with a mighty rack of antlers prepared to take me on his horns. Fortunately, the yelling and screaming of my children made him turn around and leave, while I, dumbfounded by the racket, still hadn't grasped the danger I had run. All I saw was the flash of the buck's white behind; I think they call that the "mirror."

Our life in California is really very similar to that of other Indo families in America. All things considered, we Indos who settled in this country have an affinity for and understand each other. Most of us, my family and I included, live very much the way we used to do in the Indies. We invariably walk around in bare feet at home and eat rijsttafel practically every day. The ingredients for our rijsttafel are fortunately easily available in this country. Our homes are decorated with Balinese sculpture, woven Sumba cloths, Javanese batik, and paintings by Adolfs and other Indies artists. There is always that peculiar something that shows we came from outside America, that is from *Insulinde*, the country that wraps itself around the equator, "like an emerald belt," as Douwes Dekker put it so poetically. It's an excellent description of that archipelago.

My heart is deeply attached to the land of my birth. Never a day goes by that I don't think at least once of that beautiful, special country. Nostalgia? Yes, indeed, but it is a wholesome nostalgia, which we are surely entitled to have. It's not at all a sick clinging to what used to be. Our cultural background is etched deeply into our soul and serves as our support in the development of our own identity.

Yes, we Indos are a special people, but only in-so-far as we display next to our glaring faults also the refinement of the Javanese nobleman, the social sensitivity developed while we grew up in a lushly green environment, and a droll humor that enables us to laugh at our own shortcomings. We are different in our own way, true. But the above mentioned traits enable us to adjust rapidly without becoming totally assimilated. On the whole, we have managed to keep our own identity, ideally combining in us the wisdom of both the East and the West. What richness! Yes, we Indos are rich, richer by far than we realize.

Most of us Indos who emigrated from the Netherlands now live in sunny California, with her mild winters and all that it has to offer in sea and beaches, mountains, parks, sports, and freedom of expression. I love my country of settlement, but this love doesn't diminish my affection for my country of birth. I'm grateful to the Lord, who, in his infinite wisdom, led us to this country, where Indos can finally be themselves and show what they are capable of; here they'll no longer be subjected to the indignity of being regarded as second-class Europeans, never given a chance to develop their potential.

At this time, I have lived in America almost thirty years, twenty of those as an American citizen. At age sixty-three, I stopped working, and now I get a small check from Social Security, for which I'm deeply grateful. I use it to supplement my household money.

I'm happy here, surrounded as I am by my children, grand-children, and great-grandchildren, as well as by my American friends. My own adaptability made it possible for me to make these friends without giving up my sense of identity. When I look back, my life seems to have flown past like a merry and giddy dream. My dearest memories are those of my earliest years, those that have to do with my place of birth and my grade school years. My life, like all other lives, has had its high points and its low points, but mine definitely shows a preponderance of high points.

OUR FAMILY TREE

A great deal of the information that follows has already been sprinkled throughout my life story. But I thought it would make sense to put all the family names from my side of the family (Lanzing and Geul) together in a separate chapter.

My father was Paul Guilaume Antoine Lanzing. At home, we called him Mannie. He was born in Venlo, Limburg, on 14 March 1863 and died in 1936 in Batu, Java, of a heart attack. He left for the Indies while still quite young. My father had five siblings of whom I knew one, his brother, Uncle Wim Lanzing.

Uncle Wim was married to Stien Maurenbrecher, an Indo woman. They had seven children, Paula, Louis, Delly, Hannie, Wim, Fietje, and Paul. Of those, Delly, Hannie, Fietje, and Paul are still among the living.

My mother's father was Joannes Jacobus Geul. He came originally from Brabant in the Netherlands. He was head forester in Blitar, Kediri residency, Java, the Dutch East Indies (now Indonesia).

My mother's mother was a simple Javanese woman, who adopted the name "Maria" when she was baptized in the Catholic faith. She could neither read nor write, but that didn't keep my dear little Oma from being an excellent manager of the Geul household.

Opa and Oma had fifteen children. I'll write down the names I can recall, in no particular order. Emma Louise, Lodojo, Annie, Frans, Garibaldi, Wim, Hugo, Napoleon, Eduard, and Gambetta. As far as I know, the other children died young, often of tuberculosis.

My mother, Emma Louise, was born in Blitar on 29 May 1881. We, her children, called her Moes. She married my father, Paul Guilaume Antoine Lanzing, on 2 January 1902 and had with him three children, Paul Otto Frans (Pof), Marguérite (Grietje or Rita), and Elsa Elisa Joanna (Tje). Moes died a very peaceful death when she was in her eighty-third year. She had been very frail but healthy

242

up to the day she died. The attending physician had ordered Moes to bed and told Tje, my sister, "Your mother is very weak. She might 'go' any moment now." Moes lived in a so-called old people's home in Holland at the time, where Tje happened to visit her. Sitting at my mother's bedside, Tje heard Moes call out, "Mountain! Mountain!" Tje asked, "Do you mean the Sermon on the Mount, Moes?" When my mother said, "Yes," Tje started to read her this beautiful teaching. When Tje had finished reading it, she discovered Moes had slipped away, quietly and at peace. It is a wonderful way to die and I hope I will die the same way.

Aunt Lodojo, or Do, was named for kampong Lodojo (near Blitar) where she was born. She married Fritz Hanfland, a German, and had with him two children, Marga and Fritz (Bub).

Aunt Annie (nicknamed Dickie because she was quite overweight, "fat" is "dik" in Dutch), married Charles Geul, a son of one of Grandpa Geul's brothers. Uncle Charles Geul came to Java as an enlisted man. Aunt Annie and Uncle Charles had no children.

Those of my mother's brothers whom I knew personally were Uncle Hugo, Uncle Wim, Uncle Nappie, Uncle Eddie (who was also called Uncle Baldie), and Uncle Frans. Uncle Gambetta (Cam) died before I was born and I only knew of him because of my friendship with his munchi, Aunt Kasri.

Uncle Wim (Willem) Geul was married to Aunt Dien. They had six children, Gerda, Charles (Broer), Baas, Poppy, Frieda, and Noesje. Uncle Wim joined my father for a time in running the cattle fodder mill in Pagah. Baas and Poppy have already passed away. Aunt Dien and her youngest daughter, Noesje, came to live with Henk and me for a while after the end of the Pacific War.

Uncle Frans (Frans Victor Dignus Petrus) Geul was first married to Aunt Marie, from whom he got divorced. They had two children, Do and Jan, both of whom have already passed away. My cousin, Jan, became one of my "adopted brothers." Do married Nico Celosse, who managed the plantation, Soember Agoeng, of which I have such fond memories. Uncle Frans later married Emmie (Moes) van Ligten, with whom he had no children. Uncle Frans managed the plantation, Pantjoer Anggrek, where we often stayed with the Scouts.

Uncle Nap (Jan Johannes Jacobus Andreas Napoleon) Geul administrated the Bajoe Lor plantation, where he lived with a Madurese woman, with whom he had one daughter named Coba.

243

Uncle Eddie's names were Garibaldi Eduard Urbanus Lodewijk, which distinguished him as being G.E.U.L. Geul. He also had the distinction of being known by two names, Uncle Eddie and Uncle Baldie. He managed the Blawan plantation. Uncle Eddie/Baldie lived with two Madurese women, at different times, of course. I forget the names of these aunts. With the first aunt, Uncle Eddie had two daughters, Annie and Emmie. With the second aunt, he had one daughter, Greet, and one son, Eddie. My cousin Eddie boarded with my parents on Slamet Street in Surabaya for a time, while he attended technical school there. Emmie is still among the living.

I never knew Uncle Cam. He lived with Kasri, a Javanese woman, and had with her six children, Tambora (a boy), Alex, Frans, Victorine, Loulou (from Napoleon), and Wimpie. Victorine died at a very young age of tuberculosis. Their mother, Aunt Kasri, later also died of tuberculosis. (In fact, several of my relatives either suffered severe cases of tuberculosis, not uncommon at that time, or diabetes.) My cousin, Frans, became one of my two "adopted brothers."

My brother, Paul Otto Frans (Pof), was born on 3 January 1903 in Blitar. He married a baroness, Annie van Lawick, and had with her three daughters, Emmy, Carla, and Rika. Paul has already passed away.

One of my adopted brothers, Jan Geul, son of Uncle Frans and Aunt Marie Geul, was married twice. I don't recall the name of his first wife. His second wife was an Indo woman, called Irma. She was a widow with three children. Jan and Irma had eight children together, Mady, Albert, Paul, Eric, Rita, Emmy, Elly, and another one, whose name I forget. Their eldest, a girl named Mady, has already passed away, as has Jan himself.

My other "adopted brother," Frans, son of Uncle Cam and Aunt Kasri, married an Indo woman called Nori, and they had four children together, Hans, Ilse, Winnie, and Tessa. Frans is still among the living.

My sister Els (Tje) was born on 19 July 1911 in Blitar. She married twice. Her first husband was Hans Nepveu; her second was Taco Ypma. Her first child with Hans Nepveu, a son, died when he was five months old of an underdeveloped heart. She had a daughter with each husband, respectively Anja and Ynske. Both of her husbands have passed away, but she is still among the living.

244

I was born on 1 October 1907 in Wlingi. Henk Schenkhuizen and I were married on 2 January 1935 in Malang, Java. Henk was born on 31 January 1908 in Makassar (Ujung Pandang). We had four children together, whom we gave only one name each, none of them family names on either side: Doeshka, Joy, Guido, and Pax.

Now a little bit more about my children. Three of them had blonde hair and light skin when little. Their blonde hair slowly darkened into brown. Doeshka, my eldest, was born on 15 November 1935, in Surabaya. She had large, blue eyes at birth, which slowly turned green over the years. She is married to Humphrey Schmidt, who works for the Union Bank. She herself worked until recently for Conrac, until part of the company moved and she got laid off. Now she works for her brother and seems to enjoy that.

Humphrey and Doeshka live in a spacious and hospitable house in Azusa. They have three children, all boys: Brady, who's approaching thirty, Scott, in his late twenties, and Randy, who's in his early twenties. Brady is married to Lee-An Farino, an Italian-American girl, and they have a little daughter, Britney, thus finally adding a female to the Schmidt offspring. Naturally, she's Opa Humphrey's and Oma Doeshka's darling. Brady and Lee-An now have a son, Robert Brady, who, too, is treasured.

My second daughter, Joy, was born on 4 May 1937 in Surabaya. She had hazel, almond-shaped eyes which didn't change while growing up. She was married to Jur van der Woude, from whom she is now divorced. They have four children, Monique, Marc, and twin daughters, Michelle—older by ten minutes—and Mijanou—it's a French name which is pronounced Meeschanou—all in their twenties. They all have jobs, just like their Schmidt cousins. This branch produced a third, dear, great-grandchild, Michael van der Woude, Monique's son.

Three years after Joy, Guido, our only son, was born on 11 April 1940 in Surabaya. Of all my children, he caused me the most painful and lengthy labor—seven hours. But I wouldn't have missed it for anything in the world, for I had given my husband a son to carry on the family name. His sisters were delighted with him too. Guido was born with a so-called *kulit langsep* skin, pale golden brown skin, a mop of black hair, and brown eyes like my husband, traits which have never changed throughout the years. He closely resembles his father. Guido became my support and strength after

245

Henk passed away, and he is also his sisters' trusted adviser. He is now nearing fifty and remains a confirmed bachelor.

Pax cemented the peace between my husband and myself after we reconciled. She was born on 25 July 1947 in Surabaya. She met her future husband, Patrick Couwenberg, at a dance party, and it turned out that I knew his father, John Couwenberg, from way back in Surabaya, a friend from the Scouts. Our old friendship was renewed and the two lovebirds couldn't help meeting each other regularly, either at our home, at his parents' home, or at parties. But more than one man was courting Pax, and for a time she didn't want to tie herself down at her young age.

However, finally she said yes, and the wedding took place in a lovely little church high in the mountains, surrounded by flowers and trees, and with a glorious view of the valley. Her brother, Guido, acting in his father's place, gave her away. A friend of the bridegroom married them in an original ceremony, followed by a garden party in the house the bridegroom had rented in advance. It was relaxed and merry and people stayed on until deep into the night. Patrick and Pax had two children together, Justin and Ian, now teenagers. Slowly, their marriage went awry and ended in divorce. It was all so incomprehensible and so painful. Up to this day, she hasn't remarried. Fortunately, her children stayed with her.

What more can I tell you about my children? They are normal people, each with their own weak and strong points. Doeshka is plucky, straight as an arrow, patient, and affectionate. Joy defends her relatives whenever one of them is attacked, a bit like the saying, "My country, right or wrong!" She is loyal and stubborn and insists on fairness. As his name implies, Guido is the leader who tries to keep things in balance, steadfastly holding on to his own course of action. He likes to help, especially when poor people are involved. Pax may have the sweetest character of them all. She is always good-natured, is always interested in others, and taking care of others. Pax is very easy to get along with, but, of course, she too can be hardheaded from time to time. She is very fond of children, her own in particular, and, in turn, children gravitate toward her. Because she looks and acts youthful, quite a few younger men have fallen in love with her over the years.

And Mommy just observes the goings-on from the sidelines. Every one of us is pulled in her or his own direction. Every one has his or her own preferences. This is quite understandable and that's what life is all about anyway. But we remain a close-knit family, tuned in to each other, sharing a genuine interest in each other's woes and joys, always ready to support the other spiritually as well as materially where possible. It's only to be expected that we have our share of heated arguments and fits of anger, but our affection for and devotion to each other has never failed to make things right again eventually.

Of course, besides those I mentioned earlier, I also have a lot of distant relatives, already in their twenties now, offspring of the children of my cousins, most of whom I have never even met.

So, this is the story of my life. It's now 1991. No doubt, everyone I mentioned will be several years older by the time this gets printed. This look back may perhaps serve as my legacy to my descendants and those of other Indos, to show them what sets Indo people apart, so that they in their turn may feel empowered by it to fashion their life in this new land of ours. West Covina, California, 1991. Amen.

APPENDIX

Prisoner of War Postcards

俘 侍
哇 虜
停 郵
收 便
所

爪 哇
停 俘
收 虜
所 收
檢 容
閱 所
濟

さがた便郵

Kepada Njonja M. Schenkhuizen
To

Djalan Carpentier 72

Soerabaia

1. tenteung sekali kami sekarang di idzinken oleh
   pemerentah Nippon menoelis soerat
3. Kesehatan saja baik sekali.
5. Saja harep kamoe sekalian sehat dan tida koerang saloe apa². Apa anak sehat?
   Makanan dan oewang di roemah apa tjoekoep?
   Potret dan kartoepos trima baik. Tiap² hari saja
   menginget Bibi dan anak²
   Banjak tabé tjioem dari kamoe poenja Boy

   Pengkie

250

Text

1. Oentoeng sekali kami sekarang di idzinkan oleh pemerentah
   Nippon menoelis soerat
3. Kesehatan saja baik sekali
5. Saja harap kamoe sekalian sehat dan tida koerang satoe apa[2].
   Apa anak sehat?
   Makanan dan oewang di roemah apa tjoekoep?

Portret dan kartoepos trima baik. Tiap[2] hari saja menginget Bibi
dan anak[2].
Banjak tabe tjioem dari kamoepoenja Boy

(signed) Penkie

Translation

1. Fortunately, the Nippon government has given us permission
   to write a letter
3. I am in very good health
5. I hope that you are all healthy and lack nothing. Are the
   children healthy? Do you have enough food and money?

Photograph and postcard arrived. Every day, I think of auntie [he
meant "you" but erroneously used the term for aunt/older woman,
"bibi," instead of wife of "bini"] and the children. Lots of kisses
and greetings from your boy

(signed) Penkie

251

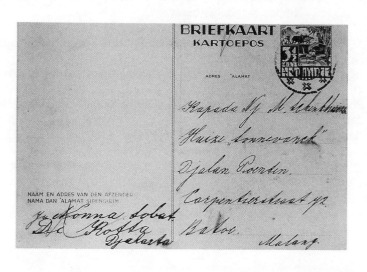

Text

Djakarta 26/11/2602

Mijn eigenste liefste

Senang² hati saja toelis soerat pada kau. Tjoemah saja harep kamoe orang dan anak² semoeanja slamat sadja. Djangan saja loepa kirimkan slamet pada waktoe. Doeschka waktoe dia poenja tahoenan tanggal 17 ini boelang. Laen dari itoe saja kasi tahoe Henk djoega slamet tida koerang satoe apa dan seger badan. Laen tida banjak tabe djoega boeat anak² dari

(signed) Penkie

Translation

Djakarta 26/11/2602 (A.D. 1942)

My very own darling

I'm very happy to be writing this. My only hope is that you and the children are all okay. Let me not forget to send my best wishes (congratulations?) now. The 17th of this month will be Doeshka's birthday. Apart from that I assure you that Henk is (I'm) in good health, too, and lack nothing, I'm physically fine. Nothing else, many greetings also for the children from

(signed) Penkie

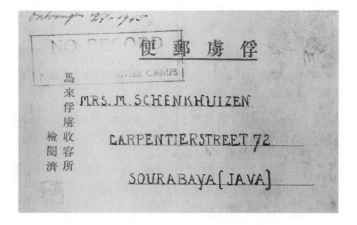

I am now in a Japanese Prisoner of War Camp, in Java.

I hope that you are all healthy and are living well. Are the children well. Have you enough money for food to keep yourselves.

I'm constantly thinking of you. It will be wonderful when we meet again.

Merry Christmas and happy new Year; I wish that next year we will soon be home together safe and sound.

(signature)

11160 H.L.A. SCHENKHUIZEN. SGT.
MALAYAN P.O.W.-CAMPS.

DEAREST VROUWKE,
BOTH SAFE AND SOUND. TAKE GOOD CARE YOURSELF AND CHILDEREN AS PROMISED. HOPE SOON WILL BE AMONGST YOU ALL.

LOVE KISSES

PENGKIE.

TRANSLATOR'S NOTE

The following bibliography was used in the preparation of this book.

Bezemer, T.J. *Beknopte Encyclopaedie van Nederlandsch-Indie.* 2d ed. 's Gravenhage: Martinus Nijhoff, 1921.

De Jong, L. *Het Koninkrijk der Nederlanden in de Tweede Wereldoorlog,* deel 11A. 's Gravenhage: Martinus Nijhoff, 1984.

Eiseman, Fred and Margaret Eiseman. *Flowers of Bali.* Berkeley: Periplus, 1988.

Eiseman, Fred and Margaret Eiseman. *Fruits of Bali.* Berkeley: Periplus, 1988.

Kloppenburg-Versteeg, J. *Wenken en Raadgevingen betreffende het gebruik van Indische planten, vruchten, enz.* 5th ed. Katwijk aan Zee: Servire B.V., 1978.

Kramer, A.L.N. Sr. *Van Goor's Indonesisch zakwoordenboek, Indonesisch-Nederlands en Nederlands-Indonesisch.* 's Gravenhage: G.B. van Goor Zonen, 1950.

Pigeaud, Th. *Javaans-Nederlands handwoordenboek.* Groningen: Wolters-Noordhoff, n.d.

Pigeaud, Th. *Nederlands-Javaans handwoordenboek.* Groningen: Wolters-Noordhoff, n.d.

Schmidgall-Tellings, A. and Alan M. Stevens. *Contemporary Indonesian-English dictionary.* Athens: Ohio University Press, 1981.

Van Velden, D. *De Japanse interneringskampen voor burgers gedurende de Tweede wereldoorlog*. 2d ed. Franeker: Wever B.V., 1977.

Williamson, Joseph F. et al. *Sunset western garden book*. Menlo Park, California: Lane Magazine & Book Company, 1972.

The following notes explain more fully a number of references made in chapter one of the text.

Page 2. Indiesman.

In the Indies, the term "Indiesman" or "Indieswoman" (*Indische*) usually referred to Indos. When applied to a totok, it describes a thoroughly acculturated person. Indos often preferred to be called Indiesman or Indies rather than Indo, and some of them still do. Until recently, there was a certain stigma attached to the term Indo. Many believe(d) it conveyed an aura of poverty and of a low educational level. Lately, however, many of the well-educated and well-situated simply call themselves Indo, perhaps thus showing a healthy measure of self-esteem.

Page 2. Javanese mother.

Of course, there are many permutations among Indos. There are a great many multiple-generation Indos. The Asian line (usually traced through the ancestress) may consist of various Indonesian ethnic groups, such as Sundanese, Madurese, Menadonese, Amboinese, to name a few, or even non-Indonesian Asian groups, such as the Chinese. On the other hand, the European line (traced through the male ancestor) may not only be Dutch—even though this predominates—but also German, Swiss, Russian or Armenian, for openers. I believe this mixed ancestry coupled with our relatively short existence as a group explains the, often decried, lack of unity among Indos. In addition, Indos lived scattered all over the former Dutch East Indies and dispersed even further after the Pacific war.

Page 5. Raising nephews.

In the Indies, people would customarily raise young relatives as their own. Often, these were children who had lost one or both parents. Sometimes, even though present, the biological parents were unable to care for their children or a childless couple might "borrow" a child from a close relative to raise as their own. Usually, the "adoptive" parents were financially better off than the biological family.

Page 13. Pechoh.

Pechoh is an Indo term, which may be spelled various ways, amongst others as petjo, petjoek, and petjoh. Until the journalist-writer-publisher-activist Tjalie Robinson popularized the use of pechoh in his humorous depictions of Indo life, many Indos shied away from it because of the attendant stigma. Society often mercilessly scrutinized and ostracized Indos for non-Dutch traits, such as speaking pechoh or so-called "broken Dutch." Indos could do nothing about dark skin or a small, rounded nose, but they could learn to speak and write perfect Dutch, and that's what many, predictably, chose to do. Ironically, their ability to speak "better Dutch than the Dutch themselves" again set them apart when, settling in the Netherlands after the Pacific War, Dutch people would express great surprise at this unexpected skill on the part of the brown-skinned "Indonesians." In the translator's view, however, the propensity to sprinkle their speech liberally with foreign terms, European as well as Indonesian, is much more widespread among Indies people than the use of pechoh. And this trait more than anything else sets them apart from other speakers of Dutch.

Page 15. Transferred.

Severe corporal punishment was virtually non-existent in Indies public schools. Young children might be scolded and shaken by the ear or receive a rap across the open palms with a ruler, painful enough as it went. More often, they would be stood in a corner with their back to the class, or set to copy one or more lines of text, say, a hundred times. Older children would be sent to the principal or given a note for the parents, or both.

GLOSSARY OF FOREIGN AND
BIOLOGICAL TERMS

Note: In Indonesian, the "c" is pronounced "ch" as in church.

Aceh. Northernmost region of the island of Sumatra.

Aduh. Indonesian term denoting pain, surprise, or frustration depending on context.

Agate garden snail. *Achatina fulica.* Giant African snail. A large snail that grows up to five inches long from foot to tip of shell. Towards the end of the Japanese occupation, it had become widespread on Java. Edible, though its meat is rather tough and chewy.

Alang-alang. *Imperata cylindrica.* Native in the Old World tropics. A fast-spreading grass with stiff, narrow, sharp-edged leaves, that may attain a height of from three to four feet, but usually grows two feet high. It may become a real scourge in gardèns, where it is difficult to eradicate. The dried leaves are used to thatch roofs. Tea made from the rhizomes is said to be beneficial to the urinary tract, especially in cases of blackwater fever.

Al. Dutch for already. Indos will often use "al" to denote a sense of finality, i.e., the case is closed.

AMACAB. Allied Military Administration Civil Affairs Branch. In Surabaya, Red Cross workers were temporarily placed under the auspices of AMACAB after the Pacific War.

Ampian. A Javanese snack. Peanut brittle made with soft palm sugar.

Angirian. Sweet roasted-rice cakes, a Javanese snack.

Anggrek. Indonesian term for orchid. *See* also **Moth orchid.**

Ani-Ani. Cross-shaped, bamboo rice harvesting tool; the half-moon-shaped crossbar has a thin razor-sharp knife edge.

Arigato. Japanese for "thank you."

Ball book. Palm-sized booklets or programs carried by women to balls, in which men could register their name for specific dances. A full ball book was a proud possession and a cherished memento.

Ban mati. Indonesian for solid tires.

Belanda. Indonesian term for European of either sex.

Belimbing wuluh. *Averrhoa bilimbi.* Origin most likely Indonesia. A small tree with large compound leaves. The small brownish red flowers and light green, cylindrical, thumb-sized fruits are born in clusters along trunk and branches. The flowers and fruits are used in herbal medicine. The very acidic fruit may also be used in the preparation of food or may be candied.

Belinju. *Gnetum gnemon.* Origin Indonesia. A tall, cylindrical, single-sexed tree. The catkins (*cenkarang*), young tops and one inch-long, slender, naked seeds are popular vegetables. The ripe nutlike fruit (*klosoh*) are pounded into thin, round crackers (*emping*), which are eaten fried as a snack or, as a side dish, with rice.

Beluntas. *Pluchea indica.* Perennial. A lush, shoulder-high shrub, on Java often planted as a living hedge. The tender tops are often used as a green vegetable and in herbal medicine (amongst others, to combat halitosis).

Bendy. Light, two-wheeled carriage for private use, drawn by a single horse.

Beo. *Gracula religiosa.* A crow-sized, glossy black bird with yellow to orange dewlaps and ears. Originally widely found on various Indonesian islands. These songbirds are prized as pets because of their uncanny ability to mimic sounds.

Bersiap. Indonesian term for the fight for independence after the end of the Pacific War. It was a very confusing time for most inhabitants of the Indies, including the Indonesians. The stringent news blackout during the Japanese occupation kept the Dutch unaware of the movement for independence among the Indonesians, and it caught them completely off-guard and unprepared to deal with it.

Biting. Javanese for the midrib of a palm leaflet. It is used in brooms and to pin closed banana leaf packets.

Blimbing. *See* **belimbing.**

Blinju. *See* **belinju.**

Blitar. Capital of the residency Kediri in East Java. A small town with about ten thousand inhabitants in 1905, among which about nine hundred Europeans (including Indos) and about seventeen hundred Chinese. Elevation 170 M.

Blondo. The full-bodied, rich, dark brown residue of coconut oil production. It is a laxative.

Blue Boy. Dutch for "blauwe jongen." Refers to an Indo.

BPM. Bataafsche Petroleum Maatschappij. Formed in 1970 from the merger of two oil companies. One was English, the Shell Transport and Trading Company of London, England. The other was Dutch, the Koninklijke Maatschappij tot Exploitatie van Petroleumbronnen in Nederlands Indie, known simply as the Koninklijke.

Bride's tears. *Antigonon leptopus.* Rosa de Montana, queen's wreath, coral vine. Perennial vine, native to Mexico but widely planted on Java. It has dark green, heart-shaped, four to five inch-long leaves and small, pink or white flowers born in profusion in long, airy sprays.

Bubur. Javanese for porridge or gruel.

Bungkil. Cattle fodder in the form of cakes pressed from some kind of residue, in this case of peanut oil production.

Ceylon. Former name of the island of Sri Lanka.

Campaka. *Michelia champaca*. Origin Southeast Asia, western Indonesia. A towering tree with intensely fragrant yellow (*C.kuning*) or white (*C.putih*) flowers resembling miniature magnolia flowers. Campaka flowers form an indispensible part of Javanese flower offerings and are often used to perfume hair oil. May also be called *kantil*.

Catut. Indonesian term for trade. During the Pacific war period applied to black market activities.

Cebok bottle. Water bottle reserved for personal hygiene set out alongside the toilet. In the Indies, water was/is used instead of toilet paper to cleanse oneself. For this purpose, only the left hand is used, making this hand traditionally "unclean" and thus taboo for eating and touching.

Celeng. Indonesian term for wild boar.

Cina loleng. Chinese street merchant, who went door to door with his wares (cottons, silks, laces, embroidered tablecloths, crocheted doilies and the like). Also called Klontong. *See* **Klontong**.

Cinchona. *Cinchona sp*. Native to South America. Hybridized, slender tree from which bark the alkaloid "quinine" isextracted, which is used in the treatment of malaria.

Congea. *Congea velutina*. Origin Southeast Asia. A perennial vine that may become rampant. It has rough-textured, finger-length, gray green leaves and mauve, scentless, silver-dollar sized, five-petalled flowers born in sprays.

Controleur. Dutch government official in the Indies who assisted a *resident* or *assistant-resident* in his duties.

Crown pen. A specific kind of triangular copper pen used to produce beautiful penmanship.

Daon kentut. *Paederia foetida.* Origin Southeast Asia, western Indonesia. Perennial vine with darkgreen, soft, from two to three inch-long leaves, which exude a strong, putrid smell when crushed, hence the name, "fart leaf". Also called *daon sembuan.*

Dawet. A flavorful, Javanese cold drink made with coconut milk and palm sugar. Also called *cendol.*

Dedek. Finely ground rice bran used as fodder.

Dendeng. A kind of jerky that is fried and served with rice. Dendeng sapi or dendeng manis, rubbed with spices and sugar, is made from beef. Dendeng celeng is salty and is made from wild boar meat.

Dermoût, Maria. Well-known Indies writer who wrote several popular novels with Indies' subjects and locales.

Dokar. A light, two-wheeled carriage drawn by a single horse; it is used for public transportation. Also called a *sado* or *dos-a-dos.*

Duku. *Lansium domesticum.* Origin western Indonesia and Malaysia. Medium-sized tree. The ovoid, walnut-sized fruit is covered with a thin, smooth, leathery, dull yellow skin. The colorless, glassy meat is succulent and sweet. Also called *Langsep.*

Dukun. Traditional, Javanese folk healers, often believed to be experts in black or white magic.

Durian. *Durian zibethinus.* Origin western Indonesia and Malaysia. Large tree. An ill-smelling but glorious tasting, football-shaped and football-sized, spiny fruit. Several species.

Emping. Javanese term for chips made from Belinju nuts. *See* also **Belinju.** It may also be called krupuk emping or emping belinju.

Es gempol. Fruit syrup served over crushed ice.

Field employee. Tuin (garden) employee in Dutch. Entry level position on the ladder for European plantation workers.

Frau Holle. German fairy tale figure, depicted as living at the bottom of a well. She creates snowstorms by shaking out her feather pillows.

Gado-gado. Javanese mixed salad consisting of various steamed and raw vegetables and hard-boiled eggs served with a peanut butter sauce.

Gambir. *Uncaria gambir.* Origin western Indonesia and Malaysia. Perennial vine. Also the dried extract of same used in *sirih* chews. At first bitter, gambir extract has a sweet aftertaste.

Gamelan. Traditional Javanese or Balinese percussion orchestra.

Gandasuli. *Hedychium coronarium.* White ginger lily, garland flower. Man-high, perennial shrub native to India with large, long, dark green leaves and foot-long clusters of deliciously scented flowers.

Gaplek. Dried cassava chips. Mostly used as cattle fodder, but also as a poor substitute for rice.

GEBEO. Acronym for *Gemeentelijk Electriciteitsbedrijf Bandoeng En Omstreken*, the municipal electric company, in Bandung.

Gedek. Stiff, sturdy, plaited-bamboo matting, often used in construction. During the Japanese occupation of the islands, both military and civilian POW camps were often fenced in with up to twelve-meter-high gedek, isolating the POW's from the outside world. Hence the slang term "put behind the gedek," meaning, "put in a concentration camp." *"Gedek-en"* (to gedek) was Dutch slang for the clandestine trade between POW's and Indonesian locals across these gedek fences.

Gendih. Pot-bellied water carafes of unglazed baked clay.

Gendoh. Young, lower-class, Javanese girl.

Gendrowo. Javanese term for tree or forest sprites.

Gentong. Knee or hip high, wide-bellied, unglazed, earthenware water container.

Gobang. Dutch copper coin worth two-and-a-half cents.

Gulden. Dutch monetary unit worth one hundred cents.

Guling. A one-meter-long, cylindrical pillow around which the sleeper drapes an arm and a leg. The original version may have consisted of open-weave cylindrical bamboo baskets reported to have been used by the Chinese in a similar fashion. A guling provides a more comfortable way of sleeping in a tropical climate. A modern-day American version is found in the so-called "body pillow," which is basically an elongated pillow rather than a cylindrical one.

Guna-guna. Black magic.

Haji. Muslim who has fulfilled the *haj*, the required pilgrimage to Mecca. Because of their purported spiritual enlightenment as a result of the haj, hajis will often rise considerably in local status.

Handkerchief tree. *Maniltoa.* Origin Southeast Asia. Large shade tree with handsome, glossy, green leaves. The pliant young tops are tinted a delicate rose-mauve and hang down from the foliage, calling to mind loosely folded handkerchiefs, hence the name.

Hansop. Basic, light cotton, baggy, child's play suit, cut straight up and down, with holes for head, arms and legs, and with a big pocket on the belly. Beloved by Indies children because it was cool and comfortable.

HBS. Acronym for *Hogere Burger School*, one of several types of Dutch high schools. The tough, five-year HBS prepared the student for higher education.

Idung pesek. Slang term for the low-bridged rounded nose as opposed to the high-bridged pointed nose.

Indies. *See* **Indo.**

Indo. Person of mixed Caucasian and Asian heritage. In the Indies, the majority of the Indos were of mixed Dutch and Javanese ancestry, but various permutations existed. In the United States, Indos usually call themselves Dutch-Indonesian. The term "Eurasian," a British term, was rarely if ever used in the Indies to refer to Indos. The archaic Dutch term was originally *"inlandsche kinderen,"* or native children. Indo culture is an amalgam of European and Asian traits.

Inggih. High (polite) Javanese for yes.

Intestinal worms. *Ascaris lumbricoides.* These roundworms live in the intestinal canal. Here, a female may lay as many as 200,000 eggs a day. These eggs may be deposited with stool in water and soil, where they may survive for months or even years.

Ja. Dutch for yes. Indos often use "ja" the way Americans use "right" or "okay," i.e. like a question mark.

Jaga rumah. Indonesian for house spirit, the benevolent guardian of a house. Also, a human house guard.

Jaksa. Javanese official who assists the prosecutor.

Jambu aer. *Eugenia aquea.* Origin South India; widely cultivated elsewhere. Midsized tree with plum-sized, glossy, white or rose-tinted, blandly sweet, juicy fruit.

Jambu klutuk. *Psidium guajava.* Guava. Originally from South America but now widely cultivated elsewhere. Midsized tree with coarse-textured dull green leaves. The fist-sized, yellow green, ovoid fruits contain numerous small, hard, round seeds and are tart-sweet. The leaves are used in herbal medicine and to color boiled eggs brown.

Jambu mente. *Anacardium occidentale.* Cashew nut. South American native. Medium-sized tree with handsome, pear-shaped, red fruit (actually, the fleshy fruit stalk), at the blossom-end of which grows the actual, green colored cashew-nut. The nut resembles a monkey's face in profile, for which it is also named *jambu monyet* (monkey). Its sap is acrid and should be avoided. The young tops are eaten raw.

Jambu monyet. *See* **Jambu mente.**

Jas tutup. Dutch colonial business costume, widely worn up to World War II. It consisted of tailored, white, heavy cotton pants and jacket. The jacket had a narrow, stand-up collar and was buttoned along the front from the neck down. Ideally, the suit was worn crisply starched and sharply creased.

Jati. *Tectona grandis.* Teak. Origin Southeast Asia. A tall tree with large, coarse-textured dull green leaves, renowned for its excellent timber.

Jemblem. Javanese snack made of ground casava, shaped into a ball around a chunk of palm sugar, and deep-fried in oil.

Jeruk bali. *Citrus maxima.* Pompelmous or pommelo. Only known in cultivation. Originally probably from Southeast Asia, Indonesia, and Malaysia. Midsized, open tree with dark green leaves. The globular, cantaloupe-sized, pale green fruits have a thick, sponge-like skin and juicy, tart to sweet, white or pink meat. The up-to-one-inch-thick skin is often used to fashion simple pull-toys and toy boats.

Jeruk keprok. *Citrus nobilis*. Mandarin. Only known in cultivation. Originally probably from Southeast Asia, Indonesia, and Malaysia. Midsized tree with dark green leaves. The up to fist-size green fruits sport a yellow orange blush when ripe. The loosely attached skin is easily peeled away from the tart-sweet meat.

Jamblang. *Eugenia cumini*. Java Plum. Origin India. Tall tree. The olive-sized, blackish purple fruits have a smooth and shiny skin and do not travel well. Its meat is glassy white and sweet. Various parts of the tree and fruit are used in herbal medicine.

Jonkok (berjongkok). To squat. Indonesians prefer to squat over a toilet rather than sit on the toilet seat. In rural areas, a toilet may consist of a hole in the ground or of a number of bamboos across a ditch on which one squats.

Juwet. *See* **Jamblang**.

Kabar angin. Indonesian term for "heard on the grapevine." Literally, message brought on the wind.

Kacong. Young, lower-class, Javanese boy.

Kain. A specific length of batikked cloth used as a wraparound skirt by both sexes. It is more formal than a sarong.

Kampong. Urban village, as opposed to *desa* or rural village.

Kankung. *Ipomoea reptans*. Origin probably Southeast Asia. Now widely cultivated. A lush, creeping vine with dark green, from two to three inch-long, arrowhead-shaped leaves, abundant in marshy ponds and along riverbanks in hot areas. The tops and leaves are an excellent vegetable, claimed to have a calming and cooling effect on the body. The roots are used in herbal medicine.

Kantil. *See* **Campaka.**

Kapok. Kapok, silk cotton, or Java cotton. The fluffy, resilient fibers surrounding the seeds in the hard-shelled, ovoid, from five to six inch-long fruits of the *randu*, *Ceiba pantandra* (silk cotton tree, native of South America), which are used as mattress stuffing.

Kebaya. A tailored, usually hip-length, long-sleeved tunic worn with sarong or kain. It is closed in front with pins.

Kedondong. *Spondias dulcis.* Midsized fruit tree, native to Polynesia but widely planted on Java. The ovoid, duck-egg sized fruits have a smooth, shiny, yellowish green skin that turns pale yellow when ripe. The seed is covered with an abundance of stiff spines, which extend into the crisp, tart-sweet meat. In order to get at the meat, the unripe fruit is smashed against floor or wall to burst it apart. After childbirth, Indonesian women often eat the leaves to purify their body.

Kemben. A wide band or sash of unbleached cotton that is worn wound around hip and belly. Part of women's traditional attire.

Kemlandingan. *Leucaena leucocephala.* A small, slender tree with light green, compound leaves. Originally from South America, it is well-known from the Hawaiian islands, where they often form great stands. On Java, kemlandingan is often planted as a living hedge, or to provide shade and green manure. The long, slender pods hold numerous flattish, tan seeds. All parts of the tree exude a pungent scent. The young pods and seeds are eaten raw as well as cooked. Children use the young, globular flowerheads in blowpipes or slingshots in warplay. Also called *Lamtoro* or *Pete Cina*.

269

Kemuning. *Murraya paniculata.* Giant orange jessamine. Origin Southeast Asia and Malaysia. A large shrub or smallish tree with an open habit. The white, bell-shaped, three-to-four-inch flowers have a powerful, jasmine-like scent. The leaves are used in herbal medicine.

Kenpeitai. Also spelled Kempeitai. A special, much dreaded, branch of the Japanese government which was in charge of political and military security. It consisted of an autonomous corps of hand-picked officers in the rank of sergeant and higher. On rare occasions, lower-ranked men were recruited. Kenpeitai men always wore a uniform with a specific insignia on the collar. Because of their wide-ranging powers, they were widely feared in the occupied territories as well as in Japan itself. The Kenpeitai ceased to exist after the end of the Pacific war.

Kentong. Hollowed-out treetrunk used to give long-distance signals. Also called *Kentongan.*

Kentongan. *See* **Kentong.**

Kerbau. *Bos bubalis.* Water buffalo. Heavy-bodied, powerful, gray-skinned cattle, often used in plowing.

Kereta setan. Indonesian for automobile, devil's car.

Keris. Traditional Javanese or Balinese serpentine-bladed dagger. It is often believed to be endowed with magical powers and is then held in high esteem. Keris are often part of ceremonial costume, especially in male attire.

Ketapang. *Terminalia catappa.* Origin Old World tropics. A towering tree with large, glossy leaves. The flattish, ovate fruit consists of a green-skinned, fibrous husk surrounding a small nut. The nutmeat is white and tasty. Nursing women like to eat these nuts, claiming that it increases the flow of milk.

Ke-te-kout-en. Indo jargon for too cold, derived from the Dutch words *te*, too much, and *koud*, cold. *Ke-kittelen* is in the same

270

way derived from the Dutch word *kittelen*, to tickle, and means getting goosebumps all over. *Ke* is Indonesian for "to be." Indos would often make up new terms on the spot this way.

Ketupat. Rice boiled into a stiff pudding in small square baskets woven of coconut leaf. Sliced into bite-sized cubes, it is served instead of the usual steamed rice. *See* **lontong.**

Klambu. Filmy, white mosquito net curtains attached to a white cotton canopy, completely enveloping the bed.

Klenkeng. *Dimocarpus longan.* Longan. Origin Southeast Asia and Indonesia. Large tree with wide-spreading crown. Small, dark green, glossy leaves. The globular, one half to one inch fruits are covered with a thin, leathery, tan-colored skin. They are born in panicles at branch-end. The meat surrounding the hard, brownish black pit is glassy white, succulent and sweet.

Klobot. Javanese term for dried cornhusks and, by extension, also the term for a cigarette made with such leaves.

Klontong. Javanese for rattle. By extension applied to the Chinese vendor who used a rattle to announce his presence. *See* **Cina loleng.**

Kodok. Javanese term for frog or toad. A large toad or frog is called *bangkong.* The term *kodok bangkong* is a *pechoh* (Indo) term denoting a huge frog or toad.

Kol Banda. *Pisonia grandis.* Widespread from Madagascar to Polynesia. A small tree with large, pliant, light green leaves which are pale yellow when young. Kol Banda leaves are often substituted for cabbage (*kol* means cabbage). It rarely flowers. Kol Banda flowers picked on a tiny island off Nusa Kembangan, south of Java, are called *Kembang Wijaya Kusuma* and are an integral part of the installation ceremony of Javanese sultans. Also called *Kol Bandang.*

Kol Bandang. *See* **Kol Banda.**

Kopi tubruk. Black coffee brewed in the glass or mug in which it is served. A wit once said that it should be hot as hell, black as midnight, and sweet as heaven.

KPM. Acronym for *Koninklijke Paketvaart Maatschappij*, the Indies ship company that used to ply the waters in the Indies archipelago.

Krempeng. Indonesian for emaciated or very thin.

Krosi males. Rattan lazy chair, a chaise longue that could be found in practically every Indies house.

Krupuk. Cracker or crackers containing ground fish or shrimp. Krupuk is served deep-fried either as a snack or as a side dish with rice.

Kuli. Manual laborer or laborers.

Kulit langsep. Pale golden brown skin, like the skin of a langsep fruit, a desirable trait.

Kumis Kucing. *Ortosiphon stamineus.* Origin Southeast Asia. Waist-high, lush perennial shrub with finger length, soft, dark green, ovate leaves, edged in purple and with purple ribs and ending in a sharp point. Its pink, long-anthered flowers— hence the name, "cat's whiskers"—appear in clusters. Also called *Remujung*.

Kuntil anak. An evil spirit often described as the ghost of a woman who died in childbirth. Deprived of motherhood, she is believed to haunt the night, especially just after sunset, "stealing" little children and/or stalking solitary men.

Kutang. Javanese for long-waisted bra or undershirt.

Kwee. Indonesian term for sweet snack or cake, often made with rice flour. Also called *kuweh*.

Lahar. Javanese for superheated volcanic mudflow. These often move down the mountain at incredible speed.

Lampu templek. Indonesian term for a small kerosene lamp with attached metal reflector, that is meant to be hung on the wall.

Lamtoro. *See* **Kemlandingan.**

Landau. Four-wheeled, covered carriage.

Langsep. *See* **Duku.**

Laut. Javanese for lunch hour.

Lebaran. The end of *Ramadan*. On the day of lebaran, Indonesian Muslims traditionally visit relatives and cemeteries and ask each other forgiveness for past offenses. Lebaran is often viewed as the equivalent of the Christian New Year's celebration. *See* **Ramadan.**

Liwit. Javanese for cooking rice in a pot rather than in a steamer.

Lontong. Javanese. Rice boiled to a stiff pudding in a tube of banana leaf. Served in thick slices, it takes the place of the usual steamed rice. *See* **Ketupat.**

Loteng. Javanese. Upstairs, attic.

LST. The acronym for Landing Ship Tank, a specific type of landing ship used by the Allied forces in Indonesia at the end of the Pacific war.

Luntas. *See* **Beluntas.**

Lupis. Javanese. Sticky rice (*ketan*) steamed to a stiff pudding in a tube of banana leaf, served sliced with palm sugar syrup and grated coconut.

Lurah. Javanese village headman.

273

Luwak. Javanese. *Paradoxurus hermaphroditus.* Common palm civet. Occurs from Sri Lanka to Celebes, common in the Indonesian archipelago. Including its bushy tail, it may attain a length of a meter. Gray to gray-brown with darker spots and from three to five black lengthwise stripes on the back. Eats insects, eggs, chicks and fruits.

Macan. *Panthera tigris.* In Indonesia, once widespread across Sumatra, Java, and Bali. Now an endangered species in Sumatra and extinct in the latter two islands. The panther, *Panthera pardus,* with black spots and rings on a yellow background, is called *macan tutul* in Javanese, while the so-called black panther is called *macan kumbang* or M. kombang. Originally widespread from Africa, through south Asia, and across Sumatra and Java, the panther is smaller than the tiger and can climb trees.

Maizena. The brand name of a commercially produced corn starch well known in the Indies. It is derived from the Dutch term "mais" for corn.

Mandi. Indonesian term for bath. The bathroom is equipped with a waist-high water trough from which the bather dips water to pour over his/her body. The trough is not meant to bathe in.

Manggistan. *Garcinia mangostana.* Mangosteen. Origin western Indonesia and Malaysia. Large tree with beautiful, round, dark reddish-brown fruits, with a circlet of green sepals at the base. A glossy, hard, leathery skin surrounds the translucent white, juicy-sweet fruit segments. A truly delicious fruit, which is harvested from November to March. People with delicate stomachs should not eat too many mangosteens at a time. The peel of the fruit contains a strong dye that can leave bad stains.

"Marigold". *Tithonia diversifolia.* Tithonia. A native of tropical America. A lush, man-high, shrubby perennial with velvety leaves and single, five inch-wide, satiny, orange flowers. Its leaves and hollow stems exude a pleasant bitter-herb scent when crushed.

May, Karl. 1842-1912. German author of imaginative westerns. His novels were very popular in the Indies.

Mbok. Javanese for mother. Used to address lower-ranked, older women.

Melati. *Jasminum sambac.* Arabian Jasmine, Pikake. Origin Southeast Asia. Waist-high, tropical perennial with dark green, glossy leaves and one inch-wide white flowers. This particular jasmine is often used in *leis* in the Hawaiian islands. Its fragrance is legendary. Melati plays an indispensible role in Javanese flower offerings, and is often used to scent toilet water. According to recent Japanese research, workers exposed to jasmine scent make fewer errors.

Melek. Javanese for being or staying awake.

Menyan. Javanese incense. The white or brown-colored, air-dried resin of the benzoin tree, *Styrax benzoin.* Its fragrance is warm and pleasant. *See* **Styrax benzoin.**

Mercon. Indonesian for fireworks or firecrackers.

Momok. Javanese for ghost.

Moth orchid. *Phalaenopsis sp.* Epiphytic orchid. Thick, leathery leaves. Long-lasting, white or pink flowers in long sprays. The white-flowered variety was most often seen in the Indies, for which this orchid is called *anggrek bulan* or moon orchid, a much more poetic name than the English one.

MULO. Three-year high school; more or less a vocational school that prepared students for entry-level office jobs.

Munci. Javanese for concubine, common-law wife.

Nasi kuning. A special and festive spread so named because the rice served with it is colored yellow with turmeric.

Naughty Boys and Sweet Girls. *Duranta repens.* Golden dewdrops, skyflower, pigeon berry. South American native. Tall, shrubby perennial, often with drooping branches, with glossy green leaves and clusters of tubular, one half inch-wide, violet blue flowers and orange fruits.

Nieuwenhuis, Rob. The pseudonym of the Indies writer E. Breton de Nijs.

Ngochop. I have been unable to verify this expression. It may be a child's corruption of a regionally used Javanese term.

Nyonya. Indonesian for mistress or madam. Before independence reserved for Europeans or wealthy Asians.

Old Shatterhand. Name of a character in several of Karl May's westerns. He was a brave and fair-minded Caucasian scout who was sympathetic to the Indians.

Oma. Dutch for grandma.

Ondeh-ondeh. Golfball-sized, sesame-studded, deep-fried rice dumplings filled with sweet black bean paste. Probably of Chinese origin.

Oom. Dutch for uncle. Nowadays the term "oom" is often used by westernized Indonesians to address middle-aged foreign men, especially those of Dutch descent.

Opa. Dutch for grandpa.

Pacar. *Lawsonia inermis.* Henna. Probably native to Iran. Tall shrub with small leaves and clusters of small, yellow, fragrant flowers. The leaves contain a red dye that is used to stain nails and as a hair dye.

Padi. *Oryza sativa.* Rice plant. Also the term for unhusked rice.

Pagah. A hamlet near Talun and Wlingi on the slope of Mt. Kelut in East Java.

Pak. Indonesian for mister or sir, derived from the term *bapak* or father. Used to address older men.

Pan bakaran. A round, legged, iron oven similar to a Dutch oven. It is set over hot coals and the flat lid is also covered with hot coals.

Pa van der Steur, Johannes. Born in Haarlem, the Netherlands, 10 July 1865. Widely known and highly respected Dutch Christian missionary who started and headed orphanages for boys and girls on Java up to the Pacific war. Besides orphans, Pa (father) also accepted and raised impoverished children with one or both parents still living. His more than seven thousand charges often became excellent citizens, who were proud to call themselves *Steurtjes*. Although already at an advanced age, Pa was interned by the Japanese in late 1943. He survived the camp period and died on 16 September 1945.

Pecil. Javanese dish consisting of various steamed vegetables served with a spicy coconut milk sauce. *Nasi pecil* as described in this book is probably a regional dish peculiar to East Java.

Pechoh. Indo creole. A specific linguistic mixture, mostly of Dutch and Indonesian terms and grammar. It was primarily spoken by less educated Indos, but also, on occasion and in our own circles, by well-educated ones. Actually, many Indos took care to speak and write faultless Dutch even among themselves and were proud of it.

Pelopor. Indonesian for troops in the frontlines. This term is specifically used for extremists or irregular fighters for independence after the end of the Pacific war.

Pemuda. Indonesian for young man. During the *bersiap* period (see there) specifically used to refer to Indonesian freedom fighters on Java. Because the bersiap period was so chaotic, the terms *pelopor* and *pemuda* were often used interchangeably by outsiders, who often could not tell the difference between the two factions.

277

Pesuratan. Indonesian for mailman.

Peté. *Parkia speciosa.* Stinkbean. Origin western Indonesia and Malaysia. Tall tree with compound leaves. The foot-long, light green pods contain the so-called stinkbeans, soft, pale green, odorous seeds which are a popular part of the Indonesian cuisine. Peté beans are eaten raw, cooked, or roasted and are claimed to have a beneficial effect on the kidneys.

Peté Cina. *See* **Kemlandingan.**

Petrea. *Petrea volubilis.* Native of tropical America. An herbaceous vine with blue and purple flower clusters, one variety of which is called Purple Wreath.

Planter. Dutch for non-Indonesian plantation worker.

Plèkat, sarong. Javanese term for striped or plaid sarong.

Plongkuh. I have been unable to verify this. The Javanese term for a yellow horse with a yellow or white mane is *plumpung*, and that for a horse with a white spot on the forehead is *petak*, while a spotted animal is called *belang*. Plongkuh may be a regional term.

Pump rods. *Cyperus papyrus.* Papyrus. Native of Africa. Tall, dark green grasslike clumps of three-angled, solid stems. The stems bear a tuft of leaves and inflorescences that resemble a gun pump rod, hence the Indies folk name.

Raksasa. Javanese term for giant.

Ramadan. The month-long ritual Muslim fast which varies from year to year following a traditional Arabic calendar and calculation involving the phases of the moon. *See* **Lebaran.** During this month, healthy, devout Muslims are prohibited from eating or even drinking during day-light hours.

Rambutan. *Nephelium lappaceum.* Origin western Indonesia and Malaysia. Tall tree with walnut-sized fruits in clusters. The fruits are covered with coarse-haired, leathery skin, which turn golden orange to dark red whenripe. The translucent white, lusciously sweet meat surrounds a bitter pit.

Rampai. The finely shredded leaves of the *pandan*, *Pandanus amaryllifolius*, used in flower offerings. Pandan leaf is also used to flavor and color snacks, drinks and steamed rice. Basmati and Jasmine rice have a pandan scent.

Rampok. Javanese term for an event in which a tiger is attacked by many men armed with wooden or bamboo lances. It also means an armed attack by a band of robbers. Also called *rampog*.

Randu. *See* **Kapok**.

Rantang. Food carrier consisting of a stack of several round metal containers with a handle on top. It is probably of Chinese origin.

Regent. The Dutch title of a *bupati*, a high-ranked, aristocratic Javanese, government office holder.

Remujung. *See* **Kumis Kuching**.

Resident. The title of the Dutch government official who was in charge of a residency in the Indies. Ranked directly below a governor.

Rijsttafel. The traditional Indies meal consisting of steamed rice served with several side dishes from the various regional cuisines in the islands. While Indonesians prefer the food of their own ethnic region over any other, Indos and totoks alike often served a mixture of regional dishes, which came to be called "ricetable".

Robinson, Tjalie. One of the pseudonyms of Jan Boon (1911-74), a well-known Indo author and publisher, also known under the name of Vincent Mahieu. He was one of the movers and shakers in the post-World War II Indo community. *See* **Tong-Tong.**

Rujak. Mixed salad of unripe fruit salad served with a spicy palm sugar sauce.

Rukem. *Flacourtia rukam.* Low-growing, native tree with thorny branches and dark red, juicy, tart fruits. Rukem make a tasty jelly or jam.

Rupiah. Indonesian monetary unit used after independence, worth 100 Indonesian cents.

Sambal goreng. A Javanese dish which is very similar to *sayor*, except that it is usually spicier and contains much less liquid; it even may be completely dry. See **Sayor.**

Sambal trasi. A dish of finely ground hot peppers to which some fermented shrimp paste (*trasi*) has been added. It is served as a condiment with rice.

Sampiran. Man-high, wooden clothes and shoe stand, primarily meant to store clothes that have been worn and temporarily taken off (for instance, while taking a nap).

Sapu lidih. A bundle of yard-long midribs of coconut palm leaflets used to smooth beds or as a broom.

Sarong. A batikked length of cloth, sewn into a tube and worn as a wraparound skirt by both sexes. It is cheaper and less formal than a kain. *See* **kain.**

Satay. Meat, chicken, or pork threaded on a bamboo stick and broiled over a charcoal fire. Often served with a peanut sauce and *lontong* or *ketupat*. *See* **lontong** and **ketupat.**

Sawah snake. *Python reticulatus.* Native to India, the Philippines, and the Indonesian islands west from Amboina. An excellent mouser, this snake can grow to ten meters long. Its skin is patterned in grey and cream. Although its prey normally consists of small mammals, humans occasionally fall victim to these giant snakes.

Sawoh. *Minilkara zapota.* Originally from Central America. Small but sturdy tree with beautiful brownish red wood. The reddish brown, ovoid, thin-skinned fruits are very sweet and juicy.

Sayor. Any kind of dish that contains vegetables and/or meat and/or seafood and a generous amount of liquid. The sauce may contain coconut milk and it may contain hot peppers, but it may also be a clear broth and/or bland.

Sayor asem. A **sayor** which does not contain coconut milk, made to taste sour by means of tamarind (*asem*).

Sènggèh. Javanese term for a long bamboo fruit picker.

Serimpi. A stately Javanese court dance. Also the performer of such a dance.

Sinterklaas. Dutch name for a mythical Spanish bishop who is said to have given presents to some starving girls. His name day, 5 December, is a popular Dutch holiday, on the evening of which people exchange presents and funny poems. Sinterklaas is depicted as arriving from Spain by ship, seated on a white horse and accompanied by his trusted black pages, who are always called "Black Pete". These pages carry switches and bags, some filled with presents and some empty. The presents are given to well-behaved children while naughty ones are stuffed into a bag and "carried back to Spain." Both Sinterklaas and Black Pete are held in awe by Dutch children.

Sirih. *Piper betle.* Origin Southeast Asia and western Indonesia. Perennial tropical vine with heart-shaped, glossy green leaves, which are used in sirih chews and herbal medicine. The leaves, which have a distinctive, peppery flavor and bracing scent, are claimed to have a warming and astringent effect.

281

Sirih box. An often ornate container holding all the paraphernalia for the sirih chew ritual.

Sirih chew. I chose to use the term "sirih chew" rather than betel-nut—as it is usually called—because it puts the emphasis where it rightly belongs, on the main ingredient—the sirih leaf—and the main action. To chew sirih, one takes a couple of sirih leaves, dabs some lime on it, adds a tiny bit of betel-nut and gambir, rolls everything together, sticks it in the mouth and starts to chew. Shortly after, a wad of tobacco is added and masticated together with the sirih. Regular use of sirih chew turns the user's teeth black.

Slendang. Carrying shawl.

Soka. *Ixora.* Flame of the Woods. Several species. Origin of most species is Southeast Asia. Some cultivated species also come from Indonesia and Malaysia. Tall, lushly foliaged, perennial shrub with leathery, dark green leaves and small, tubular, red, yellow or orange, scentless flowers in compact clusters.

Soos. Dutch term for country club, peculiar to the Indies. Most towns had a "soos" where any European was welcome, either as a member or as a guest. In small towns, it served as the center of social life, much like recreation halls in the United States. Perhaps because liquor was available and often consumed in great quantities, Indonesians rarely became soos members. As Muslims, they are forbidden to consume alcohol.

Southeast Asia. The countries of Myanmar (Burma), Thailand, Cambodia, Laos, Vietnam, Malaysia, Brunei, Indonesia, the Philippines, and Singapore.

Spekkoek. Literal translation is bacon cake. A kind of spice cake baked in alternate dark (spiced) and light (vanilla) layers resembling bacon. It is very rich and flavorful.

Srampangan. Pecoh for careless.

Srigaden. *Nyctanthes arbor-tristis.* Originally from India. A tall, woody, perennial shrub with rather coarse-textured leaves. The one inch-wide white flowers have an orange red heart and last only one night. Powerful fragrance. Also called *Srigading.*

Srigading. *See* **Srigaden.**

Sudah. Indonesian term for already, done, finished, settled. It is also often used by itself as a term of resignation.

Sumpil. **Lontong** served with a shrimp and vegetable **sayor.**

Stormking lantern. Gasoline fed pressure lamp.

Styrax benzoin. Towering forest tree found on Sumatra, Java, Borneo and on the Asian continent. The resinous sap is air-dried into white or brown-colored benzoe, *menyan* in Indonesian, and is used as an incense and in herbal medicine. *See* **Menyan.**

Talun. A village in East Java, located on the slope of Mt. Kelut on the highway that connects Blitar to Wlingi.

Tani. Javanese term for peasant.

Tante. Dutch for aunt. Nowadays often used by Westernized Indonesians to address middle-aged foreign women, especially those of Dutch ancestry.

Tètès. Indonesian term for raw molasses.

The Lords XVII. The Lords Seventeen, the wealthy and powerful underwriters and board of regents of the Dutch East India Company, the *VOC* (*Verenigde Oost Indische Compagnie*).

TKR. Acronym for Tentara Keamanan Rakyat, the name of the official Indonesian army between 5 October 1945 and 25 January 1946.

Tobat-tobat. Indonesian expression of dismay.

Tong-tong. *See* **kentongan.** Also the name of a magazine started by Tjalie Robinson (Jan Boon), after he settled in the Netherlands after World War Two. It has since been renamed *Moesson.*

Totok. Indonesian term for Europeans of either sex, usually but not exclusively applied to Holland born and raised individuals. In the Indies, the term "totok" was rarely or never applied to Chinese people. Rather, Indies-born Chinese were called *Orang Cina* and foreign-born ones were called *Baba* or *Singkek.*

TNI. Acronym for Tentara Nasional Indonesia, the present Indonesian army. The name dates from 3 June 1947.

Trasi. Indonesian-style fermented fish or shrimp paste.

Trengguli. *Cassia javanica.* Senna. Origin West Indonesia. A tall tree often used to shade streets. It bears scentless yellow or pink flowers in foot-long clusters. Its brown, tubular pods can grow up to two feet long and contain flat seeds surrounded by a sweetish, dark brown pulp. Flowers in October and November.

TRI. Acronym for Tentara Republik Indonesia. The name of the official Indonesian army between 25 January 1946 and 3 June 1947.

Trommel. Dutch term for a rotating reading club to which people could subscribe in the Indies. At regular intervals, members received an assortment of magazines in a wooden box, or *trommel*, hence the name.

Tuan besar. Indonesian for top executive, head of the household. During colonial times, reserved for Europeans.

Tukang kèplèk. Javanese term for night watchmen. On their rounds, they would announce their presence by rapping on a

284

hand-held length of hollow bamboo or, in towns, on (metal) telephone poles.

Udet. Javanese. A long, narrow, multi-colored, woven band that is wound around the waist to hold up sarong or kain.

ULO. Dutch four-year high school after World War II. It prepares students for entry-level office jobs.

Upet. Javanese term for a twist of coconut fiber used as a slow burning fuse, which people would take along at night to light their way.

Veluwe. The name of an undeveloped, heather covered region in the central part of the Netherlands.

Wajan. Round bottomed Asian frying pan of Chinese origin, which the Chinese call a *wok*.

Waringin. *Ficus benjamina.* Native to the Asian continent and Indonesia. Towering trees with a wide spreading but elegant crown and with massive trunk and main branches. The small, glossy, dark green leaves are produced in abundance and are often used in street and room decorations. Often planted in town squares, the Javanese consider it sacred and set out offerings at its foot. A small-scaled hybrid of Ficus benjamina is now widely available as a pot plant in southern California and is often seen in sidewalk planters.

Waru. *Hibiscus tiliaceus.* Widespread throughout the tropics of the world. Midsized tree with an abundance of hand-sized, heart-shaped, soft, dull green, heavily veined leaves and dull pink, hibiscus-like flowers.

Wayang. Javanese and Balinese shadow puppet theatre.

Wlingi. A village near Blitar in East Java.

Winnetou. The name of a noble Indian chief and warrior, one of the principal characters in several of Karl May's westerns. *See* **Karl May** and **Old Shatterhand.**

MONOGRAPHS IN INTERNATIONAL STUDIES

Africa Series

ISBN Prefix 0-89680-

38. Wright, Donald R. *Oral Traditions From the Gambia: Volume II, Family Elders.* 1980. 200pp.
084-9 $15.00

43. Harik, Elsa M. and Donald G. Schilling. *The Politics of Education in Colonial Algeria and Kenya.* 1984. 102pp.
117-9 $12.50

45. Keto, C. Tsehloane. *American-South African Relations 1784-1980: Review and Select Bibliography.* 1985. 159pp.
128-4 $11.00

46. Burness, Don, and Mary-Lou Burness, eds. *Wanasema: Conversations with African Writers.* 1985. 95pp.
129-2 $11.00

47. Switzer, Les. *Media and Dependency in South Africa: A Case Study of the Press and the Ciskei "Homeland."* 1985. 80pp.
130-6 $10.00

48. Heggoy, Alf Andrew. *The French Conquest of Algiers, 1830: An Algerian Oral Tradition.* 1986. 101pp.
131-4 $11.00

49. Hart, Ursula Kingsmill. *Two Ladies of Colonial Algeria: The Lives and Times of Aurelie Picard and Isabelle Eberhardt.* 1987. 156pp.
143-8 $11.00

51. Clayton, Anthony, and David Killingray. *Khaki and Blue: Military and Police in British Colonial Africa.* 1989. 235pp.
147-0 $18.00

52. Northrup, David. *Beyond the Bend in the River: African Labor in Eastern Zaire, 1864-1940.* 1988. 195pp.
151-9 $15.00

53. Makinde, M. Akin. *African Philosophy, Culture, and Traditional Medicine.* 1988. 175pp.
152-7 $13.00

54. Parson, Jack ed. *Succession to High Office in Botswana. Three Case Studies.* 1990. 443pp.
157-8 $20.00

55. Burness, Don. *A Horse of White Clouds.* 1989. 193pp.
158-6 $12.00

56. Staudinger, Paul. *In the Heart of the Hausa States.* Tr. by Johanna Moody. 1990. 2 vols. 653pp.
160-8 $35.00

57. Sikainga, Ahmad Alawad. *The Western Bahr Al-Ghazal Under British Rule: 1898-1956.* 1991. 183pp.
161-6 $15.00

58. Wilson, Louis E. *The Krobo People of Ghana to 1892: A Political and Social History.* 1991. 254pp.
164-0 $20.00

59. du Toit, Brian M. *Cannabis, Alcohol, and the South African Student: Adolescent Drug Use 1974-1985.* 1991. 166pp.
166-7 $17.00

60. Falola, Toyin, ed. *The Political Economy of Health in Africa.* 1992. 254pp.
168-3 $17.00

61. Kiros, Tedros. *Moral Philosophy and Development: The Human Condition in Africa.* 1992. 178pp.
171-3 $18.00

62. Burness, Don. *Echoes of the Sunbird: An Anthology of Contemporary African Poetry.* 1993. 198pp.
173-X $17.00

63. Glew, Robert S., and Chaibou Babalé. *Hausa Folktales from Niger.* 1993. 136pp.
176-4 $15.00

Latin America Series

9. Tata, Robert J. *Structural Changes in Puerto Rico's Economy: 1947-1976.* 1981. xiv, 104pp.
   107-1 $11.00

11. O'Shaughnessy, Laura N., and Louis H. Serra. *Church and Revolution in Nicaragua.* 1986. 118pp.
   126-8 $11.00

12. Wallace, Brian. *Ownership and Development: A comparison of Domestic and Foreign Investment in Colombian Manufacturing.* 1987. 186pp.
   145-4 $10.00

13. Henderson, James D. *Conservative Thought in Latin America: The Ideas of Laureano Gomez.* 1988. 150pp.
   148-9 $13.00

14. Summ, G. Harvey, and Tom Kelly. *The Good Neighbors: America, Panama, and the 1977 Canal Treaties.* 1988. 135pp.
   149-7 $13.00

15. Peritore, Patrick. *Socialism, Communism, and Liberation Theology in Brazil: An Opinion Survey Using Q-Methodology.* 1990. 245pp.
   156-X $15.00

16. Alexander, Robert J. *Juscelino Kubitschek and the Development of Brazil.* 1991. 429pp.
   163-2 $25.00

17. Mijeski, Kenneth J., ed. *The Nicaraguan Constitution of 1987: English Translation and Commentary.* 1990. 355pp.
   165-9 $25.00

18. Finnegan, Pamela May. *The Tension of Paradox: José Donoso's The Obscene Bird of Night as Spiritual Exercises.* 1992. 179pp.
   169-1 $15.00

19.   Sung Ho Kim and Thomas W. Walker, eds., *Perspectives on War and Peace in Central America.* 1992. 150pp.
172-1 $14.00

20.   Becker, Mark. *Mariategui and Latin American Marxist Theory.* 1993. 214pp.
177-2 $18.00

21.   Boschetto-Sandoval, Sandra and Marcia Phillips McGowan. *Claribel Alegria and Central American Literature: Critical Essays.* 1993. 263pp.
178-9 $20.00

Southeast Asia Series

47.   Wessing, Robert. *Cosmology and Social Behavior in a West Javanese Settlement.* 1978. 200pp.
072-5 $12.00

56A. Duiker, William J. *Vietnam Since the Fall of Saigon.* Updated edition. 1989. 383pp.
162-4 $17.00

64.   Dardjowidjojo, Soenjono. *Vocabulary Building in Indonesian: An Advanced Reader.* 1984. xviii, 256pp.
118-7 $26.00

65.   Errington, J. Joseph. *Language and Social Change in Java: Linguistic Reflexes of Modernization in a Traditional Royal Polity.* 1985. xiv, 211pp.
120-9 $20.00

66.   Binh, Tran Tu. *The Red Earth: A Vietnamese Memoir of Life on a Colonial Rubber Plantation.* Tr. by John Spragens. Ed. by David Marr. 1985. xii, 98pp.
119-5 $11.00

68.   Syukri, Ibrahim. *History of the Malay Kingdom of Patani.* Tr. by Connor Bailey and John N. Miksic. 1985. xix, 113pp.
123-3 $12.00

69. Keeler, Ward. *Javanese: A Cultural Approach.* 1984. xxxvi, 522pp., Third printing 1992.
121-7 $25.00

70. Wilson, Constance M., and Lucien M. Hanks. *Burma-Thailand Frontier Over Sixteen Decades: Three Descriptive Documents.* 1985. x, 128pp.
124-1 $11.00

71. Thomas, Lynn L., and Franz von Benda-Beckmann, eds. *Change and Continuity in Minangkabau: Local, Regional, and Historical Perspectives on West Sumatra.* 1986. 363pp.
127-6 $16.00

72. Reid, Anthony, and Oki Akira, eds. *The Japanese Experience in Indonesia: Selected Memoirs of 1942-1945.* 1986. 411pp., 20 illus.
132-2 $20.00

73. Smirenskaia, Zhanna D. *Peasants in Asia: Social Consciousness and Social Struggle.* Tr. by Michael J. Buckley. 1987. 248pp.
134-9 $14.00

74. McArthur, M.S.H. *Report on Brunei in 1904.* Ed. by A.V.M. Horton. 1987. 304pp.
135-7 $15.00

75. Lockard, Craig Alan. *From Kampung to City. A Social History of Kuching Malaysia 1820-1970.* 1987. 311pp.
136-5 $16.00

76. McGinn, Richard. *Studies in Austronesian Linguistics.* 1988. 492pp.
137-3 $20.00

77. Muego, Benjamin N. *Spectator Society: The Philippines Under Martial Rule.* 1988. 232pp.
138-1 $15.00

79. Walton, Susan Pratt. *Mode in Javanese Music.* 1987. 279pp.
144-6 $15.00

80. Nguyen Anh Tuan. *South Vietnam Trial and Experience: A Challenge for Development.* 1987. 482pp.
141-1 $18.00

81. Van der Veur, Paul W., ed. *Toward a Glorious Indonesia: Reminiscences and Observations of Dr. Soetomo.* 1987. 367pp.
142-X $16.00

82. Spores, John C. *Running Amok: An Historical Inquiry.* 1988. 190pp.
140-3 $13.00

83. Malaka. *From Jail to Jail.* Tr. and ed. by Helen Jarvis. 1990. 3 vols. 1,226pp.
150-0 $55.00

84. Devas, Nick. *Financing Local Government in Indonesia.* 1989. 344pp.
153-5 $16.00

85. Suryadinata, Leo. *Military Ascendancy and Political Culture: A Study of Indonesia's Golkar.* 1989. 250pp.
154-3 $18.00

86. Williams, Michael. *Communism, Religion, and Revolt in Banten.* 1990. 356pp.
155-1 $14.00

87. Hudak, Thomas John. *The Indigenization of Pali Meters in Thai Poetry.* 1990. 237pp.
159-4 $15.00

88. Lay, Ma Ma. *Not Out of Hate: A Novel of Burma.* Tr. by Margaret Aung-Thwin. Ed. by William Frederick. 1991. 222pp.
167-5 $20.00

89. Anwar, Chairil. *The Voice of the Night: Complete Poetry and Prose of Anwar Chairil.* 1993. Revised Edition. Tr. by Burton Raffel. 180pp.
                                                           $17.00

90. Hudak, Thomas John, tr. *The Tale of Prince Samuttakote: A Buddhist Epic from Thailand.* 1993. 275pp.
174-8 $20.00

91. Roskies, D. M., ed. *Text/Politics in Island Southeast Asia: Essays in Interpretation.* 1993. 321pp.
175-6 $25.00

ORDERING INFORMATION

Orders for titles in the Monographs in International Studies series may be placed through the Ohio University Press, Scott Quadrangle, Athens, Ohio 45701-2979 or through any local bookstore. Individuals should remit payment by check, VISA, or MasterCard.* People ordering from the United Kingdom, Continental Europe, the Middle East, and Africa should order through Academic and University Publishers Group, 1 Gower Street, London WC1E, England. Orders from the Pacific Region, Asia, Australia, and New Zealand should be sent to East-West Export Books, c/o the University of Hawaii Press, 2840 Kolowalu Street, Honolulu, Hawaii 96822, USA.

Other individuals ordering from outside of the U.S. should remit in U.S. funds to Ohio University Press either by International Money Order or by a check drawn on a U.S. bank.** Most out-of-print titles may be ordered from University Microfilms, Inc., 300 North Zeeb Road, Ann Arbor, Michigan 48106, USA.

Prices are subject to change without notice.

*   Please include $3.00 for the first book and 75¢ for each additional book for shipping and handling.

** Please include $4.00 for the first book and 75¢ for each additional book for foreign shipping and handling.